Charlie's Good Tonight

THE LIFE, THE TIMES,
AND THE ROLLING STONES:
THE AUTHORIZED BIOGRAPHY
OF CHARLIE WATTS

Charlie's Good Tonight

Paul Sexton

HARPER

An Imprint of HarperCollins*Publishers*

HarperCollins books may be purchased for educational, business, or sales promotional use. For information, please email the Special Markets Department at SPsales@harpercollins.com.

Originally published in the United Kingdom in 2022 by Mudlark, an imprint of HarperCollins UK.

FIRST U.S. EDITION

Library of Congress Cataloging-in-Publication Data has been applied for.

ISBN 978-0-06-327658-1

22 23 24 25 26 LSC 10 9 8 7 6 5 4 3 2 1

To the memory of Mum and Dad,
with eternal gratitude for their
love and encouragement

Contents

Acknowledgements

This biography has only been made possible with the kind and enthusiastic help and support of Charlie's family, friends and collaborators. I would like to give special thanks to his daughter Seraphina, granddaughter Charlotte and sister Linda for taking part in it with the grace that runs throughout the Watts family. Huge gratitude, too, to his oldest friend Dave Green for going beyond the call of duty with photographic and documentary research; to the Rolling Stones' team (including Joyce Smyth, Paul Edwards, Bernard Doherty, Dave Trafford, Carol Marner, Rachel McAndrew and Sarah Dando) for encouragement and endorsement; and to all of those other contributors (Bill Wyman, Tony King, Jools Holland, Glyn Johns, Lisa Fischer, Chuck Leavell, Don McAulay and many more) who also loved Charlie as much as I did. And of course I am indebted, as so often over the past several decades, to Mick Jagger, Keith Richards and Ronnie Wood, both for their historical contributions and for giving up their time during rehearsals for the *SIXTY* tour, when the Stones rolled with undiminished splendour into the summer of 2022. They took the spirit of Charlie Watts with them, as we all do.

Foreword
by Mick Jagger

Charlie was an incredibly open-minded musician, and there was a real subtlety about his playing. He was so catholic in his taste, through jazz, boogie-woogie, blues, classical, African music, dance, reggae and dumb pop songs that just happened to be good. People always say he was a great jazz fan, but he wasn't just that. It's over-simplifying his musical tastes, and what he liked to play.

It's a bit of a myth that Charlie didn't go out. Of course he did. We used to go to watch sport, and to lots of fashionable places, to eat and to hear music. In the studio we would often play just on our own, every kind of music, after everyone had gone home or before people turned up. Sometimes he'd play these African beats, and some of the things he did were amazing. He wasn't super-technical, but he was very adaptive, so when he got a new beat, he got very excited about it.

He was a classical music fan, too. He liked Dvořák, Debussy, Mozart, and he and I used to listen to Stockhausen and Mahler. We listened to modern composers and tried to figure out what the hell they were on about.

He was intelligent, and softly spoken, but he could be direct and say what he thought. He would keep his private life very private, but we understood each other's thought processes. Charlie was a very quiet person, but he had a great sense of humour and we laughed all the time. I miss him in so many ways.

Mick Jagger
June 2022

Foreword
by Keith Richards

Every time I think, 'I'm going to talk about Charlie Watts,' you realise the essential man wasn't something you put into words. Charlie was a presence, and when you were with him, that was it.

With Charlie and me, it was basically structured around humour. We took the piss out of people without even talking. We had a sort of visual sign language, necessary between a rhythm guitar player and a drummer, because you have to communicate in certain ways. But we developed a language to a finer art where it could encompass irony, being pissed off, or on stage: 'OK, now we're flying, how do we land?'

Charlie's humour was incredibly dry and understated, but I knew certain key words, which I'm not going to release. I didn't do it often, but there were a couple of words I could say that if he was in the middle of an airport, he would lie down and start laughing with his legs in the air. The odd time that I got him in that position, luckily, we were in hotel rooms, because sometimes you'd get hysterical laughter, and he'd let it all out in one big go. And God knows what the joke was. As usual with that sort of laugh, whatever kicked it off was not really that funny.

He was a very private man. I always had the feeling that I wouldn't necessarily step over or enquire about something, unless he wanted to talk about it. There was no side on him, there was no act to follow. Charlie was just what you got, which was Charlie. He was the realest guy I ever met.

Keith Richards
June 2022

Prelude

The first time I met Charlie Watts was on Eel Pie Island. It was a Wednesday, first day of May. I had seen the Stones live for the first time the previous Sunday at the Station Hotel in Richmond. I had not spoken to him – I may have nodded at Mick and Keith but I only spoke with Brian Jones, at the time the group's designated spokesman.

I'd been overwhelmed by the band at the Station Hotel. I had no idea what it really was, except that it had changed my mind about so much, and I wanted in. By the following Wednesday I was hustling on behalf of myself and my landlord, the agent Eric Easton, who rented me a room and phone on Regent Street. The gig had ended, and I was nervously hanging around wanting to pass the audition and get on with it.

I was standing next to Charlie and his kit. I had no idea what to talk about, so I offered to help him schlep his kit. He smiled and declined my offer; he already knew better and that my skills lay elsewhere. He had mesmerised me at the Station Hotel, as had they all.

In my first autobiography *Stoned*, I wrote: *The drummer appeared to have been beamed in, and it seemed you didn't so much hear him as feel him. I enjoyed the presence he brought to the group as well as his playing. Unlike the jacketless other five, he had the two top buttons of his jacket done up meticulously over a just as neat button-down shirt and tie, unaffected by the weather in the room. Body behind kit, head turned right in a distant, mannered disdain for the showing of hands waving at 78rpm in front of him. He was with the Stones, but not of them, kinda blue, like he'd been transported for the evening from Ronnie Scott's or Birdland, where he'd been driving in another Julian 'Cannonball' Adderley time and space. He was the one and only, all-time man of his world, gentleman of time, space and the heart. His rare musical talent is an expression of his bigger talent for life: I'd just met Charlie Watts.*

Our last sessions together were 'We Love You' and 'Dandelion'. As happened on many a Stones tune going in, there was no pre-arranged ending – better to see if the meat and potatoes were in place before applying the veg. The ending was a mélange of Nicky Hopkins and Brian Jones on keyboards and woodwind, Keith and Mick on hallowed vocals and Charlie leading the fray with improvised fills. At the time I thought the fills were just for me. They were not, they were just Charlie-appropriate.

In the '80s Charlie dropped by for something in New York during one of his solo jazz jaunts. I made the mistake of playing him something I had been working on. He was just not interested. 'Andrew,' he said, perhaps by way of an explanation, 'I just don't care about what the Stones are about. I'm only interested in what I play.' Fortunately the rough patch faded, the get-over-it, get-on-with-it yell prevailed and the band played on. I saw him last in Seattle in 2005, exactly the same fellow I'd said hello to on Eel Pie Island.

In the movie world they talk about the golden era. Ours was Charlie Watts. All the great bands have one thing in common: a different drummer.

Andrew Loog Oldham
June 2022

INTRODUCTION

A Man Out of Time, Always in Time

Madison Square Garden, New York, November 1969. As 'the greatest rock 'n' roll band in the world', newly anointed thus by tour MC Sam Cutler, ease out of Chuck Berry's 'Little Queenie' and into their most recent No. 1 'Honky Tonk Women', Mick Jagger offers a conversational observation: 'Charlie's good tonight, innee?'

Of course he was, and he always would be. The very mention of Charlie Watts's name, in the context of this biography or however it may arrive in the conversation, is enough to have fellow musicians and fans alike practically standing to attention. Which is exactly the sort of eulogy he would have run a mile from, as he did throughout a truly singular and unlikely life.

Charlie was the proof that not all rock stars are created equal, and that clichés are there to be avoided. Such as the one that, in his mind, he was a rock star at all. He was the global celebrity who hated attention and once said that he preferred the company of dogs to humans; the car enthusiast who didn't drive; the horseman who didn't ride; the man of wealth and taste who grew up in a prefab; the drummer who toured the world for five and a half decades and spent all of them yearning to be back home; the jobbing musician who thought the Stones would be finished in a year, and ended up as their pilot light with a whole-life tariff. If you made him up you would find few believers.

To be writing about him in the past tense is innately sad, but he would probably have avoided reading this book in any case. I can imagine he might have looked to see which photographs we had chosen of him in his besuited elegance, but that would be it. It is, I hope, a gentle tale of a life well lived and certainly well loved. If you're looking for controversy, you're looking under the wrong Stone.

After the great joy of 30 years of interviewing him and all of the Rolling Stones, I was approached in 2020 about the idea of working with Charlie on his autobiography. It was an idea that was simultaneously exciting and doomed; the very notion of him writing about himself was fundamentally flawed.

He openly admitted that the Rolling Stones' music was not really his cup of tea, and he hardly ever listened back to any of it, unless he had to approve a reissue or some such. But he was never less than entirely gracious whenever he was wheeled out for promotional duties. In time, you learned how to weave in and out of his unpredictable thought processes and the way he expressed himself, and to look forward to that warm, beaming smile. This despite the fact that there were times when his brain and his mouth ran at different speeds, and he sometimes had the distracted look of a man trying to remember whether he'd left something on the stove.

To document his life in the third person feels entirely more appropriate, and the speed with which his friends and family offered their approval and involvement says everything about him. It mirrored the extended, worshipful cheering that would follow his introduction by Mick Jagger at every Stones show in memory, and the global cascade of affection triggered by his death at the age of 80 in August 2021.

From young drummer for hire to the steady pair of hands with an aura beyond his age, and from bedrock of the glory years to silver-haired style icon and retainer, Charlie Watts lived all those lives, but left it to others to make a noise on his behalf. Exhibitionism? Not him. He just yearned to be home and wondered what all the fuss was about.

When he died, almost every tribute and obituary made reference to the silent Stone, the backbone of the band, the man who never missed a show in 57 years (not strictly true: he did miss one, at least, in 1964, because he got the date wrong, as we will learn). But there was considerably less talk about the inveterate collector, the munificent gift-giver, the man with an old-world sense of style that often made him feel he was born in the wrong century.

Charlie had the ability, both intentional and otherwise, to sum up a story, a situation or a life with a crisp uppercut that was rivalled only by his friend Ringo Starr with his hard-day's-nights and tomorrow-never-knows malaprop-isms. 'Five years working, 20 years hanging around' was among Charlie's most famous one-liners, but there were many more. To have been there to hear some of them, to witness his square-jawed stoicism, that granite face break-ing into his dazzling grin, those stop-start, splintered speech patterns and insouciant asides, was worth even more than the price of admission to what the Stones have given the world: the greatest show on earth.

It's not unusual to meet world-level rock musicians for whom the adulation of millions does not inure them to sometimes excruciating self-doubt. But it's collectibly rare to hear any of them say anything specifically self-effacing. Almost every time we met, Charlie would mutter something about not rating himself as a drummer, or not coming close to par with any of his percussive heroes.

This might hint at a lack of self-awareness, but it was founded on a sense of English reserve and humility that was better developed than anyone's. Brian Jones, even as he began his slalom of substance-based deterioration, described him as 'probably the most detached and well-adjusted person on this whole pop scene'.

In the opening couplet of 'If You Can't Rock Me', the first track from *It's Only Rock 'n Roll*, Mick sings: 'The band's on stage and it's one of those nights ... the drummer thinks that he is dynamite.' He certainly wasn't talking about Charlie. To him, arrogance was simply uncouth. He knew who he was, and with the exception of a relatively short period of narcotic madness in the 1980s, which he saw off without any of the clichéd dramas of rehab and was clear-minded ever after, he didn't change.

'His philosophy is "I only need so much,"' the Stones' early manager Andrew Loog Oldham once said of him. 'He has settled for that and not digressed for the bullshit.' Even in his first flush of fame, Charlie was telling the music press: 'I give the impression of being bored, but I'm not really. I've just got an incredibly boring face.'

It may seem implausible to cite the words of an American basketball coach, but Oldham's latter-day email signature, recognising the wisdom of the late John Wooden, seems apposite. 'Talent is God-given, be humble,' he said. 'Fame is man-given, be grateful. Conceit is self-given, be careful.' Charlie was born with the first, had the second hurled at him and was intrinsically incapable of exhibiting the third.

This biography is not intended as yet another exhausting re-tread of the legend of the greatest rock 'n' roll band in the world, but as a portrayal of the life and times of a singular human who made them better, as he did all of us who met him. It is told chronologically, but also with periodic *Backbeat* interludes to focus on specific aspects of Charlie's world, especially his enduring marriage to his beloved Shirley.

Yes, it is a tale of sticks and Stones, but also of someone whose like we won't see again, who almost seemed to belong in another epoch altogether: a man out of time, but always perfectly in time.

1

A Prefab Childhood and a Comrade in Jazz

Mozart knew what he was talking about.
But he should have had a good drummer.
Keith Richards, 2011

The Human Riff was actually explaining to me about the synthesis of hillbilly and black music that customised the recipe for rock 'n' roll, putting the match to the kindling for the nascent Rolling Stones and the generation of hopeful oiks they represented. But that payoff line has always felt like a playfully succinct overview of the man who sat behind him for 58 years. In a parallel timeline, you could imagine Wolfgang Amadeus looking up to Charlie Watts. Everyone else did.

Charlie was not only the most reluctant star in all of music, he was the least likely candidate to fill the seat for so many decades with rock 'n' roll's most global representatives. Even after he acceded to the band's repeated overtures to join their number, neither he nor anybody else thought that the Stones or their rhythm and blues racket would last more than a year.

In early June 1941, with the *Bismarck* sitting at the bottom of the Atlantic, Germany was preparing for its invasion of the Soviet Union with troops three million strong. In a terrible portent of 2022, tank battles soon raged near Kiev. The Proms had just been bombed out of their headquarters at Queen's Hall and were rehomed at the Royal Albert Hall, while Churchill's Board of Trade announced the introduction of clothing coupons. Since they had yet to be printed, margarine coupons from ration books had to suffice: sixteen for a raincoat, seven for boots. But at University College Hospital in Bloomsbury, Lil Watts had other things on her mind.

Just turned 20, Islington-born Lillian Charlotte Watts, daughter of Charles and Ellen Eaves, was married in 1939 to Charles Richard Watts, a month her senior, who served in the RAF, as ground crew and as a driver for officers. When demobbed, he became a lorry driver for the London, Midland and Scottish Railway, a job he was still doing as the Stones conquered Britain. On Monday 2 June 1941 Lillian gave birth to their first-born; like Bill Wyman and Brian Jones, he would share his father's name. Charles Robert Watts took his first beat.

At the time, the British record charts were still a decade from formal inception, but the Andrews Sisters were providing a tonic for the troops with 'Boogie Woogie Bugle Boy'. Soon, Glenn Miller and plenty of others, including our Vera, were forecasting bluebirds over the White Cliffs of Dover. Wireless sets of the day also warmed to the comedy programme *It's That Man Again*, to Deanna Durbin's 'Waltzing in the Clouds', the Ink Spots and Bing Crosby, while Noël Coward politely enquired, 'Could You Please Oblige Us with a Bren Gun?' At the pictures, Abbott and Costello were among the top new movie stars, with their third film just released, Universal's *In the Navy*, co-starring Dick Powell. Joan Crawford, later to feature in the collage of art for *Exile on Main St*, was still filling the 1s 9d's in George Cukor's newly issued *A Woman's Face*.

As a toddler, Charlie spent some time living with each of his grandmothers, while his father was serving in the RAF, but he would remember little about the war years. He later said: 'I heard bombs exploding in the neighbourhood. I remember the mad rush from the house into the air-raid shelters. I was very young. War was something of a game to me – I don't think I ever really and truly got frightened.'

Not only his father, but his grandfather (Charles A. Watts), uncle and cousin also shared his forename, so his mum and dad would often call him 'Charlie Boy'. The youngest Charles attended Fryent Way Infant School in Kingsbury, north-west London, and as the war ended, he met Dave Green, nine months his junior. They would become friends, and were bandmates in many of Charlie's jazz projects on stage and in the studio for the rest of his life.

Despite being nine months younger, Dave's war memories are more vivid. 'I was born in 1942 in Edgware, and we lived in Kingsbury. My dad was in the Royal Engineers. He went over to Germany on D-Day, and I remember – I must have been two – the Doodlebugs coming over. One came down in our street, about 60 houses up, and completely destroyed the house. I remember my mum put me under the stairs. That was government advice, I think.'

Dave remembers his mother listening to *Music While You Work* on the wireless, and she later said that he would sing along to the bass lines of popular songs, an early sign of what would become his career-long prominence as a double bass player. He shares his memories with such warmth and generosity that he soon becomes someone you feel you've always been friends with. About to turn 80 when we spoke for this book, he retains a self-effacing joie de vivre that would have endeared him to Charlie.

In 1946 they became neighbours and, soon, conjoined musical spirits.

Courtesy of the Luftwaffe, the two families were about to have new addresses in Pilgrims Way, Wembley, in the 'prefab' housing offered to so many British households affected by bomb damage. The pre-built maisonette modules seem basic in retrospect, but in hard times they were a thing of wonder to the Green family.

'When we were at Brampton Road, Kingsbury, the prefabs weren't very far away, and I remember going up there to look at them,' says Dave. 'The road wasn't even a road, and there were great piles of mud everywhere. But my mum loved these prefabs. The kitchen was fantastic, very modern, self-contained, fridge, everything. She put her name down for one, and when they were finished, we moved in.'

Charlie and his parents were at No. 23, and the Greens at No. 22.

In 1944 Lillian gave birth to Charlie's sister Linda, to whom he was always close, especially so before he left home. The interview that she and her husband Roy Rootes gave me for this book is the first she has ever granted about her brother. Indeed, Linda has maintained such a low profile that many people don't realise Charlie had a sister at all.

'No, they don't, because I never pushed myself to the front,' she says softly, sitting with me and Roy in their home in Buckinghamshire. 'That's not my nature, and I know it's not what he would have wanted. But you'd be out at the front of the show and someone would say, "Oh, you're Charlie's sister. You must be so proud," and I'd say, "Yes, I am proud of him." He was never one to go over the top. One-to-one was ideal for him, because he was quite a reserved man. He was like my mum, and I'm like my dad. He would sit there and not say a word.'

She speaks with nostalgic warmth about those years at home with her brother and their parents, and the sense of community they shared in that compact homestead. 'Dad decided that because they liked sport and billiards, they would buy a half-size snooker table,' says Linda. 'If you wanted to play a shot, you had to open the window,' says Roy drily. 'That brought everybody in, and my dad loved that,' Linda adds. 'My mum was a bit more reserved, but she was all right because she was in the kitchen.' Roy, one year older than Charlie, went on to marry Linda in 1965.

Says Dave: 'I think the first time Charlie and I met was when I was four and we moved there. Our mums became very good friends, that was the thing, and as we grew older we became very close. It was just remarkable, really, that we had this same interest in jazz, and developed it in tandem.'

'Up to when we were ten we'd be playing in the garden,' Charlie told me, 'because it was all one thing with a little fence at the back, and we had a hole in the fence to go through. Our mums and dads were friends. Then he started to play with skiffle groups and so did I. We played in our first jazz band together, played our first records together, and I always use him if I do anything outside of the Rolling Stones.' Then, his deadpan sign-off: 'I wouldn't encumber him with them.'

'My dad played a bit of piano, but not jazz,' Dave explained. 'He used to play Les Paul and Mary Ford, stuff like that, and we had a radiogram, so it started from that kind of thing for Charlie and me, when we were about nine or ten. Of course we went to the same school, Fryent Junior, but he was a different year from me. And then we went to secondary modern school at Tyler's Croft in Kingsbury, still living in the same place.' A near-contemporary there was actress Shirley Eaton, the Bond girl in *Goldfinger*; another was William Woollard, the longtime presenter of *Tomorrow's World*.

'Funnily enough,' says Dave, 'I don't remember [Charlie] at school. I didn't see him much there. But we started collecting 78s and going to record shops together, and then LPs, by Charlie Parker and Jelly Roll Morton, which I'd never heard. Listening in his bedroom, or sometimes in mine.'

Bill Wyman's splendidly detailed *Rolling with the Stones* places Charlie, aged all of seven, in a satin suit at his Uncle Albert's wedding in Holloway. 'My dad bought me suits and I wore them as smartly as I could,' said Charlie. 'A kind of Little Lord Fauntleroy, I suppose. But I do remember that I didn't like jeans and sweaters in those days. I thought they looked untidy and I didn't feel somehow as good as I did in my little suits with the baggy trousers.' So much never changed.

When Dave's parents' marriage failed, he was sent to live with relatives in Yeovil, but returned to London after two years of bucolic bliss and reconnected with Charlie in 1953.

'My mum was offered a council house while she was in the prefabs, a new build back in Kingsbury, so we moved down there. I remember the fog – pea-soupers – and the bus conductor walking in front of the bus. You just couldn't see, the fog was incredible. Many people died.

'We stayed down there a year in this new-build place, and my mum reapplied to go back to the prefab,' Dave remembers with a laugh. 'She missed them so much, and Lil Watts and everything. They were a wonderful concept. Everybody had exactly the same place, and more or less exactly the same size garden. It was utopia, it was like a community, and my mum missed that. We couldn't go back to living next door to Charlie, so we lived just down the way.'

The boy Watts became a teenager in June 1954, as Doris Day shouted from the highest hills and told the golden daffodils about her 'Secret Love'. At Tyler's Croft, in a class of 40, Charlie began to develop his interest in art, more so than performing and studying music, which was hampered by a teacher that no one could understand. He also excelled at both football, as a nippy right-winger, and cricket, even having a trial for Middlesex. 'He was a big boy with strong legs,' said Lil. 'We often thought he would become a foot-baller.'

'My earliest memory would be of him playing cricket,' says sister Linda. 'He was really a very good cricketer, and in the loft we've got medals that he got. He always had a good build, and mum and dad always helped him with whatever he wanted. It was only a two-bedroom prefab, so my brother had the big bedroom, which should have been my mum and dad's bedroom. I had the smaller one, and mum and dad had a put-you-up in the front room, for a good few years.'

Soon afterwards, Charlie took his first faltering steps as a musician, on the banjo. He would say that in his extended family no one played anything except the gramophone, but that wasn't strictly true. An unlikely branch of the family tree grew in the Migil Five, the British jazz combo that Charlie went on to dep with on occasion, and who later followed the Stones' path into R&B-edged pop, making the UK top ten in May 1964 with 'Mockin' Bird Hill'.

That group was originally fronted by Charlie and Linda's uncle, Lennie Peters, with whom Charlie played in his early drumming days. 'He was the only blind person I've ever known who could hang wallpaper,' says Linda nonchalantly. 'And change a lightbulb.'

After years of solo toil on the London pub circuit, and neglected singles for labels such as Oriole and Pye, Uncle Lennie became part of Peters & Lee, remembered by survivors of the 1970s as chart-topping archetypes of pipe-and-slippers pop. With glorious incongruity, their signature No. 1 'Welcome Home' shared space in the British Top 20 in September 1973 with the Stones' 'Angie'.

Back with that banjo, Charlie didn't care for the dots on the neck, so he pulled the thing apart. 'At the same time I heard a drummer called Chico Hamilton,' he said, 'who played with Gerry Mulligan. I wanted to play like that, with brushes.' With his first home-spun drum kit lacking a snare drum, he put the banjo head on a wooden stand that he made, turned the head around the other way and played the round skin with wire brushes.

Thus he made ends meet until, for his Christmas present in 1955, Charlie's father and grandmother took pity on him and bought him his first proper set, a second-hand Olympic kit acquired from a fellow who played in the local pub. It arrived complete with beer stains on the skins and cigarette burns on the bass drum. 'I remember finding it in my auntie's bedroom,' said Charlie Boy. 'Can't remember anything that gave me greater pleasure, and I must say the neighbours were great about the noise I kicked up.'

As Linda remembers, he was prepared to put the work in too. 'He used to sit in the kitchen with two Sorbo balls, and that's how he strengthened his wrists,' she says. 'You'd be sitting looking at him and my mum used to say, "For goodness' sake, put those things down!" But they did him proud. When that drum kit came in, I thought, "Goodness, what are the neighbours going to think?" Luckily, they were OK. He and Roy used to go to London together, with another friend, Andrew Wren. I think he got the bug then.'

By that time, his friend Roy Rootes's technical know-how as a television engineer was coming in handy. 'I was the one who started Charlie off with playing in the bedroom,' he says, 'running wires everywhere from the radiogram in the front room into his bedroom. I put a speaker up, so that he got the music in his bedroom while he was playing the drums.'

And, oh, the records. Charlie's first passions as a listener included Earl Bostic's 1951 US R&B No. 1 'Flamingo', which his uncle bought, and which would be played at his mum and dad's parties at home in the prefab. On it, the alto sax man from Tulsa led a supremely swinging version of a tune first cut a decade earlier by Duke Ellington and his Orchestra. It provided a perfect early taste of sophisticated jazz with rhythm and blues seasoning. Charlie Parker's 'Out of Nowhere', recorded back in '47, began Charlie's lifelong love affair with the masterful saxophonist and the diaphanous drumming of Max Roach. A certain 21-year-old Miles Davis was on that session, adding trumpet.

'I am what I am, thanks to this man,' Charlie said of Parker. 'Every drummer that's got any ears would want to be Charlie Parker's drummer.' Indeed, 'Bird' flew into the imagination of the future Rolling Stones more than once. Over in Cheltenham, it was hearing a Parker record that compelled Brian Jones to ask his parents to buy him a saxophone. As we shall hear, one Charlie would become the inspiration for a book by another.

Charlie's conversion to drums was enhanced by the hands of the aforementioned Chico Hamilton, the Los Angeles native whose deft brush style emerged when he joined baritone saxophone sorcerer Gerry Mulligan's quartet. Their *Volume 1* LP of 1952, also featuring Chet Baker on trumpet, contained Mulligan's own composition 'Walkin' Shoes', a marvel of restrained elegance by Hamilton and the entire group. The discs mesmerised the young Charlie. He needed to play like Chico Hamilton. More than ever, he knew that the drums were where he wanted to sit.

Charlie and Dave (always 'David' to his friend) filled the prefab with the contemporary sound of skiffle, Dave gamely accompanying on his homemade tea-chest bass. But Charlie essentially taught himself drums by listening to those early jazz heroes, while achieving distinctly average qualifications at school. When he left at 16, his only 'O' level was in art, and his only other reward two cups for running. His gift for graphic design led him to enrol at Harrow Art School.

'When I was younger, I'd find it very difficult to sleep, so I'd draw,' he later reflected. 'I did it for therapy, and probably as a way of keeping me out of trouble.' Says Dave: 'He was a tremendous artist. I know he had aspirations to be a graphic illustrator, but he failed one of the exams or something. I don't know how, because he was very good. So that was a bit of a setback to him, I think. That's when he started getting more into the playing thing.'

Meanwhile, the friends continued their sonic education, both in Pilgrims Way, Wembley, and up west. 'We learned from playing records, and we used to go to clubs,' says Dave. 'We went to the 100 Club together to see Humphrey Lyttelton's band – that was in about 1958. Later on I joined Humph, in '65, and stayed for 18 years. Charlie loved Eddie Taylor's drums in that band, and it was Brian Brocklehurst on bass. We sat there avidly. You listen and you watch the relationship between the bass and drums, and you're playing records, and you copy. Charlie would play along with the record, as I did.'

'I was brought up on this thing of looking at certain people play,' Charlie explained. 'When I used to go to local dance halls I never danced; I used to go and stand near the drummer and watch him play. And my favourite ones were invariably black Americans, and they played a music called jazz. That's what I wanted to play like.'

Charlie's in-built self-doubt came through when he talked about those days on *Desert Island Discs* in 2001. 'I'm a halfway-there person,' he said. 'When I was young I should have had lessons, I should have learned to read properly, but I preferred the glitter.'

By 1958 they had gigs of their own. North London jazz outfit the Joe Jones Seven were looking for new recruits after their bassist and drummer were called up for National Service. Jones lived at Meadowbank Road, Kingsbury, not far from Charlie and Dave in Pilgrims Way. His real first name is Brian, not to be confused with the Stones' original leader and co-founder, nor with the American drummer Jo Jones, whose definitive work with the Count Basie Orchestra was much admired by Charlie.

'I knew a scale of B flat,' remembers Dave, who'd been playing in a skiffle outfit. 'I got this real bass, started learning it, and then we heard about this band doing auditions. It was a Dixieland mainstream band, and we'd been listening to those kind of records anyway. So we just turned up. We didn't ever think we'd get through it. But as Brian recently told me, nobody else came anyway. It was either us or nobody, so we got the gig.

'Neither of us were interested in doing solos,' he adds. 'We just wanted to sit there and swing for the band. That attitude never changed in him, and basically in me neither. We're both team players. Any band I play with, I play for the band, for the music, to fit in. That's what Charlie did.'

Jones, aged 83 in 2022, tells me: 'We put an advert in the *Melody Maker* saying we were doing a gig at a pub called the Upper Welsh Harp in west Hendon. They read it and came along, and they were the only two that turned up. But being a semi-pro band, they were good enough for what we wanted at the time, because we were all learning. So they joined the band. I think that was Charlie's first job.

'He was a dapper young man, always very smart and stylish. He was a good timekeeper, which is the main thing you want, but that's about all he was at that early stage. He wasn't a child prodigy. He used to play on the beat, which drummers must never do, really. But not for long. He cured himself of that.'

Jones, who shared Charlie's particular admiration for Louis Armstrong, adds: 'Charlie's mum and dad were very nice people, and we used to practise round at their house, in the prefab. We had a pianist in our band, but they didn't have a piano in the house, obviously, and electric piano hadn't been invented yet. So we just had drums and bass, sometimes a guitar player, and with a three-piece sax, trumpet and trombone front line.

'I think his parents were glad he was doing something and not hanging around,' Jones continues. 'A lot of mums and dads were like that – they'd put up with the noise rather than have him wandering the streets. It was a good period. We'd be round there for a couple of hours on a Sunday, and the band would come to do rehearsals in my house as well.'

'They all used to come to the prefab,' adds Linda, 'and the noise you would hear would be jazz. It was never rock 'n' roll or pop. Charlie used to like Billy Eckstine, which is what my mum and dad listened to. But apart from that, it was jazz.' Johnnie Ray and Nat 'King' Cole were on the phonograph too. 'They were very much into the Perry Comos and that,' said her brother, who went to see Eckstine at the London Palladium. The stylist from Pittsburgh combined all of Charlie's musical loves, as a sophisticated jazz and pop vocalist, a swing and bebop bandleader and trumpeter. Charlie raved about his 1940s group featuring Dizzy Gillespie, Charlie Parker and Art Blakey.

With Charlie and Dave in the lineup, the Joe Jones Seven got a weekly residency at the Masons Arms in Edgware. In a wonderful 1959 photograph of the group at that venue, featuring their teenage recruits, bassist Green is wearing any old sweater while drummer Watts is pristine in Ivy League jacket, hair nearly parted and a handkerchief in his top pocket.

'He had this sense that we were going out to play and you've got to look the part,' Dave continues. 'My dad used to run us up there sometimes, or we'd get a cab to the station and get the train, me carrying the bass as well, get off at Canons Park and get a bus. Get to the gig, and do the same thing on the way back. I just turned up in what I was wearing. Charlie changed for the gig. Never saw him in jeans.'

Sterling research by Jones's wife Ann has uncovered a letter to Brian, or 'Joe', on Mecca Dancing letterhead ('world's largest ballroom organisation'). 'We had travelled to the Streatham Locarno in August 1958 to compete in one of the heats of the National Amateur Jazz Band Championship,' says Dave. 'This was a big deal for us and I remember very well playing on the revolving stage.'

He points up another early example of his mate's sartorial flair. 'Brian organised a band uniform for the event, and he remembers that Charlie wore a bright coloured tie instead of the one that was chosen for the uniform. Ann also remembers coming across one of the judges who was in the bar instead of being in his place listening and judging the various bands.'

The band assumed that their appearance in the heat had even failed to excite any of the judges who were at their correct station – until the Locarno manager admitted in the letter to a judging error, advising Jones that his group had actually come second, behind the Jack Bayle Quartet. Dave completes the story neatly: 'Nothing came of it,' he says, 'because we didn't bother to go and play in the final.'

Recalls Jones: 'There was a lot of jazz then. You could play in pubs all over London, and we were doing little dance band things as well – anniversaries, weddings, things like that, and playing a few pop songs of the period. None of us were out and out mouldy figs, as they used to call [purist] jazzers. If there was a gig coming up, you could earn ten bob. If it was a really good one, 30 bob. That Masons Arms gig, I don't think we even got paid – we got free beer. Charlie was drinking orange juice.'

At an August 1959 date at the Edgware Jazz Club, Charlie was on drums and Dave on bass as the now-renamed Joe Jones All-Stars worked through a set containing George Gershwin's 'Summertime', bluesy staples such as 'St James Infirmary Blues', 'St Louis Blues' and Woody Herman's 'Goosey Gander'. Sometimes, it would be Charlie's dad driving them, with a double bass and a drum kit in the back. On other occasions the friends got the bus, cramming their equipment in the luggage hold and on the platform. One time the drum rolled out and down the road. A charitable conductor stopped the bus to let them retrieve it.

As the '60s arrived there was room among the gigs and the records for Charlie to devote time to the opposite sex. He attended Jones's 21st birthday party. 'My brother-in-law was there,' says Jones, 'and he said to me, "That Charlie Watts, he asked me if I was going out with that girl, because he said if I didn't want to, he would."'

The band broke up after about a year, after Jones got married and moved with Ann to Luton. 'They went their different ways,' he said, 'but they did come up and see me a couple of times and we'd play with some local musicians.' Bedazzled by his favourite players of the day, Charlie said that in his imagination he was bespoke New York drummer Art Taylor, playing, as Taylor did, with genius pianist Thelonious Monk. Charlie had left art school in July 1960, but not before, for a class project ('as practice for a career in graphic design', he later explained), he had written and drawn a small but meaningful book in tribute to Charlie

Parker, calling it *Ode to a Highflying Bird*. He drew it, lovingly, at home, with inks and a brush. 'The inks ran into each other, and I never cleaned the brush properly, so they've got very strange colours,' he explained with his customary attention to detail.

Once the Stones made the A-list, the pocket-sized volume was published by Beat Publications in January 1965, with a cover price of seven shillings. Charlie said drily: 'This guy who published *Rolling Stones Monthly* saw my book and said, "Ah, there's a few bob in this!"' Dave Green, by then on his own jazz trajectory and out of his friend's orbit, told me with a laugh: 'I remember seeing that book in the kiosk at Kingsbury station. I didn't buy it because I couldn't afford it.'

The 36-page, five-by-seven-inch *Ode to a Highflying Bird* may have been the proverbial slim tome, and with its simple but beautiful handwriting and drawings could have been a children's book – except that it was as cool as the music it depicted. It deserves to be dwelt on as the first, and perhaps definitive, manifestation of Charlie's twin passions, for jazz and art.

The teenager drew Parker as a real bird, in sunglasses, describing his rise and all-too-sudden fall with stark grace. 'This story was compiled by one Charlie to a late and great Charlie,' he wrote as a preface. The book detailed how Bird's parents 'made nest' in Kansas and how Parker, realising he was different from other chicks, practised hard on his 'whistle', but found himself out of step with other birds and sought refuge in 'bad seeds and rye drinks'.

He finds acclaim in New York, but never shakes his bad habits. Over five pages of affecting illustrations the bird wastes away, smaller in size on each page, going, going and finally gone. Parker died of his excesses in 1955 at just 34, but with the body, it was said, of a 50- or 60-year-old man. 'Flown,' concluded Charlie eloquently, 'but not forgotten.' In 1991 the book was reprinted, newly accompanied by the handsome mini-album *From One Charlie*, on which Charlie modestly helmed a hand-picked quintet, including Dave.

In 1960, out of college, and perhaps with the first iteration of his book as an endorsement, Charlie took a job for £2 a week as a tea boy at London graphic design firm Charles Daniels Studios. He and his workmates would be glued to *Hancock's Half Hour* on the radio the night before, and repeated all the best lines of The Lad Himself in the studio the next day.

Andy Wickham, subsequently a notable industry publicist and executive who was central to the Laurel Canyon-fuelled expansion of Warner Brothers Records, said: 'I worked next to Charlie in the studio. He was just about the smartest-turned-out artist in the department. He used to help all of us with our drawing if we were in trouble. But you should have heard him talk about jazz. He was like a walking encyclopaedia.'

Charlie's dual fascination for design and jazz would later endear him to a rising photographer who would help shape the Stones' visual dynamic: one David Bailey. 'I got on very well with Charlie because he had worked as a graphic designer,' he said. 'He knew who [storied American photographer] Irving Penn was and a little bit about my own work. And of course he was more jazz-oriented, and I had been listening to a lot of jazz – when I was fourteen I really wanted to be Chet Baker.'

Charlie rose to the level of visualiser, designing posters, and could have pursued a highly successful career in design, but his love of playing wouldn't leave him alone. He left the job because he simply had to drum, keeping his hand(s) in with sets in a coffee bar twice a week, then landing a spot from September 1961 at the Troubadour in Earl's Court, where his prowess brought a staging-post meeting with Alexis Korner.

Paris-born Korner had arrived in London, not yet a teenager, during the Second World War, and in 1949 joined Chris Barber's band, where he met the perennially undervalued harmonica player Cyril Davies. Their combined energies as artists and scene-makers were immensely important to the development of London's rhythm and blues uprising, especially when they formed Blues Incorporated in 1961.

Charlie often reminisced with me about those early club days as both punter and performer, with instant recall on those he had played with decades earlier. He worked for the likes of Art Wood, Ronnie's older brother, and in the band Blues By Six, but really in any configuration that suited. 'You made a living,' he said. 'You played where you were asked to play. David, because he played a bass, and was extremely talented, I might add, he played with a certain crowd of people. I used to play in Art's band, and Art Themen [later with Stan Tracey] was the tenor player.'

Later he noted: 'I remember when I first started to play, you had modern jazz and traditional jazz, and they were totally split. The people that went where I went, to see Georgie Fame, looked totally different, with their haircuts and everything, to the ones that went to Cy Laurie's club [in Great Windmill Street] and danced, which is where my [future] wife went.

'That's how Alexis started, through the kind and amazing guy Chris Barber, through his instigation,' he explained. 'Harold Pendleton owned the Marquee, and Alexis got a Thursday night there. It became bigger than the Johnny Dankworth night, which was Sunday night. I used to go Sunday nights, I used to see [Scottish jazz drummer] Bobby Orr and people like that playing there.' By now he was spending more time in Soho, also going to watch Phil Seamen at both Ronnie's and the Flamingo, and buying records from Ray Smith, owner of the jazz mecca that was Collet's Record Shop in New Oxford Street.

Korner's attempts to add Charlie to the Blues Incorporated fold were thwarted by the drummer's offer of some graphic design work in Denmark, where he lived in Randers on the Jutland peninsula. While he was there he played with multi-instrumentalist Holger Laumann in the band Safari Jazz, and prestigiously with Don Byas, the tenor sax man of swing and bebop repute who had worked with Basie, Ellington and Gillespie.

Charlie returned to the UK in February 1962 to a day job in design for the advertising agency Charles Hobson and Grey. But he played briefly with Dudley Moore's trio, forming a friendship with the pianist and emerging comic that would resurface in later years. For now, though, Blues Incorporated finally got their man.

'I'd got this message saying Alexis Korner – and I said "Who?" – wants you to play in his band,' recounted Charlie. 'I spoke to Alexis a bit and turned up and I didn't know what the hell they were playing. Blues to me was "Parker's Mood". I'd never heard Chicago blues. And I was never into rock 'n' roll, really. Fats Domino was about the nearest, him and Little Richard. I thought they were wonderful, still do.

'I hated Elvis. Keith Richards turned me on to Elvis Presley, and the greatness of his Sun days. I like up until "All Shook Up" and those things. I think he'd have been even worse, now, if he'd lived, because I hate the last period of his life, the show. I loved it when he had Scotty Moore and D. J. Fontana, that little band. He must have been something else then. It must have been incredible to see him on one of those barn dances.'

Thus, at two quid a gig, Charlie became part of a training ground for British prospects that was surely rivalled only by John Mayall's revolving door of talent that would soon emerge in the Bluesbreakers. 'A great magnet,' was Charlie's apt description of Korner. Blues Incorporated incubated such names as Jack Bruce, Ginger Baker, Graham Bond, Long John Baldry, Paul Jones, American Ronnie Jones (no relation), Davy Graham and Dick Heckstall-Smith, and gave early opportunities to another young pretender then often still known as Mike Jagger.

'I sometimes wish I had percentages of all the people who got started with me,' Korner told *Melody Maker* in 1966. 'The Stones, for example. Charlie Watts was in my band and Mick Jagger used to sing with me. I'd have kept him on, but Cyril Davies objected.'

Jack Bruce once told me: 'When I got to London, I started to get more work, and thankfully a more interesting musical situation, because I never really was a big fan of trad – that was very formulaic, second-rate music. When I met Dick Heckstall-Smith and joined Alexis Korner's band, with all these great people like Ginger and Graham Bond, Charlie Watts and all the amazing people I met in the very early '60s, that's when I started to develop.'

'Jack's a fine musician, always has been from the age of 16, or younger,' said Charlie. 'When I first met him, he was a wonderful bass player, in a band with Ginger and Dick. He's one of those musicians that can just turn up, which I can't do. Well, I can, but there's areas I can't cope with it, where Jack can. When I first played with Alexis, Jack played upright string bass, when I first knew him. He changed to electric very early.'

One local gig that was very much to Charlie's distaste involved another local act, the early 'shock-rock' novelty turn Screaming Lord Sutch, when he played near the Wattses' home with his band the Savages, featuring their friend Andrew Wren on piano. Astute historians will know that the under-celebrated Wren had replaced the Savages' original pianist Nicky Hopkins, later a vital ingredient of so many classic recordings by the Rolling Stones and dozens of others. Wren, in turn, was soon to be briefly co-opted for both piano and vocal duties by Brian Jones in the embryonic rehearsals of what became the Stones, to be swiftly replaced by one Mike Jagger.

'We played a cricket match. I played for Charlie's company that he worked for down at Hayes,' remembers Roy Rootes. 'We were driving back and he said, "Andrew Wren's playing at Southall Community Centre, shall we go down and have a look?" So we did, and Lord Sutch was on, playing "Great Balls of Fire" and that sort of thing.' You must picture Sutch in his regular stage outfit, modelled after American eccentric Screamin' Jay Hawkins, of buffalo horns glued to a crash helmet with a wig on top, and a leopard-skin jacket with the sleeves cut off, borrowed from his auntie.

'Lord Sutch is running across and Andy Wren had a big fire bell,' says Rootes. 'There was so much smoke and rubbish on the stage, and all of a sudden [Wren] ran across and hit Lord Sutch across the head. His face was one mass of blood. It was only when we saw an ambulance outside that we realised it wasn't part of the act.' Charlie was suitably horrified.

Charlie was on duty for Blues Incorporated's first gig at the Ealing Club on 17 March 1962, alongside Korner on electric guitar, Davies on harmonica, Dave Stevens at the piano, Andy Hoogenboom on bass and Dick Heckstall-Smith on tenor saxophone. Korner and Davies had previously run their London Blues and Barrelhouse Club at the Roundhouse pub at the junction of Wardour Street and Brewer Street, where Davies earlier held the London Skiffle Club.

The Ealing Jazz Club, opened in 1959 at 42a The Broadway, opposite Ealing Broadway tube, now became the first true home of British rhythm and blues. Charlie was there again the following week when he met the 'other' Brian Jones (then a trad jazz fan living in Cheltenham), who in turn, two weeks later, was introduced to Mick and Keith. Seeds were being sown.

Fully 60 years on, and during preparations for the European tour that marked this anniversary, Mick and Keith are reminiscing with me about their very first memories of their lifelong friend. 'Yeah, the Ealing Club,' says Keith. 'Mick and I had driven up there because we'd heard about this club, and we're going, "Wow, rhythm and blues in London! We've got to check this."

'I couldn't see down to the other end of the stage, and I'm hearing this drummer. I'm trying to find a space to look at the stage, and there's this one little triangle between somebody's elbow and somebody's ass, and all I can see is this left hand on a perfect backbeat. And that was my introduction to the left hand of Charlie Watts, and listening to it and desperately trying to see what was on the other end of it.

'Finally I did get to see the little bugger, and Mick and I looked at each other and thought, "If we can pull some other strings, this is the man we've got to have." Alexis sometimes also played with Ginger Baker and Phil Seamen and some very well-known jazz drummers. But they didn't have that thing that Charlie had, that unique touch.'

Remembers Mick: 'I just watched him play at the Ealing Club. I'd never heard of him or any of those people. I'd never heard of Alexis Korner. I just went on Saturday night because it was a band you could go to. Charlie would be one of the drummers, there were others. That's how I met him.

'It was a very nice idea. You come in and bring your instrument and hope to play on three numbers. I would try and sing every Saturday, get at least two numbers. I'd play with him. I'd sing on my own, or Keith and I would do a number, but they frowned on that because it was too rock 'n' roll. But it was obviously the most popular thing of the evening, because it was the most danceable. Then I would sing with Brian doing 'Dust My Broom', or not.'

As usual, Charlie would underplay his own credentials and those of Blues Incorporated. At the same time he remembered the swift impact of those Ealing Club nights, and of a group that he would describe as 'a cross between R&B and Charles Mingus'. About 100 people turned up for the first one, in a 200-capacity room, but within four weeks they were turning people away. 'Alexis had the record in the club within about a month of playing, and I don't know why, because it wasn't a very cohesive band,' Charlie said.

'It was playing things that nobody in the band had heard. It was a totally different set of minds, really. It was only Cyril Davies and Alexis that really knew the songs we were playing. The rest of us were going blind at it. It was amazing, really, but people came.' Then from May, Blues Incorporated secured a Thursday-night residency at the Marquee, in the interval of the Chris Barber Band's show.

Away from the stage, Charlie turned 21 on 2 June 1962 as Elvis Presley continued to rule the British charts with 'Good Luck Charm'. Charlie marked his landmark birthday by throwing a party at the Green Man pub in Kingsbury. Sixty-plus years later, Brian 'Joe' Jones still had the letter that came with his invitation. It read (and the punctuation and other errors are Charlie's):

Dear Joe,

    I'm enclosing this note hoping you and Anne can make it on Saturday June 2nd all the Boys will be there.

    I would also like you to extend this invatation to your Mother and Father and to Terry and his Girl, as you can see its only at the Green MAN.

    Charlie.

PS – There will be a band there but if you want to bring your horn and have a blow later in the evening you quite welcome. See and hear from you soon.

Jones wrote back to say that he and Ann (without the 'e') were unable to attend because she had given birth to their daughter Sara only four days earlier.

Meanwhile, at the helm of Blues Incorporated, Korner and Davies were arguing about the precise direction and sound of the group – the latter favouring a Chicago blues style – and inevitably about money. 'I wasn't going to sit in the middle,' said Charlie. 'I was just the drummer ... I couldn't even join in the arguments because I didn't have a clue what they were talking about.

'I was playing with Cyril Davies, who was a straight Chicago, Jimmy Cotton, blues harp player. I'd never played with a harmonica player. The first time I played with Alexis I told him to keep quiet, because he had an amplifier about nine inches square and he hung it above my head in this coffee bar called the Troubadour. Still there, in Earl's Court. Very bohemian. I couldn't stand the noise. Ginger Baker was there that night, I remember.'

Some weeks later at the Marquee Club, on 12 July 1962, Blues Incorporated had to forfeit their now-headlining gig when they were offered a spot on the BBC's *Jazz Club* programme. Stepping into the gap were the formative Rollin' Stones, with Brian (going by the name 'Elmo Lewis' at the time), Mick and Keith, joined by stalwart pianist and, soon, beloved road manager Ian 'Stu' Stewart. With Dick Taylor on bass and either Mick Avory or, more probably, Tony Chapman on drums (depending on whose memory you rely on), they made their epoch-starting live debut.

'I knew them all,' said Charlie, 'because I'd played with Mick a few times with Alexis, who never had a [regular] singer. He had Ronnie Jones – an American guy – Paul Jones I think sang with Alexis then, and Mick did a few gigs. Keith sat in with us at Ealing, I remember that, and Brian I played with a few times.'

Charlie was there, as a punter, that July night and was able to look in on the world in which he would soon be entwined for a lifetime. After the *Jazz Club* show he headed to 165 Oxford Street, the original home of the Marquee. 'We [Blues Incorporated] did a radio broadcast, and I remember coming from Broadcasting House and going down the back stairs, or the side actually, of the Marquee, and standing in the doorway looking at Brian doing his Elmore James stuff with the slide.'

For all that, not everyone was overwhelmed. Harold Pendleton was the canny north of England businessman and trad jazz fan who established the Marquee. I interviewed him at a spry 89 in 2014, three years before his death. He recalled: 'Years ago, the BBC came to see me and said, "Someone asked me, when the Rolling Stones first appeared at your club, what did you think of them?" I said, "I was in the pub." We weren't licensed, and the real band, Cyril Davies's group, all went to the pub, and I went with them. The Stones were the interval group.' With the Jagger–Richards songwriting axis still far from realisation, the set list that night didn't feature a single original. There were covers of inspirations such as Jimmy Reed, Robert Johnson,

Muddy Waters and Chuck Berry. They drilled down even deeper for material by Little Willie Littlefield, Jay McShann and Billy Boy Arnold. The non sequitur was a version of 'Tell Me That You Love Me', a 1957 B-side by teen heart-throb Paul Anka.

This was a group still distinctly green around the edges, for whom 'Stu' would be taking bookings from his day job at ICI for some time to come, since none of the Stones were on the telephone. They gigged and rehearsed, augmenting their weekly Ealing Club residency with south London dates in Sutton, Cheam and Richmond, and a few further afield. All the while they were searching for a regular drummer, as the sticks passed from the unfavoured Tony Chapman (from the group Bill Wyman was playing in, the Cliftons) to Carlo Little, from Screaming Lord Sutch's outfit. Some gigs had no drummer at all.

Brian Jones was chasing Charlie, who held out, holding on to his semi-pro status and the income from his day job. Decades on he was still deflecting the suggestion that he had ever been in demand and, ultimately, head-hunted by the Stones. 'I've got no idea about that,' he said, one time I mentioned it. In another interview, he said he had been 'looking for a job … I was what actors call "between engagements".'

Not a bit of it, says Keith, thinking back to that first sighting. 'After that, of course, it was months of trying to persuade Charlie to throw in his lot with us,' he remembers. 'He said, "Look, I'd love to, but I need at least one steady gig a week, just to cover the costs." So then we scrambled for a few weeks until we managed to rack up another spare gig, and we proudly presented it to Charlie, "We have *two* gigs a week!" And he was in.'

Mick explains: 'We saw Charlie play with Alexis and said, "He'll be good." But he had a lot of little gigs. Alexis had a lot of drummers and he let everyone have a go, Ginger Baker or whatever. But we didn't have enough gigs, and we couldn't give anyone any money. As soon as we got a regular gig, like Richmond and Ealing and Ken Collier's, Charlie joined. He was just waiting for us to get enough. It took a while, but not that long. People like to mythologise all this stuff, but it was really that simple.'

Mick and Brian moved into one of the most famous fleapits in rock history, their flat in Edith Grove, Chelsea, soon to be joined by Keith. It's not always remembered that Charlie was with them too, for a while, in that 'beautiful dump,' as Keith called it. 'I used to live with Mick and Keith and Brian,' said Charlie, who would still go back to his parents' at weekends. 'It was in London, in the centre, it was easy, and it was a bloody laugh, actually.'

By mid-December 1962, after impressing the embryonic Stones at rehearsals with his amps more than his playing, Wyman was aboard, and Charlie was giving up his Blues Incorporated gig, characteristically claiming that he wasn't up to their level of musicianship. Come the new year, he had recommended another future drumming legend to be his replacement, and taken the plunge to join the

Rolling Stones. This despite the fact that his friends thought he'd gone mad, and he wasn't sure what his dad was going to say.

2

'Do You Think I Should Join This Interval Band?'

Peter Edward Baker first figured in Charlie Watts's life in the late 1950s. Already known by his nickname of 'Ginger', he was older by two years and had been drumming since 1954. They would not only have an important influence on momentous turning points in each other's careers, but formed a friendship that lasted until the very end.

Charlie and Ginger met at the revered folk club the Troubadour in Earl's Court, when the Stone-to-be was playing in a quartet there. 'He came in glaring at me,' Charlie told *Melody Maker* years later. The notion of Ginger being able to start a fight in an empty room will ring true to those of us who practically had to watch the documentary *Beware of Mr. Baker* from behind the sofa.

'He really is good,' Charlie continued. 'He was the nearest thing I have seen to a completely American player. Americans put it down the way they think it should go, and so does Ginger. He sounded more to me like Elvin Jones than Elvin does.' That was praise indeed: Charlie held the post-bop jazz drummer, best known as part of John Coltrane's quartet, in the highest regard. Charlie and a fellow A-lister and friend, Jim Keltner, even performed a 12-minute 'Elvin Suite' on their adventurous and imaginative 1996 collaboration *Charlie Watts Jim Keltner Project*, co-writing the piece with the Rolling Stones live band member and *Holland*-era Beach Boy, Blondie Chaplin.

'The relationship they had goes back to before I was born,' says Ginger's daughter Nettie, née Ginette. 'It was around the time my mum [Liz, who became Baker's first wife] and dad were first seeing each other, which was 1958. Charlie knew of my dad around the jazz scene, and they moved in the same circles.

'They lived close by, and they used to travel backwards and forwards on the Bakerloo Line [now in a section of the Jubilee Line] with my mum, all going from town back out to the suburbs. Charlie was in Kingsbury, they were in Neasden, so they took the same route and used to chat. They had that mutual adoration. No one could say a bad word about Charlie in our house.'

Like Charlie, Baker had forsaken an interest in graphic design to follow his beat. 'So they had a lot in common,' says his daughter. 'There was something about those early times that definitely bonded them, and that's very rare for my dad. I was walking around the sites of some of the old London clubs, and I knew that Dad had carried his drums in and out of Cy Laurie's, for example. It's important to know that Charlie was right there in those times as well.'

Baker lands in Charlie's story at this juncture because, when Charlie left Blues Incorporated, he recommended

Ginger as his replacement. As we've heard, Charlie felt he was struggling to keep pace with his bandmates. 'I left Alexis because he was heading off in a different direction,' he explained, 'and I could feel that I wasn't up to it. I said, "Ginger Baker should do this," and he took over from me. Ginger was seriously strong in those days. I remember the drum kit he used to play with Alexis – he had made it himself out of clear blue plastic, very avant-garde.' Charlie even helped Ginger set up his kit at his first rehearsal.

There was another reason for Charlie's departure, adds Nettie. 'He said to my dad, "It's not a secure future," and Dad said he thought that was hilarious. But that's when he gave him the Alexis gig.' The mutual appreciation was soon working the other way around too, when Ginger recommended Charlie to Brian Jones. 'My dad liked Brian, because he said he was a good musician,' explains Nettie. 'He said, "Your drummer is absolutely dire, Brian. Why don't you get Charlie Watts?" So he definitely repaid the compliment. With Charlie, my dad knew he had good jazz roots and maybe he thought he would bring something to the Stones. He did say, "I could see they were going to be very successful from the first time I saw them."'

Nettie was always aware of the unlikely friends' contrasting personalities. 'What can you say about someone who's just a really nice person?' she muses candidly. 'My dad is famously *not* a nice person, and yet they had this incredible close friendship. It was the same thing with Eric Clapton. He said, "Ginger never told me to fuck off, so that's why I got on with him. He was never like that to me." So they saw a completely different side of him. And I don't think being a nice person is a prerequisite for being a good artist.'

The nascent Stones lineup of Jagger, Richards, Jones, Ian 'Stu' Stewart and Dick Taylor knew who they wanted. 'We said, "God, we'd love that Charlie Watts if we could afford him,"' wrote Keith in *Life*. 'Because we all thought Charlie Watts was a God-given drummer. Stu put the feelers out. And Charlie said, "I'd love any gigs I can get, but I need money to hump those drums on the tube." He said, "If you can come back to me and say you've got a couple of solid gigs a week, I'm in."'

Ronnie Wood recounted the conversation between Charlie and Ronnie's older brother Art, with whom Charlie was also drumming at the Marquee. 'He said to Art, "I've got an offer to join this interval band called the Rolling Stones. What do you think I should do?" Charlie thought it would only last a week or two or something, but Art said, "Yeah, go for it. If you want to join this band, we'll give you a hand over with your drum kit."'

So it was that, even in the knowledge that his bank balance might take a hit, Charlie ultimately couldn't resist the Stones' offer. 'I was earning a comfortable living, which obviously was going to nosedive,' he said, as quoted in Bill Wyman's *Rolling with the Stones*. 'But I got to thinking about it. I liked their spirit and I was getting very involved with R&B. So I said OK.'

Dossing weekdays amid the squalor of the Edith Grove flat, Charlie was finding himself oddly seduced. He had given up his job at Charles Hobson and Grey Advertising, a newly fortified organisation after the 1962 purchase of Charles Hobson and Partners by the powerful New York firm Grey Advertising. But he was less and less inclined to make his living in art. 'I'd get up in the morning, and Brian and Keith would be snoring away, and I'd think, "I'm not going to an interview today. We're playing tonight anyway." Suddenly, I was in this band where everybody was clapping.'

A lifetime later, as the Stones' (mere) 50th anniversary approached in 2012, Mick Jagger made it clear that he had been doing a bit of personal research on the band's early chronology, back to that July 1962 starting point. He told me: 'I said to Charlie, "When was your first gig?" and he said, "January the year after."' Spot on. Tony Chapman was given the bad news after their gig at the Ricky-Tick in Windsor on the 11th, and just 24 hours later, back at the Ealing Club and with the group now six in number, Charlie was in the drum seat for the very first time.

Keith's diary entry about Charlie's debut performance expressed reservations. 'Maybe due to my cold but didn't sound right to me, but then Mick and Brian and myself still groggy from chills and fever!!!' (Even such a mundane thought was expressed in a song title: 'Chills and Fever' was a 1960 R&B track that had recently been covered by Jet Harris, and would provide Tom Jones's debut release.) Keith concluded: 'Charlie swings but hasn't got right sound yet. Rectify that tomorrow!' When I remind him of his comments, nine months after the drummer's passing, he cackles: 'What cheek!'

A few days later, Keith's diary records: 'Charlie swings very nicely but can't rock. Fabulous guy though ...' Keith added in his 2010 autobiography *Life*: 'He had not got rock and roll down at that time. I wanted him to hit it a little harder. He was still too jazz for me.'

The answer lay in the records of Jimmy Reed, the Mississippi bluesman whose impact on the Stones started early and never left: they covered him not just in the earliest days, but played 'The Sun Is Shining' at the infamous Altamont gig of 1969, his 'Little Rain' on the back-to-basics 2016 chart-topper *Blue & Lonesome* and 'Shame Shame Shame' at the December 2021 wake for Charlie at – where else? – Ronnie Scott's.

'Keith and Brian Jones and I, we used to sit and listen to Jimmy Reed numbers all day long when I first joined the Stones,' Charlie told me. 'I learned all the subtleties of the Reed stuff from hanging around them.' In 2003's *According to the Rolling Stones*, he added: 'I learned that Earl Phillips was playing on those records like a jazz drummer, playing swing, with a straight four.

'Freddy Below, on the other hand, played shuffle, which is what they did in Chicago. So on a lot of the Chuck Berry songs, which we turned into "straight eight" rhythms – which is what Chuck played – Freddy Below was playing four, four, swing, and the mixture when it hits right is incredible, but if it doesn't, one of you is going to be out of sync. So we learned to play the Freddy Below way.'

Keith was impressed at the style with which his new bandmate instinctively got himself in their groove. 'Amazingly, he started to listen to a lot of Chicago blues, necessarily, hanging with us,' he says. 'But with his intuitive pickup of what he was listening to, and what he was playing before, jazz and free, I was amazed that within a couple of weeks, he'd not only found the right things to do, but he was enjoying it. It was like he was learning something by joining the Stones, which was a pretty weird school.'

After an October 1962 tryout at a Highbury studio owned by session guitarist Curly Clayton, March 1963 had the group cutting demos for a second time, now under the aegis of their contemporary Glyn Johns. Beginning a lifetime in music in which he has consistently reaffirmed his standing as one of Britain's finest producers and engineers, Johns was working at IBC Recording Studios in Portland Place and was allowed to bring in the Stones to record in downtime. As he remembered in his *Sound Man* memoir, they were already cooking, thanks in no small part to the rhythm section.

'I thought the results were tremendous,' he wrote. 'I had finally got to record the music that had inspired me so much on my American pal Pat's Jimmy Reed album. They sounded like the real deal. I remember being particularly impressed by Brian Jones's harmonica playing, and the extraordinary feel and sound that Charlie and Bill got, and it goes without saying, Stu's piano playing.'

In Charlie's first six months the Stones played live 91 times, across London from central gigs like Soho's Flamingo, the Scene Club and Marquee, north to Harringay Jazz Club, south to the Red Lion in Sutton and Guildford's Wooden Bridge Hotel, and west to the Ricky-Tick in Windsor and Twickenham's Eel Pie Island. One famous early residency had a particular place in his memory. 'The time I must have really been impressed must have been when we used to do the Crawdaddy when it moved from the pub,' he said. 'This is looking back so I could completely be wrong, but we moved from the pub to the athletic thing [when the club upscaled to the Richmond Athletic Ground in June 1963]. I can remember Mick dancing in there, we used to play every Sunday.

'We used to play at Ken Colyer's club opposite Leicester Square tube station, and we'd go from there to the athletic club. They were our two gigs. That kept us going, actually, for a while. But we always got more and more people. We're very fortunate like that.' It was at the Crawdaddy, he recalled, that the Stones became 'a cult', whipping up the crowd with sets that ended, he said, in a 'gyrating riot'.

In May 1963 the group signed to Decca Records, and within weeks their rudimentary but exuberant cover of Chuck Berry's 'Come On' was their debut Decca single, even if its connection to their live sound was tenuous at best. 'We never did it as good as Chuck Berry, nobody ever does,' Charlie remembered. 'His is a very hip version, actually. The rhythm is great. It's like a New Orleans rhythm he plays, it's fantastic. We played it straight, like a Liverpool beat group. When we were young, we played things bloody fast. You never thought about it then,' he added with a laugh.

Before the 45 was even out, *Record Mirror*'s Norman Jopling wrote the first, influential national music paper piece on the group, reporting that they were packing them in at the Station Hotel in Richmond. This was where the 'hip kids throw themselves about to the new "jungle music" … and the combo they writhe and twist to is called the Rollin' Stones. Maybe you've never heard of them – if you live very far away from London, the chances are you haven't.' The drummer, wrote the pop weekly, was Charles Watts. He was weeks from taking the next plunge: turning professional.

Bill Wyman, sitting in his front room in Chelsea in 2022, speaks about his friend with palpable veneration. 'When Charlie joined, he was a jazz musician, and he always talked about the jazz people,' he says. 'The only jazz people I knew at that time were Fats Waller, who I loved, and still do, and Dizzy Gillespie and Gerry Mulligan. I'd heard a few things, and they were OK, but it wasn't my forte. But at least we could talk about that. He went much deeper into other jazz musicians I wasn't aware of at the time. So there was a bit of a gap. But musically, we just hit it off right away.'

Charlie was no rock 'n' roll devotee, but it didn't matter. 'He wasn't, but he could do the shuffle, and that was so important in our stuff,' says Bill, 'because all the other bands were playing eighths and 16ths, da-da-da-da, Bits-and-Pieces, She-Loves-You, they're all like that. And we're playing da-dum-da-dum, "Down the Road Apiece" and all that stuff. Charlie was brilliant at that, because he was a jazz drummer, and so we were streets ahead of anybody that ever wanted to imitate us. They never could quite get the feel we had.

'When we started,' he goes on, 'it was the three Bs, wasn't it – Chris Barber, Acker Bilk and Kenny Ball. They were the traditional jazz, and that was everywhere, in all the clubs. We were the first band that went into those clubs *not* play-ing traditional jazz, and that's why the traditional jazz people didn't like us. And when we started to get a bit more applause than they were getting, we got banned from every jazz club in London, and we had to go to Richmond, and Twickenham, and Windsor, because there was nowhere else to play in London. The Jazz Federation just blocked us. But we were bloody good in those days. We were better live than any other band, and we continued to do that.'

'He was playing very much like black drummers playing with Sam and Dave and the Motown stuff, or the soul drummers,' wrote Keith of Charlie in *Life*. 'He has that touch. A lot of the time very correct, with the sticks through the fingers, which is how most drummers now play. If you try to get savage you're off. It's a bit like surfing: it's OK while you're up there. And because of that style of Charlie's, I could play the same way. One thing drives another in a band; it all has to melt together. Basically it's all liquid.'

Charlie went on to reflect on the contrast between the crossover appeal of the Stones' early recordings and their personal taste for deep, down-home blues. 'We did a lot of terribly commercial things on record. You know, "Money", "Come On" were never in our agenda, if you know what I mean, that we played in clubs. That was much more Bo Diddley stuff, and Muddy Waters.'

The big money was still some way off, but the new addition to the group's kit from July 1963 was a map of England. This was when they set off for the Alcove Club in Middlesbrough to begin a gruelling three-month spell of 78 shows in 76 days, now not just across London but up and down the UK, from Morecambe to Margate, Prestatyn to Peterborough, and Wisbech to Woking. Often, on their return, it was all back to Charlie's, who was still living at home at weekends.

'When he came home,' says his sister Linda, 'I'd get a knock on the door: "The boys are staying," Keith and Bill and that. They were all very friendly. They'd all be sitting down eating bacon sandwiches and having cups of tea. Dad and I had to go to work the next morning, and Charlie's asleep until about lunchtime.'

By November, with 'I Wanna Be Your Man' gifted to them by Lennon and McCartney for their second single, the Stones' rapid rise was such that *Record Mirror* was running a weekly 'A Rolling Stone Writes' on each member in turn. As they continued their first big UK tour, with Little Richard and Bo Diddley, Charlie's entry had him describing Bill Wyman's birthday party, at which the entire gathering 'had a great session with Jimmy Reed records'.

In an era in which many such columns were, of course, ghost-written, there's a certain ordinariness about the tone of Charlie's piece that makes it sound rather believable. 'I cannot work out whether I had had too much to drink or not,' he shared, 'but I could not believe my eyes when the coach driver proceeded to eat a glass at the party. Still, strange things do happen.' More solemnly, he updated readers that the name plate from their van had now disappeared completely.

In May 1964, their star now soaring, *Record Mirror* reader Graham Prout wrote from Aberdeen to share the result of the Stones' popularity contest he and his friends had held locally. Mick came top, but only narrowly ahead of Charlie. Keith came last.

In no time, Charlie's unassuming partnership with Bill was making them a rock-solid rhythm section, and they formed an unbreakable bond on and off the pitch, so to speak. Bill was frank with me in his assessment of their friendship. 'I'm OCD,' he said. 'I have to have things in the right order. All my records have to be alphabetical. Everything I do has to be either numerical or alphabetical. You know, because you know about my archive. And Charlie was even worse.' ('I am fastidious,' Charlie told *Esquire* in 1998, 'but not as fastidious as Bill Wyman.')

Charlie's sister Linda recalls visiting him decades later at his London residence, when his granddaughter Charlotte was also there. 'She had a tangerine,' she says. 'She peeled it, and the peel was on the table. In two seconds, he picked it up. They used to call it St Vitus' dance. My gran used to say, "He's got worms, that boy." It's just how he was made.' Adds her husband Roy: 'We were there one Sunday, and someone delivered a CD. The shelf was full, and he must have spent 25 minutes trying to find a space for this CD. Move this one, move that one, and we're all standing there looking at him.' 'He was a bit like that at home,' says Linda. 'He was never untidy. You hung your coat up, you never put it on a chair.'

Mick Jagger explained amusingly that at the end of a show, his bandmate would only join him, Keith and Ronnie stage front to take a bow when he had finished fiddling with his drumsticks, arranging them into a neat row before he would leave the stool. When he was the victim (the word is used advisedly) of *Desert Island Discs*, he said a friend had pointed out that his would be the neatest island ever.

Laughs Charlotte: 'What should have been a ten-minute walk in the countryside would turn into half an hour because he'd be tidying the side of the road. Like twigs, and pushing pebbles off the side, and put them in the under-growth. I'd be like, "*Come on*!!"

'I always believed that he had OCD. It was really enter-taining,' she continues. 'We would mess with him. I can remember getting home and going down to the dressing room and moving one pair of socks and swapping it over with another pair. They'd be colour-coded. You'd time how long before you heard "Who's touched my stuff!!" from down the stairs. "Oh no, it wasn't me." I broke the espresso machine once and wrote a note in bad handwriting saying sorry from my stepdad. "Sorry I broke the coffee machine, from Barry." So much fun.'

Charlie was entertainingly forthright the first time his relationship with Bill Wyman came into our conversation, in 1991. 'Bill's got a wonderful sense of humour. But certain things bother him that I (a) wouldn't even think about, and (b) would have forgotten about. I don't know half of what he's talking about. If Bill says on the 4th of August 1963 we weren't paid for playing at wherever, well the bloke still owes us the money, and it irks him. For 30 years, he's harboured this resentment.' He added with clear affection: 'He's an angry young man, that one.'

'I don't know why,' reflects Bill, 'but then we became this great rhythm section that everybody admired, and we were always on time, always ready, always available, always sober, and they could always rely on us. We were the bedrock that they just went loony on, basically. If you ever see any of the videos, you can see me and Charlie at the back laughing at them, when they're doing all that crazy stuff they used to do, jumping off beds and going through walls and things.'

But as Bill remembers, the Stones' first British itineraries, especially outside London, were nothing short of an ordeal. 'Whenever we were doing gigs in London or coming back from a concert in, I don't know, Sheffield or Nottingham, we'd end up in London late, and then the boys would go on to the Ad Lib or somewhere, but Charlie and I would go home. I had a little boy, Stephen, eight months old when I joined the band, and I was in south London, so I had to go down there. Charlie was in the prefab with his parents in Wembley, and when he married Shirley, of course he had a flat. He'd go back home to her, and we wouldn't be partying all the time.

'So we were always pretty level headed, and I think that was very good for us. I think that's why neither of us got into drugs. In those days, sometimes it was almost impossible to stay awake, because we'd be driving in that bloody Volkswagen van of Stu's all over England. Sometimes we wouldn't eat, we wouldn't sleep, we'd travel from Lowestoft to bloody Llandudno, overnight, so you never got any sleep, you never got any food, because there weren't places open in those days.

'And you'd end [up] there early in the daytime, you had nothing to do, you had to play that night and then go up to Manchester after that gig, overnight again, to do *Top of the Pops* or one of those bloody things, and you'd sleep on the floor in one of the rooms. You'd ask the guy to let you in, he'd say, "It's closed, it doesn't open until 9 o'clock," and we'd say, "Yeah but we need sleep, *please* let us in and just let us sleep in one of the rooms," and we used to just lay on the floor and get three hours' sleep before we got woken up.

'It was insane, and you'd finish that and then you'd have to drive all the way back down to London, then drop them off one by one, and then finish with me down in Beckenham at like six in the morning. It was like that day after day after day. It was a nightmare, and I got so drawn, my features got really sunken, if you see all those early pictures. But we had such a friendship, me and Charlie.'

We know the script of the Stones' insanely intense year of 1964: 206 gigs in all, with four British tours, their first two in America, the debut LP, endless TV and radio sessions (including a slot on the first-ever *Top of the Pops* with 'I Wanna Be Your Man'), and three UK singles, including their first No. 1s with 'It's All Over Now' and 'Little Red Rooster'. 'That was the only blues record ever to make No. 1,' said Charlie with a certain pride in 2013, 'which I never knew, but somebody said it, someone like Bill Wyman. It's amazing when you think about it. I don't know how many blues records I play and love, and they're nothing in chart terms.'

In January they flew to a gig for the first time, to play Barrowlands in Glasgow. But the next night they played 275 miles away in Mansfield; the next, another 100 to Bedford; the next, a mere 85 to Swindon. But with every gig the Stones enhanced their reputation as the most exciting live attraction in the UK and, soon, far beyond.

'If you ever saw the Beatles, there was nothing about projection with them,' said Charlie. 'It was like four guys standing there … it was nothing to see, you just went for the name. Even when we played in Richmond, we used to have a stage as big as the carpet, but Mick's always been able to project, and you need that.'

Adds Bill: 'I still say the Beatles wrote better songs than us, and they sang better than us, but we were so much better than them live. And they were always nervous about going on the same venue as us, like at the [September 1963] Pop Prom at the Royal Albert Hall, and the *NME* [Poll-Winners' Concert, April 1964]. They used to talk about it later, and tell us. We were nervous of them, because we knew the massive adulation they had. So there was a mutual admiration society really, and that's why we were such good friends. And the music was totally different, so we weren't in each other's way.'

March 1964 brought the collector's item that latter-day commentators often overlook: the one Rolling Stones show that Charlie definitely missed. It happened after the completion of a sprawling British tour that they looked to have outgrown even when it started, in the middle of a bill headlined by John Leyton, whose biggest hits with 'Johnny Remember Me' and 'Wild Wind' were more than two years old, and Mike 'Come Outside' Sarne, whose chart shelf life was also expiring fast.

On 7 March, after the last of 33 exhausting dates, two shows a night, Wyman recalls that he and his family had a few days off in the New Forest, while Mick and his steady, Chrissie Shrimpton, went to Paris. Charlie and his girlfriend Shirley Shepherd went on holiday to Gibraltar. All very well deserved, except that the drummer was still there when the next gig, at the Invicta Ballroom in Kent, relentlessly arrived just eight days after the last. At least, that was the band's version. Charlie's was more convoluted.

'I missed one show because I got the wrong date,' he said in *The Rolling Stones: A Life on the Road*. 'The others all say no, I didn't, [that] I stayed on holiday an extra day, but I didn't. Micky Waller [who had played with Cyril Davies and Marty Wilde, and later recorded with Rod Stewart, among others] played the drums, really well, much to my chagrin. I remember distinctly walking in and someone saying, "Where were you?" I said, "I was in Gibraltar last night." We'd been in Catford or somewhere and everyone was raving about Micky.'

Later in the year it seems Charlie was also missing for most of an impromptu club set by the group while they were back in Liverpool, for two shows at the Empire and others in the surrounding area. *Mersey Beat* editor Bill Harry wrote of an evening at the city's Blue Angel nightspot at which they were moved to play spontaneously, with Charlie's absence covered by Brian Low, drummer with Scottish group the Blue System.

Harry wrote: 'A close friend of [the Stones'], Denny Flynn, told me that Charlie was at an antique dealer's house in West Derby discussing antique guns, of which he's a collector.' It's an excuse that certainly has the ring of truth. 'At the sound of the music, everyone from upstairs came down to watch, and later on Charlie Watts came into the club. He sat down near the front of the stage listening for a moment, but the excitement of the music was too much and he took his place on the drums.'

The editor also asked Low what it was like to take Charlie's part. 'It's great to play with them, of course, but it's difficult to explain,' he said. 'What they're doing is comparatively simple, it isn't highly technical, but the feeling is so fantastic that you find yourself being in it. They're not fantastic musicians but you're playing with fellows who feel inside and it makes *you* feel inside, too. Let's face it, they all know what they're doing. It's great. Their music just has a great, great feeling.'

Keith Richards was sounding almost impossibly innocent when he (or perhaps it was a ghostly Andrew Loog Oldham) told *Beat Instrumental* of the Stones' on-stage cohesion. In the November 1964 issue, with Charlie on the cover, he wrote: 'It's just one big circle really. But the one person who mustn't make a mistake is old Charlie at the back. If he got confused and gave us the wrong beat, we'd be up a gum tree!'

He went on: 'You see, we never do a song exactly the same way twice. Mick is a great improviser. He sings every number exactly the way he feels it, and that means that if he sings one number seven times in one week, it comes over seven different ways. That's why I often turn to face Charlie in the middle of a number. He's always stuck at the back of the stage and with the fantastic "whoosh" of sound coming from the audience he has to lip read what Mick is singing most of the time.

'When I think he can't possibly know what Mick is doing, I turn round and give him the beat so that he's OK for the next bar. Like I said, it's a big circle. Charlie takes his cue from Mick; Brian, Bill and I take it from Charlie and Mick takes it from the lot of us.'

One of my favourite of the many beautifully described (if probably embroidered) stories that Keith has told me was not directly about Charlie, although you can well imagine his part in it and think how much you would have paid to see it. In the madness of those early tours, in 1964 and again in 1965, the Stones' schedule took them to the ABC Cinema in Chester. By now, the fan hysteria at their gigs was both deafening and dangerous. Keith recalled that the screams drowned out their music to the extent that they amused themselves by playing 'Popeye the Sailor Man'.

Ever more intricate tactics had to be employed to get the group out of the building and away in one piece, as rabid teenage girls forced them into a hasty retreat. 'It was madness,' said Keith. 'In the middle '60s, it would be, "How are we getting into the theatre?" and "How are we getting out?"

'We knew on stage it would last maybe ten minutes at most, before it became a shambles, a riot, and the Red Cross is there with these stretchers for these poor girls, sweating with all their dresses up in the air. And you wonder what the hell you're doing there. It's like some Hieronymus Bosch painting in front of your eyes, and that's the *audience*.

'This one time in Chester, it was the Chief Constable of Chester, in full regalia, with the ribbons and the medals and the swagger stick. Show's finished earlier than he expected. The whole theatre is surrounded. Mayhem. Maniac teenage girls, bless their hearts. "Right," he says. "The only way out, up the stairs, over the rooftops, I know the way!" Suddenly you're in his hands, because he's got a few constables with him.

'So we get up on the Chester rooftops, and it's raining. The first thing that happens is the Chief Constable almost slides off the roof. A couple of his bobbies managed to hold him up. We're standing in the middle of this rooftop saying, "I'm not too familiar with this area, where do we go?!"

'He pulled himself together, and in a shambolic sort of way they managed to finally get us down through a skylight and out of a laundry chute, or something, I don't know. That was what happened every day, and you took this as normal. Everything was a Goon Show. Spike Milligan and the Pythons would have loved to be there.'

There are many similar quaint stories of these gangling first days of stardom. At the Stones' show at the Odeon in Cheltenham in September 1964, the 'merch' opportunity was a chap in a sports jacket outside hawking black and white photographs of the group for two shillings and sixpence. Trevor Lewis delivered fruit and veg for George Vic's local greengrocery, and managed to corner Charlie, Brian and Bill on their way in to the Odeon. He got their autographs, but only on a paper bag from the shop. Lewis cycled back to Vic's with his prize, put it aside while he visited the bathroom, only to be told on his return that the shop assistant had filled it with a pound of tomatoes for a customer.

Bill recalled another episode of fan-dodging at which Charlie's obsessive tendencies came to the fore. 'When we used to run off stage, we had to get out while they were playing "God Save the Queen",' he said. 'They all had to stand, and we had, like, two minutes to get out to the police car, or the Black Maria or whatever was getting us away. We'd all go tearing down the corridors, and I'd run behind Charlie. The others are way ahead of me, and we're going down three steps, and he stops and comes back up, and I go arse over head because he wanted to do the steps again. I went flying and they had to carry me out. And there were so many moments like that.'

Sometimes, at least, it was possible to hide in plain sight. In the spring of 1966, with the wildfire of Stones mania crackling worldwide, their time in Hollywood for recording sessions at RCA Studios had untamed fans searching frantically for all five group members – completely missing Charlie, as *KRLA Beat* reported, sitting in the big glass window of a restaurant, having a Coke with his friend, composer and arranger Jack Nitzsche.

Almost every aspect of Charlie's unique personality revealed him to be the precise opposite of the rock hero he represented to millions. There may never have been another musician of such global stature who spent so long stoically putting up with the very trappings of global success that most artists dream of. On our first meeting in 1991 I naively asked him whether he got excited on the eve of a tour. His unvarnished answer was the one he had no doubt been giving for all the decades past, and certainly for those to come.

'No, never am. I hate it. I've always hated it,' he said, without rancour. 'For 30 years I've never liked to get up in the morning. My idea of working is to get up and go across the road to Ronnie Scott's, play till three in the morning, come home and go to bed. That to me is doing a job. This sort of two-hour Wembley Stadium job, I've never ever liked it. *Doing it* is wonderful. The feeling of having that many people there is wonderful.

'One of the horrors for me is, two days before you leave, looking at that suitcase and deciding what's going in it. Actually it's not two days, it's a week I have to sit there and decide what's going in the bloody thing. But there is no way I can play the drums at home. I can't sit with the piano and work out scores. Whatever I do is in front of X amount of people, two, or 10,000, and you get paid ten shillings or whatever. A lot of other instruments you can, but sitting there whacking about on drums, I can't think of anything more boring in my life.'

Therein lay the quandary of being trapped in a bubble of unrequested adulation and, for so long, endless months away from home. 'It always amazes me that (a) people want to go and (b) that we're bothered to do it,' he told me. 'But for me, it is my living.'

Keith's take on that compromise was typically thoughtful and eloquent. 'We're musicians, and at the same time you've got to deal with other people just looking on you as some pop star, and you've got to try and reconcile the two things,' he said. 'You've got to say, "We asked for it, we put our arses and faces out there and they went for it," so you've got to deal with that.

'But we ain't here just to stay famous, for Christ's sake. I had enough of that. To me, and probably Charlie, it's a price you willingly pay for being able to do what you want to do. The fact that we're all still stuck here together and still enjoying it, I'll take that as a blessing.'

Brian Wilson certainly wasn't the only integral contributor to pop culture who just wasn't made for these times. Charlie often came across as a bemused but benign traveller making the best of a most unexpected life, swatting away unwanted attention as politely as his good manners would always demand.

Backstage in Amsterdam in 2006, halfway through the 147-date *A Bigger Bang* tour that was two years from start to finish – albeit with some parole for good behaviour – Charlie described his daily routine of attempted sanity. 'Normally I try and get out, but if you can't get out the front door, it's very difficult,' he said.

'Show days are the worst. Other days aren't so bad. It used to be autographs, now it's "Can I take a picture with the mobile?" It's endless, and I'm one that walks out the front door and walks along streets, see. So you've got all of them trooping after you. It's easier to stay in. But I usually get up early and go out then.'

By then, he had already had more than four entire decades on the run. All those years of music's quintessential trade-off. As he explained: 'A long time ago now, I call it the Beatle period, when people used to scream at you – I used to hate that. Nothing worse for me. I used to hide in bakers' shops, girls running down the road. Used to drive me mad. But there's nothing like walking on a stage and the whole place is full of screaming girls leaping up and down.'

BACKBEAT

Shirley Is My Darling

Shirley Ann Shepherd, born in London on 11 September 1938, was a student of sculpture at Hornsey College of Art when she met Charlie Watts on his return from Denmark early in 1962. He had taken up Alexis Korner's offer of a rehearsal with Blues Incorporated, and Shirley, nearly three years older than him, came with the band's bassist Andy Hoogenboom and his wife Jeanette. Hoogenboom and pianist Keith Scott were her fellow students at Hornsey. She became Charlie's greatest constant and, quite simply, the love of his life.

Nettie Baker, daughter of Charlie's great friend Ginger, says that her mother would recall how the young Charlie would confess his fears to her. 'He used to say, "Oh, no one will ever go out with me, *for me*. Will I find the right girl?" My mum used to say, "You'll be fine, Charlie."' She was right.

Shirley was in and around the Rolling Stones' gigs and rehearsals from the early days, as their great studio compadre Glyn Johns recounts. 'My earliest memory of Charlie is the Stones doing a radio broadcast for the BBC, which I attended for some reason or other,' he says, laughing. 'There'd been a bit of an upset between Shirley and Charlie, and I remember very clearly sitting with him and trying to calm him down, and doing the same thing with Shirley, trying to appease the situation. I don't know why I remember that particularly, but I do. I was terribly fond of both of them, I have to say.'

These were the days when – as John Lennon also knew from his relationship with *his* art college girlfriend Cynthia Powell – pop stars were always advised to be, or appear to be, single and available to their female fans. Charlie may have feared the wrath of Stones kingmaker Andrew Loog Oldham, but he and Shirley were both devoted and determined.

On 14 October 1964, three days after the completion of yet another Stones UK tour at the Brighton Hippodrome (and as 'It's All Over Now' came to the end of its three-month chart stay), they were married at Bradford Register Office. The ceremony was witnessed by Andy and Jeanette Hoogenboom, and after a champagne lunch at a country pub near Ripon, the newlyweds came back to London by train.

'He didn't want the band to know because he was scared of Andrew and all that,' says Bill Wyman, 'so they kept it secret for about three weeks, [then] the press released it. He still denied it for the first couple of days, and then he owned up and that was all right.'

Early Stones associate Jimmy Phelge, quoted in Oldham's *2Stoned*, said that when that news seeped out there was trouble. 'When Mick, Keith and Andrew were confronted with it they stood stunned in near-disbelief. The band was going from strength to strength and news of the marriage could jeopardise this success for everyone concerned.

'There was still a considerable stigma attached to pop stars who were married – many people thought this heralded the beginning of the end. Keith saw Charlie's marriage, to begin with at least, as a treasonable act. After the initial shock, the final verdict was that the deed was done and that the only sensible course of action was to live with it. Andrew hoped that having two married Stones [Bill having previously tied the knot] would not adversely affect the group's fortunes.' The beautiful irony of the situation was that, just a month earlier, Oldham had disappeared for a few days to Scotland, and come back married.

Bill recalls that it was a reporter from the *Daily Express* who asked Charlie outright whether he and Shirley were married. 'I emphatically deny I am married,' he replied. 'It would do a great deal of harm to my career, if the story got around.' But the new Mrs Watts, when it was her turn to speak, could not tell a lie. 'We have wanted to marry for about a year, and just didn't dare,' she confessed. 'The months went on and we decided we could not live separately any longer.

'I'm terribly happy being Charlie's wife. It's just wonderful,' she went on. 'I really don't know what it's like being married to a Stone yet. We have only spent five days together in all and then we couldn't be seen out together. My parents like him an awful lot. I intend to finish my college course and, in about 18 months' time, I may teach. It's all a bit up in the air at the moment.'

Thankfully, if there ever had been any appreciable damage to a group's marketability caused by the shocking concept of marriage, it was already becoming an outmoded idea. As it happened, Shirley ended her formal studies but continued with her sculpture, as the couple moved into a flat in Ivor Court, just off the south-west side of Regent's Park. They soon gave it the look of an artist's studio, reflecting their tastes.

When photographer Bent Rej came to the apartment to take pictures in May 1965, he found a happy scene, even if the couple were only able to make all-too-brief time for themselves in between the Stones' latest tours of America and the UK. Rej wrote: 'Shirley and Charlie are very much in love, they confess. So much that she follows him around the world most of the time. That is why you find four ready-packed trunks in one of the rooms.

'"They are always ready for us," Charlie explains. "When we are at home we can't waste time packing and unpacking. We want to relax and enjoy being at home. We are always longing for London and what I look forward to most of all when we are touring is Shirley's cooking."' Added the photographer: 'His favourite dishes are oriental and even if he is not much of a cook himself you will always find him with his nose in the pots when Shirley is preparing dinner. The only thing he does himself, whether at home or on the road, is the tea.'

Shirley was in the party for some early Stones tours, such as the Scandinavian shows in March and April of 1965 during the band's first European jaunt, when the couple would often go exploring on their own in between gigs. On his own in a shop in Copenhagen, Charlie bought Shirley horse figurines, an early reflection of the equine passions that would lead to her becoming a breeder of Halsdon Arabian horses in later years on their 600-acre stud farm in Devon.

That began with Charlie, too: 'He showed me a photograph of an Arab stallion and I fell in love,' she told *Horse & Hound* in 2002. 'Charlie bought me my first Arab, which was a part-bred, and it spiralled from there.' At one time the herd grew to nearly 300. 'The original intention was to have 20,' she told *Arabian Horse Times*. 'I'm not good with maths.' Charlie mentioned the number to Stones keyboard player Chuck Leavell, who observed: 'Man, that's a lot of hay.'

There were, inevitably, many times when Shirley wasn't on the road with Charlie. He would still go shopping, as in Paris in 1964 when he ducked into an art store and started looking through Picasso and Buffet prints to take back. But as his equally well-behaved bandmate Bill Wyman remembers, the drummer's sadness without his wife was tangible.

'He'd spend all his money on the early tours in the '60s, when we didn't earn hardly anything, on phone calls home,' he says. 'His phone bills were massive. Phoning from Australia, for three hours every night, it was ridiculous in those days. You'd go home with $7,000 each or something at the end of the tour and he would have spent $10,000 on phone calls.'

'She is an incredible woman,' Charlie once said of his wife. 'The one regret I have of this life is that I was never home enough. But she always says when I come off tour that I am a nightmare and tells me to go back out.' Wrote *Rave* magazine in 1966: 'His three obsessions in life are his drumming, his antique collection (which mostly consists of old guns) and his wife Shirley. No wife had a more devoted husband.'

Shirley's early quote about loving life as Charlie's wife hinted at a meekness that she was soon disproving. She was very much her own woman, and indeed on one occasion in the early 1970s her feistiness got her arrested, at Nice airport, allegedly for hitting customs officers. She received a suspended sentence.

In an early 1967 interview with *Melody Maker* Charlie was clearly pleased to reveal her fearless character. 'You know, I think my wife Shirley was the first woman ever to answer Mick intelligently. It was quite a funny incident. Mick has very strong ideas about politics and philosophy, and he'd never taken much notice of girls' opinions before. It was quite funny to see him when Shirley answered back. It was one of his ideas smashed.'

* * *

Tony King has had a vividly colourful life, the like of which the music business couldn't possibly create anymore. When Charlie and Shirley's daughter Seraphina was born in 1968, King was already a significant wheel in the machinery of the British music industry and such a close family friend that he became her godfather. Starting at Decca Records in 1958, he was a promotions manager while he was still in his teens, going on to work with visiting notables from Roy Orbison to Phil Spector. King was in the Rolling Stones' milieu through his friendship with Oldham, who appointed him head of promotion when he launched his independent label Immediate Records.

He later became general manager at the Beatles' Apple Records and an executive at Rocket for Elton John, whom he later rejoined. Via other important roles, and having already known all of the Stones for more than 20 years, he arrived in Mick Jagger's orbit during the singer's solo sojourn of the 1980s. This led King back to the Stones, with whom he was a vital facilitator on and off the road for the next quarter-century, the public face of the band who would guide the interviewer's way to rehearsal space or hotel room.

Soon after turning 80 in 2022, and completing work on a must-read memoir to be titled *The Tastemaker*, King talked about his long personal history with Mr and Mrs Watts. 'They were a huge part of my life as a family, from the word go, when I first met them in Ivor Court, when they were along the corridor from Andrew,' he says. 'Then they moved to Lewes to the Old Brewery House, and I used to go and visit them at weekends. We were starting to become friends, and Shirley and I got on very well. I think it was more Shirley and me to start with. Charlie thought I was the gayest man he ever met at first – he told me that later on.'

The friendship continued as Charlie and Shirley moved just outside Lewes to Peckhams in Halland, which had belonged to John Peckham, Archbishop of Canterbury, in the late 13th century. 'They used to have lots of costume [parties], and I remember one with Chrissie Shrimpton when she was going out with Mick. Then Mick came down with Marianne [Faithfull] one day. He had his electric guitar out on the lawn and was playing, Charlie was drumming and Marianne was sitting talking to Shirley. It was lovely.

'One weekend I was down there and we had an Elizabethan fancy dress party. Mick came, and Mick Taylor came, and they ended up with the same outfit. We had a really great time. Charlie got so drunk, he ended up with his arms around the toilet.'

King remembers one particular example of Charlie's brilliantly deadpan humour. 'The next day, he had to go up to London to record with the Stones in Barnes, at Olympic. The car came to pick him up and I was standing outside the house, and he went past and wound down the window and said to me, "Hi ho, hi ho ...". That's all he said. He didn't have to say the rest. He knew the impact.'

Charlie and Shirley's 1971 move, with three-year-old Seraphina in tow, was to La Bourie, a farm in Massiès near Thoiras, a small village between Anduze and Saint-Jean-du-

Gard in the Cévennes region in the south of France. It may have been visited upon the family because of the band's parlous tax affairs, but the property became a cherished retreat, and one that they kept and returned to for the rest of Charlie's life.

The mayor of Saint-Jean-du-Gard, Michel Ruas, said of him: 'Charlie and his wife were very approachable. We could easily talk to them. His daughter Seraphina was even educated in Saint-Jean-du-Gard. The locals all knew they had a home here in the heart of the Cévennes.'

'It was a converted goats' farm – they made chèvre in there,' says King. 'It was a beautiful, idyllic paradise, and I used to go there on holidays and have wonderful times. Then of course they came back to England and ended up in Dolton in Devon. So I've travelled with them through all the different homes and years. Seraphina came along and she meant everything to them. Then of course later on along comes Charlotte. Everybody loved her.'

In the post-*Steel Wheels* era of gigantic stadia and audiences by the scores of thousands, the Stones' tours ballooned to two-year epics, the prospect of which Charlie found traumatic. 'They took him away from home, and he didn't like that,' says Bill. 'He said, "I'm not touring anymore" and they said, "You are." It took a while to get him to say all right, and then he'd go. But he didn't like it.'

In 2002, just ahead of the band's 40th-anniversary *Licks* tour, which played over 100 shows across more than a year, Charlie told me how the process regularly began, and

Shirley's part in it. 'Mick or Keith will usually say something, I'll discuss it with my wife, and then we have a meeting and say we'll go, and it's usually a year away,' he said, noting his close involvement with all of the tour visuals. 'The work will start nine months before with stages and then merchandising, and it builds up and builds up. Now there are books of stuff you have to OK.'

Lisa Fischer was a fabulous addition to the Stones family when she came on board as backing singer on albums and tours, and Mick's exhilarating vocal and visual foil, circa *Steel Wheels* in 1989. She also had to show plenty of mental resolve as the only woman in the performing band. When I tell her about Charlie spending a fortune on calls home in the old days, it strikes a chord.

'That so makes sense to me,' she says, 'because he was not the hanger-out. You would never see him downstairs at the bar. It wasn't his thing. He would just disappear to his room and that would be that until the next day. He just seemed like whenever Shirley came to a show, he was as happy as he could be. They were like two little schoolkids. He'd take her hand, and she'd be beautiful and demure with those blue eyes. Just beautiful.

'I would look at his ring. It was silver, and it was a man and woman entwined, but you wouldn't know it unless you looked deeply at it. I believe that was his wedding ring, and I just thought it was so romantic. So subtle, but so sensual at the same time. It was like two people being water together.'

King agrees that when the Watts family came out on the tour, his whole demeanour changed. 'Shirley would show up, and Seraphina, and many years hence, [granddaughter] Charlotte. There was always a different feeling when Shirley arrived. Charlie was always very relaxed. He used to draw everything, he's got his books of drawings of everything, doorknobs and telephones. When Shirley arrived, he would draw her lying on the bed reading *The Sunday Times*, or something like that.

'If Shirley showed up, he was always happy to see her, and if Seraphina showed up, sometimes with Shirley, it was always a happy occasion, usually in somewhere like New York or Los Angeles. I was living in LA in the '70s and when they played the Forum, I remember there was this whole big line of mariachi dancers going down the aisles. Shirley said, "What's all that?" and I said, "They're showing Bianca to her seat."

'Sometimes Seraphina would go on her own and Shirley would get very cross, because Charlie would spend a lot of money on her. She said, "He mustn't spend all this money on her. He's spoiling her." But that's what he was like.'

In 1982, ready to move from Gloucestershire, their home of six years, and searching for a large property in England, Charlie and Shirley were exploring the country lanes of Devon when they saw a signpost to Halsdon. 'It seemed the end of the world then,' she said. 'The woods, the river, the valley – it was utterly enchanting.' In the village of Dolton, they found Halsdon House, also known as Halsdon Manor, a 16th-century property that had been owned by Devonshire squires for hundreds of years.

'We fell in love with the place instantly,' Shirley explained. 'There were, of course, no barns or paddocks then, but we knew it was a natural fit. Devon became our heaven and we have never looked back.' A writer for the online archive for nearby Bideford recorded at the time: 'Mr Charles Watts, I hear, has bought Halsdon House at Dolton. The six-bedroom property is a Grade II listed building standing in a lovely park and woodland of 14 acres. Estate agents Michelmore Hughes stated no official announcement regarding the buyer has been made.'

Shirley became owner, breeder and an expert in husbandry of her beloved Halsdon Arabian horses, named for the stud farm where they resided. Under the stewardship of Shirley and her team they grew from a small number of riding horses to the 'universally esteemed breeding powerhouse of over 250', as the Tom Arabians website described it.

She never granted interviews as a rock wife, but Shirley spoke in huge detail to the site about her daily life in the stables of Halsdon. She said of her philosophy: 'It is not rocket science, it is simply paying attention to the needs of each horse, both physiologically and psychologically. This understanding involves awareness, which can only be achieved through daily contact with the horses and intimate appreciation for the unique nature of each horse.'

She also discussed what she enjoyed most about her noble Arabians, and her answer was revealing about the peace that she and her husband had found far from the madding music industry. 'Just being among them,' she said. 'I love to feel the heat of their bodies, to listen to the rhythmic cadence of their breathing, to relish in the quiet satisfaction of belonging.

'Horses always give you the intention of what they feel towards you. I so enjoy this interaction, as each horse has its own unique personality and approach towards human interaction. To find that acceptance with horses is the most satisfying. They make us feel like we belong.

'The Arabian horse has taught me so very much in life, humility most of all,' she concluded. 'One experiences the entire spectrum of emotions in a life with horses, from great joy and overwhelming exhilaration to deep sorrow and tragic loss. I feel more alive to have experienced life alongside the horse. There is so much pleasure to be had each day. It is the great circle of life. It is a bond unlike any other.'

This passion made headlines in 1995, when it was widely reported that Charlie paid $740,000 for an Arabian stallion from Australia. Marion Atkinson of the Simeon stud farm in Sydney stated that this was a record for the breed in Australia, and that the couple bought the horse, Simeon Sadik, after seeing him in a video.

Meanwhile, back in the house, Charlie would always say that he never listened to the Rolling Stones' records, but that his wife certainly did. 'She's a great fan of the Stones,' he said. 'I'm not; it's what I do. Mick and Keith and Ronnie are my friends and the band is a very good one, but that's it. But Shirley actually plays our records.'

As the *Forty Licks* compilation of 2002 gave the old hits yet another lap of honour and united the ABKCO releases with those of their later, more lucrative deals, Charlie said: 'Listening to yourself playing 40 years ago, if you're not Louis Armstrong ... I never play our stuff anyway. I wasn't aware you couldn't buy them together, I was told that. I wouldn't know, because I'm not that interested in knowing.

'When I go to a record shop I can always see racks of our stuff. But I never play it, except when I get them [early] and I'm asked to comment. My wife will play them, and I'll hear them on the radio occasionally. That's interesting.'

Says Tony King: 'He and Shirley loved soul and Motown. When I lived in America I used to make tapes and send them off to them in La Bourie in France. They loved them. Shirley used to say we loved "Do It Again" by Steely Dan and "Love Train" by the O'Jays. Great songs I used to send them.'

In a 1998 exchange with *Esquire*, Charlie told Robin Eggar: 'My wife has kept me very sane. I'd have probably ended up a drug addict nutter in Soho if I'd been single all the way through. It's very difficult to keep a romance alive for 35 years. The only good side about touring is the absence makes you realise how much you miss someone.'

Five years later Charlie reflected on what was soon to be 40 years of marriage to Shirley. 'I've always had the fortune of a solid home base,' he said. 'We first met on the day I started playing in Alexis Korner's band, even before I became a member of the Stones. My wife has known Mick and Keith for as long as I have. She's a sensible woman. She has always kept well away from the Stones.'

The couple also knew another of the great friends who confided in Tony King: Elton John, who once name-checked Shirley herself. In 1974 he confided: 'Bette Midler said my new album should be called *Fat Reg from Pinner*. I wanted to call it *Ol' Pink Eyes Is Back*, but I had a rebellion on my hands, the band didn't like it. Charlie Watts's wife had the best one. She wanted to call it *Ol' Four Eyes Is Back*.'

The Wattses were much respected among their neighbours in Devon; on Charlie's death, a parish councillor revealed that in 2011 they made a generous contribution to the refurbishment of the village hall. Shirley was invited to the reopening ceremony, and to everyone's surprise brought her husband along. Charlie had a car on standby outside in case he didn't enjoy himself, because the cricket was on the television. They were the last to leave.

Charlie and Shirley's daughter Seraphina, after growing up in France until she was eight, later moved away for many years, in America and elsewhere. But in the early 2000s she turned on the television and saw something that struck a hilarious chord. 'My parents were a bit Sharon and Ozzy of

Devon,' she says. 'When I saw that show I was like, "Oh my gosh." He walked around the house going "Shirleyyy".

'I said to my godfather, Tony King, "Have you seen that show?" and he went, "I know." I said to them, "This is you two." And I was like stroppy Kelly. All the dogs and everything. "This is you!" They were horrified, but I said, "It is!" They were an incredible team.'

'Shirley had the best taste and she knew so much about so many things,' says King. 'She was a totally brilliant lady. She arranged everything. But if you went down to his house, he was always doing the washing up, always making cups of tea, always swearing at the dogs, always cleaning up the shit and the piss if they did that in the house, always doing all the menial tasks. He was thoroughly domesticated.

'Shirley always kept him in line. He was never allowed to get too big for his boots if she was around. She would very quickly call it. She didn't flinch about saying something to pull the rug from under his feet. I remember she wrote me this brilliant letter in the early days when they were touring America, around Altamont time. She said, "Charlie came home at the weekend, full of conceit about being a member of the Rolling Stones. So I made him clean the oven."'

Charlie's drum tech of his final decade, Don McAulay, fondly shares a much more recent memory of the couple. 'The last time Shirley saw Charlie playing the drums that I know of was at the Hyde Park show in 2013. She sat right next to my work area and was so happy to be there watching him again. And he just couldn't keep his eyes off her. I just felt that it was really special for both of them, since it was also how they first met, when she would go and see him play.'

'I can't emphasise enough that his marriage and his child and grandchild were the bedrock of his life,' concludes King. 'He loved the Rolling Stones and everything that went with it. But at the end of the day he loved his family.'

3

Home Thoughts from Abroad

The Rolling Stones' national and international conquest had everything to do with the far-sighted management of Andrew Loog Oldham. Another war baby, a month younger than Keith Richards, he steered the band's business and creative affairs like a maestro, in an unprecedented age in which rock managers really were making it up as they went along.

His was the ruthless decision to tell Ian Stewart that his face didn't fit the group frontline, whereupon 'Stu' assumed the glamour-free troubleshooting role too modestly described as 'road manager'. As the group became pop's prototype bad boys, Oldham's was the brilliantly pugnacious question: 'Would you let your daughter go with a Rolling Stone?' He fed the line to Ray Coleman in *Melody Maker*, who changed 'daughter' to 'sister' in his on-the-road report of March 1964. Either way, the irony was that the answer in the case of the largely unassuming Charlie Watts would surely have been an unequivocal 'yes'.

'He was the best, Andrew, I liked him,' said Charlie, who became his neighbour when the drummer, already a pop star and 23 years old, finally moved out of his parents' house for good in the summer of 1964. His new four-room flat was in Ivor Court in Gloucester Place, and the all-remembering Wyman records that his rent was just over £54 a month. Moving straight there from home, Charlie never lived alone. 'My mum wrapped us up in cotton wool,' says his sister Linda. 'Even when he left home, he'd bring his washing home for my mum to wash and iron.'

After their marriage in October 1964 he and Shirley soon had the apartment reflecting their penchant for the visual arts; his brief time working in Denmark also gave him a great fondness for Danish pine furniture, with which the place was filled. An English Chesterfield adorned the abode, which featured other furniture acquired with the keen eye he would now always keep while on the road.

'When Andrew got his office in Regent's Park, I used to live down the hall – my apartment was at one end of the hallway and his office was at the other end,' Charlie remembered. 'Andrew was very smart. He used to wear all those little suits with tiny, short jackets. We all got on with him and we all liked what he was saying. He was very good at channelling our feelings. And he could see the possibilities, otherwise we'd have still been schlepping round the clubs, playing in Bournemouth forever and never moving on.'

The management of the Stones' image was deft, capitalising on their long hair and supposedly loutish behaviour that simply willed young fans to adopt them as a daring antidote to the clean-cut Beatles. As the national press and the moral majority raged about these rumpled cavemen, a Wrexham schoolteacher denounced parents who allowed their children to wear morally lax corduroy trousers in tribute to their heroes. Charlie, meanwhile, was getting his first solo magazine cover, inappropriately in a June 1964 edition of *Mersey Beat*.

Oldham placed a Christmas 1964 notice in the *New Musical Express* wishing the best of the season to starving hairdressers and their families. The *Tailor & Cutter* trade periodical beseeched the group to start wearing ties to save tie-makers from ruin. They weren't looking closely enough: Charlie was routinely modish in his appearance, and, if he could have been bothered to care, would have had every reason to be offended when the same magazine, years later, named not him but Mick among its list of best-dressed men. Indeed, when the group were refused service in the restaurant of the hotel they were staying in for being too scruffy, Charlie was reported to be wearing a jacket and tie. 'I suppose they'd serve me,' he said, 'but I'm not going in there alone.'

There were times when Charlie did join in with the fun of the band's collective misbehaviour, notably when they guested on a July 1964 edition of the weekly pop show *Juke Box Jury*, on which panellists voted new releases a 'hit' or a 'miss'. Perhaps it wasn't quite on the Bill Grundy vs Sex Pistols scale of a dozen years later, but BBC thoroughbred and host David Jacobs had his hands full. Wrote Oldham in *2Stoned*, the second volume of his estimable autobiography: 'With no prompting from me, they proceeded to behave as complete and utter yobbos and in 25 minutes managed to confirm the nation's worst opinion of them once and for all.

'They grunted, they laughed amongst themselves, were merciless towards the drivel that was played and hostile towards the normally unflappable Mr. Jacobs. This was no planned press move. Brian and Bill made some effort to be polite but Mick, Keith and Charlie would have none of it. Eventually the two Bs had to join in, put up and go with the flow.' The *Daily Mail* said they had 'scandalised millions of parents'; Oldham said it was 'excellent press fodder'. A week later, 'It's All Over Now' was No. 1.

Such disruption was, of course, largely out of character for Charlie. For the most part, he and Bill maintained an air of studied, mildly amused indifference whenever possible. A *Rave* magazine group profile in the same month as the *Juke Box Jury* kerfuffle got about as controversial as recounting how the group made fun of Charlie the night he forgot his own telephone number. But his band personality was already well defined.

'Charlie Watts is the studious one,' the piece observed. 'He reads books on the American Civil War. Has many classical albums among his LP collection. The well-dressed Stone, he often spends £50 at a time on clothes. The silent one. Of the five Stones, Charlie is the one who says the least.'

'There is something about drummers,' wrote Coleman with tangible frustration in that 1964 *Melody Maker* story. 'They are all wary of questions and are not very keen to get involved. Charlie, a devout jazz fan, asked when Stan Getz was opening in London, then drifted out of the room.' Charlie would play jazz to the group, with little expectation of conversion, although Mick's admiration at the time did go as far as Charles Mingus and Jimmy Smith.

'There's no question that it is the strangest dilemma, really,' says Glyn Johns, the Stones' respected studio side-man through the 1960s and beyond. 'He ends up being recognised as one of the great rock 'n' roll drummers, and in fact his passion was jazz. If he had been – and frankly he was, on occasion – given the opportunity, he would have picked jazz way over rock 'n' roll. It's very strange.'

Few are better qualified to judge Charlie's musicianship than Johns, as the group's engineer and confidant for the first 13 years of their existence. 'There are a lot of musicians who are one-offs, and Charlie was certainly a one-off,' he says. 'He and Bill, for me, are as responsible for the Rolling Stones' success as anyone else. However, it's more sublimi-nal than the obvious writing the songs and prancing about looking sexy. The combination of Bill Wyman and Charlie Watts is a remarkable thing. One without the other and they're still great musicians, but it ain't the same as the two of them together.

'I did spend a huge amount of time with Charlie on our own, based on the fact that he would always get to sessions well before everyone else,' says Johns. 'I'd always be there setting up, or whatever. So he and I spent many an early evening on our own chatting about the weather or anything else. We talked about the family, we didn't necessarily talk about music at all.

'He was a modest man in every respect, really. I never had a conversation with him where we discussed his ability as a drummer. It wasn't necessary, to be honest. I don't think Charlie was insecure in any way, but equally he had no ego either. He did what was required of him, invariably without anybody making any suggestions. I can't ever remember anyone, Mick or Keith or anyone else, come to that, suggest he changed his part. Certainly not me. Wouldn't dream of it.'

The Stones' first two American visits, in early summer and autumn of 1964, were followed by two more in 1965, when they also toured Australia and New Zealand, the UK and Ireland twice each, Scandinavia twice, and made new inroads into France, West Germany and beyond. An unavoidable duty of such globe-conquering was the dreaded press conferences, at which the infamous five would be assembled against their will to be confronted by the inanities of the local media. Bill Wyman's memories of them capture their full absurdity.

'You'd be in a row, in Denmark or Germany or Australia, wherever it might be, and of course they all direct the questions at Mick. After Mick's had four questions he says, "Ask someone else," so they'd ask Brian, then they'd ask Keith. Me and Charlie used to be up the end, having a cup of tea and talking about cricket, or where we're going to go on holidays, all that kind of stuff.

'Then one of the people who ran the fan club, one of the young girls in Adelaide or wherever, came over to Charlie at the end as they were breaking up, as we were getting off our seats and going to walk away. She said, "Mr Watts, can you give me something to take home as a memento?" He said, "What do you mean?" and she said, "Anything, just anything so I can remember this." And he got up and passed her the chair, and walked away.'

His memory jumps to the 1986 Grammys, at which the Stones' old mate Eric Clapton presented them with their Lifetime Achievement Awards. 'It's live on bloody satellite TV to America, and Eric's coming down and giving us all our things and congratulating us. He's talking and Mick's talking, Eric gets down to Charlie and gives him his award, and Charlie says, "Where's the wheels? It hasn't got any wheels!" And we all crack up because it was just bizarre. Time and time again, he was hilariously funny without really meaning to be.'

Those OCD traits that bonded Bill and Charlie could manifest themselves in the most mundane circumstances, especially on their early British tours. 'He had these weird habits,' says Bill, affectionately. 'We'd stop off at a café to have a bite to eat on the way up north, Glasgow or some-where. We'd stop on a side road somewhere, then we'd come outside to get in the car and then we'd say, "We'd better all go to the loo, because we're going to be in the car for the next two hours."

'So we'd go to this outside toilet. I'd go in, I'd come out, and then Charlie would go in and then he'd come out.' He stands and goes to the door to demonstrate. 'That's the door of the toilet. He'd come out, shut the door, check the handle, start to walk towards us. We're all waiting for him. Stop, go back, check the handle again, ten paces. We'd say, "Come on Charlie!" and he'd do it three or four times.'

A bookmark of the Stones' early embrace of American culture, and one that stayed with them forever, was being on a fabulous bill (Chuck Berry, Marvin Gaye, the Beach Boys, you name it) at the late 1964 *T.A.M.I. Show*. The special went down in history for featuring the performance by James Brown that brought his utter genius as both a singer and dancer to a pop audience. The memory stayed forever with Mick, who told me about 40 years later that he still sometimes played *Live at the Apollo Vol. 1* to get in the mood to go on stage. Charlie was also talking about it decades on.

'He was unbelievable on that. They called him the Hardest-Working Man in Showbusiness, and he certainly was. And the band he had, no one was ever that good. When I was young and I saw black musicians play, it's not a racial thing with me, it's just that I immediately acknowledged the fact that, for me, my finest hours of listening pleasure have been Ben Webster, Bobby Womack and the great drummers I've seen. Phil Seamen and Ginger Baker, shut your eyes and they're black, the way they play. That's a term of endearment for me.'

After more than two and a half years of fulfilling almost sadistically relentless UK tour schedules, the group arrived in Denmark for their first European dates in March 1965. The opening date in Odense was preceded by a press gathering at the Royal Hotel in Copenhagen, of which Danish photographer Bent Rej wrote in his collection of striking images of the time, *In the Beginning*: 'I spotted who the jokers in the band were and quickly established a rapport with them: Charlie and Brian.' He added that when Charlie was asked who wrote their answers, he said, 'Ringo.'

Charlie's reward for enduring such dreariness was his new ability, wherever the group were in the world, to visit jazz clubs to see some of his heroes, especially in the States. 'When I first went there I wanted to go to New York and Birdland and that was it,' he said. 'I didn't care about the rest of America. New York was the home of what I dreamed I wanted to be, which was a black drummer playing in 52nd Street. Of course, I'm not black and the scene had gone by the time I got there, but New York was still a very hip jazz centre.

'One of the first bands I saw when I got to New York was Charles Mingus's, with Danny Richmond on drums, and [saxophonist] Sonny Rollins had just come out of hibernation and had his trio. Those were the days when Sonny used to start playing in his dressing room and then play to the walls all round the stage. It was fantastic.'

There would be a memorable teaming with Rollins much later, when he provided the inspired tenor solo on the formidable 'Waiting on a Friend', from the Rolling Stones' 1981 *Tattoo You* album. 'I had a lot of trepidation about working with Sonny Rollins,' Mick said later. 'This guy's a giant of the saxophone. Charlie said, "He's never going to want to play on a Rolling Stones record!" I said, "Yes, he is going to want to." And he did, and he was wonderful.'

'Mick said, "Shall we get a saxophone player on 'Waiting on a Friend'? Who's a good saxophone player?" I said, "Sonny Rollins," thinking that he'd never get hold of him, and there he was in the studio. He said about trumpet and I said "Miles Davis," but I don't quite know where that one went to. [Sonny] was marvellous. We've had some wonderful sax players play with our band, Trevor Lawrence, Ernie Watts ... the best saxophone player is a man from Texas called Bobby Keys, without a doubt.'

Charlie not only brought his first musical love to bear on Stones' sessions and gigs when he could, but confessed that when a certain intro allowed, he would sit and imagine he was one of his idols, such as Kenny Clarke or Ray Lucas. He would go to some lengths to catch his favourites in concert, whether it was stepping out in Copenhagen on that first European jaunt to see the Oscar Peterson Trio, Ella Fitzgerald and Erroll Garner, meeting the latter swinging pianist and his bassist Ray Brown backstage, or rushing home the night after a gig in Vienna later that year because he was going to see Count Basie and his Orchestra.

Sometimes he had a bandmate travelling with him. 'A lot of our conversation was about jazz,' says Mick. 'I quite like jazz, and Brian did. Keith never liked it much, because for him it represents all these Dixieland bands, like Chris

Barber. Charlie and I would go to jazz clubs a lot. In the early days he would go out a lot more, so if there was so and so playing in Europe – because quite a lot of musicians from America lived in Europe – we'd go to Denmark, say, and meet up with them and have a coffee or a drink with them. Then we'd go and see Miles Davis. Charlie was so in awe of him. Miles would be really difficult – or not, he'd be the nice Miles.'

Another of Oldham's audacious gambits was to hire a film crew to record the group's second visit of 1965 to Ireland, as an ultimately unsuccessful means of encouraging funding for a Rolling Stones movie. The documentary, wrote their manager, 'was to be a sort of trial run, get-your-celluloid-legs together for any forthcoming feature film and an effort on my part to keep the Stones interested in the idea of film. It would be titled *Charlie Is My Darling* based on the fact that he was.'

Under the direction of Peter Whitehead, the results, restored in 2012, are a compelling piece of socio-realism that show five young men going about their business in a sort of *Harder Day's Night*: jamming in a Dublin hotel room, catching a train to Belfast and flying back to London, talking all the while about the success and lifestyle that they had expected to end by now.

In the vox pop of young Irish fans outside the show, a young girl says, 'I like da fella that plays the drums.' Charlie, facing the camera almost certainly under duress, says, 'I just took up the drums. I can't read, I'm not a musician of that calibre. Maybe it's just standards I'm looking at. Maybe it's an inferiority complex. Maybe I'm great after all.' He manages a smile.

More than half a century after it was made, the film evokes sadness in the way that, amid industrial levels of smoking, it bottles almost a final moment of relative innocence and togetherness in the group, including the train journey on which they all sing 'Maybe It's Because I'm a Londoner' and discuss Max Bygraves. Charlie, in cool shades, just reads his magazine. Backstage, Mick and Keith work on the new song 'Sittin' on a Fence' (soon to be recorded in the *Aftermath* sessions but given away to pop duo Twice as Much) and strum the Beatles' 'From Me to You' and 'I've Just Seen a Face'. Charlie sits alongside, dour and inscrutable.

The documentary was all the more engrossing because it captured a riot at the Dublin show, filmed with safety-endangering *verité* and none of the cosy packaging we have come to associate with old rock footage. Here too, Charlie was apparently unflappable. 'Bill Wyman was forced to hide behind Ian Stewart and the grand piano on stage,' wrote Oldham. 'Keith managed to make a run for it, and Charlie Watts just kept on playing.'

A newspaper report of the time confirmed: 'Mick Jagger was dragged to the floor, Brian Jones was wrestling with three punching teenagers and Bill Wyman was forced back against a piano at the side of the stage. Keith Richard [no 's' on the end in those days] managed to escape onstage. And implacable Charlie Watts carried on playing stone-faced as bedlam raged around him.'

Later in the film Charlie muses: 'I can afford to do exactly what I want … but then again I haven't got much time to do what I want.' Oldham concluded: 'Charlie, and Charlie alone, was the only member of the group who managed to be natural on camera, and in that reality-verité mode, reasonably unselfconscious and true.'

In 2012 Oldham told the *Los Angeles Times*: 'After I saw, and edited with Peter Whitehead, the interviews, I just had this dream [a filmmaker] would call me and go, "Charles Bronson couldn't turn up for this movie in France and could Charlie [Watts] come over and do it?" I thought he was wonderful. He had a great presence.' The comment echoed an *Evening Standard* report in 1964 that said Charlie was 'considered by his manager to have the bone structure of Steve McQueen and therefore a great future in films'.

It was all the more of a pity, then, that the Stones never got to make that feature film promised by Oldham around the same time, *Only Lovers Left Alive*. Even with the British music press reporting that filming would begin within weeks in the autumn of 1966, it fell foul of its financiers. Charlie coulda been an improbable contender.

Back home, and in the brief time they seized between tours, public life for the drummer and the group was becoming equally challenging, if a little less dangerous. In the spring of 1965 Keith told a music paper that he, Charlie and Bill could generally remain undisturbed by fans when they were out at the Ad Lib Club, which had opened the previous year above the Prince Charles Cinema, just off Leicester Square.

'People are mistaken when they think we live a cloak-and-dagger existence,' he said, 'always going out in mufflers, dark glasses and hat pulled down right over our eyes. If we want to go out, we go out, but we often prefer to stay at home and either sleep, listen to records, or in my case, take the dog out for a walk. I'm not keen on walking, but the dog seems to enjoy it.' His name, for the record, was Ratbag. But more often, Charlie and Shirley were opting for the quiet life. Bent Rej photographed them in their Ivor Court retreat, and wrote in May 1965 of their cherished days there. 'Whenever Charlie settles down with his records, Shirley settles down to her art,' wrote the Danish snapper at the time. 'She will go into her studio to work on her sculpture. So far she hasn't tried to live from being a sculptress; all of her pieces of modern art go to friends and family – or stay at home. It's because they not only love each other, but they also love art.'

Looking at the Stones' touring schedule for 1965 alone makes those idyllic days sound even more like stolen moments. Still playing two shows per city at the beginning of the year, they did well over 200 gigs in that 12-month period, never mind studio sessions at home and abroad for the *Out of Our Heads* and *Aftermath* albums, and epochal singles such as 'The Last Time', '(I Can't Get No) Satisfaction' and 'Get Off of My Cloud'.

In June of that year, as Rej recalled, he went with Charlie and Shirley to view a property they were thinking of buying, the 16th-century Old Brewery House in Southover Street, Lewes. The manor house had survived when the Verrall & Sons brewery building was demolished in 1905. It was exactly what they wanted in an East Sussex town far removed from the wild West End (and indeed the Wild West) of London.

They made an offer immediately and by October had moved in. Charlie's dad wasn't so sure. 'We can't understand why he prefers an old place like this to something modern,' he said. But the couple were very happy with their new location, where Shirley could begin another of her life-long passions, breeding horses. He spent much of his time rummaging in antique shops, both in Lewes and Brighton. The only reported downside was the girls who worked in the nearby perfume factory standing on the roof in their lunch hour, hoping for a glimpse of their reticent hero.

In a filmed 1966 interview, Charlie sits on a bench outside the house, answering a series of laboured questions delivered in terribly-terribly received BBC English. His yearning for it to finish is palpable, but he fields enquiries politely and with his customary modesty. 'We're selling our music back to American boys who've probably never even 'eard of the people we copied half of it from,' he says. 'This is in the beginning. We're selling our influences back, our way of doing it. Maybe it's more acceptable, the way we do it. Although I can't very well answer about that because I'm just part of the thing, I don't actually create the songs or anything.'

As their dog waits patiently with his ball and we see Shirley on her horse, in headscarf and chic jacket, Charlie muses about how success may have changed him. 'I no longer think, unfortunately, about spending £5,' he says. '£100, I do. That really is the only difference it's made to me. If something is £5 and I like it, I buy it. But it really probably isn't worth £5, although it is to me.' Asked if it has changed his attitude to people, he answers sagely: 'No, I think it's changed people's attitude to me.'

His very idiosyncratic way of looking at the world came out as he continued: 'Before, I'd sit in a café, when I was working ... you had a luncheon voucher and threepence to spend. Now, if I had a luncheon voucher and threepence to spend, it would be such a ridiculous thing in people's eyes, for me to go into a place and say, "I'll have three cheese sandwiches with mustard and pickle." They would think, "What's he doing? He's probably only doing this to meet people." I don't know, I get that feeling. Maybe it's a silly thing. But really, it's changed people's attitude to me. Success the way I'm talking about it is money. Not adulation, because I really don't consider that anything.'

As the album format came of age and made many bands begin to question the very validity of the 45rpm single as a means of expression, the Stones achieved self-governance with 1966's *Aftermath*. It was their first LP composed entirely of originals by Jagger and Richards, who were finding new highlands of imagination with such songs as 'Lady Jane' and 'Mother's Little Helper'. Charlie was ever-present with a steadfast and creative beat, and was soon able to augment his essential contribution with several pieces of work that drew on his teenage vocation.

Somewhere in the breathless touring diary of 1966, as Mick would recall decades later with slightly weary mirth, he witnessed the debut of what became perhaps the hoariest of all unimaginative media questions: '*Could this be the last tour?*' Yes, really,' he said. 'I distinctly remember that. I've always dated it.'

In June and July the quintet launched into a typically exhaustive North American tour, a 32-date caravan that included shows at the Washington Coliseum and the Hollywood Bowl. The concert programme that was produced for the itinerary included a comic strip by Charlie that recalled the slightly esoteric narrative style of *Ode to a Highflying Bird*. It deserves to be viewed far and wide as a fascinating summation of his own view of the group's rise.

Titled *A Biography by Charlie Watts*, the comic strip – which now resides in the collection of the Rock and Roll Hall of Fame Museum in Cleveland – had the subtitle *It's the Same Old Story (If Not the Song)*, with the Jagger figure singing on a stage that grows higher with each drawing.

In the first he is at the Crawdaddy, as a man in a hat comments, 'He's very good ... if only he'd have his hair cut.' As the stages expand along with crowds, Charlie draws him singing the Stones through the years, doing 'Walking the Dog', 'Time Is on My Side', 'Satisfaction' and 'Lady Jane' ('but he's still got holes in his vest'). Hilariously, in the final illustration, Mick is at the top of a skyscraper, singing 'Have You Seen Your Mother, Baby, Standing in the Shadow?' Down below, the same little man, standing in what is now a big crowd, is still saying, 'He's very good ... if only he'd have his hair cut.'

The Stones' 1966 Christmas card was also a Watts original, with cartoons offering festive wishes, 'However you spend it whether it be on your feet, your knees, your back or simply floating.' Then he was on similarly inspired form again for January 1967's *Between the Buttons* album. Faint but perceptible harmony vocals on the chorus of 'Please Go Home', with its Bo Diddley beat and Brian Jones's theremin, were by none other than Shirley Watts.

The front cover of the record, a definitive group image of the era shot on Primrose Hill by Gered Mankowitz, was complemented by Charlie's six-panel cartoon based on a title that he had misinterpreted. Andrew Loog Oldham, producing the Stones for what turned out to be the last time, instructed Charlie to do the illustrations and, when asked about the title, used a piece of slang meaning 'undecided'. Charlie took him literally. 'He told me the title was between the buttons,' he explained in *Melody Maker*. 'I thought he meant the title was *Between the Buttons*, so it stayed. It was my fault because I misunderstood him.' But the crossed wires produced the spark for some illustrative inspiration.

He showed himself to be entirely plugged in to the group's public image, and how sharply they divided opinion. Above the line drawings was the advice: 'To understand this little rhyme, you must tap your foot in time. Then the buttons come much nearer. And the Stones you see much clearer.'

In the first caption, Charlie writes 'Between the Buttons started as a laugh but pretty soon turned into a farce,' as crowds shout 'We want the Stones!' In the second, figures berate the group's popularity with such comments as, 'In all my years in showbusiness' and 'Wait till I tell my wife ...', and in the third, 'Say is that a boy or a girl?' Then, 'You know they ain't so bad after all ...', 'Well, I like it ...', 'Well, I don't know ...' and finally, 'What do they think they're up to now ...'.

Charlie was up, or down, to his usual prosaic calm in *Rave* in December 1966, in which Mike Grant wrote: 'Charlie Watts is the classical exception of a person removed from the work he does. The hysteria, the screaming dramatics and the frenzy of a pop existence all sail over Charlie's cool head.

'He rarely speaks because he finds it is a way of avoiding undue attention – he hates fuss and prefers not to receive personality treatment. If someone asked me who I thought would ever be the first to leave the group I would say Charlie, simply because he has so little to lose. "It's just a job," says Charlie, "which pays good money!"'

* * *

After a spring tour of Europe running to 27 shows, 1967 brought relief from close to four years of living like actor Richard Bradford in *Man in a Suitcase*, the new private eye TV series of the day. Charlie was hardly an early adopter of the Summer of Love and later confided that he hated Flower Power, even if he told the press at the time that he liked it. But he was pleased to have time to catch a new guitarist who really was the talk of the town. Thinking back on the occasion, he laughed at the technical limitations.

'I remember seeing Jimi Hendrix at the Saville Theatre, and it was the week *Sgt. Pepper* came out, which he played,' he remembered with admirable accuracy: the show was on 4 June, just three days after the release of the Beatles album, and Hendrix did indeed start his set with the title track, a cover that Paul McCartney later described as one of the greatest honours of his career. The concert also featured Procol Harum and, in another performance of which Charlie spoke highly, former Moody Blue and future Wings man Denny Laine's Electric String Band.

'It was amazing, the sound [Hendrix] had,' Charlie went on, 'and it was the first time I'd ever seen, they'd mic'd Mitch [Mitchell]'s drums up – in other words, they put the mic over the top of the drum, and the sound was fantastic in this little theatre, with this bloody great stack. Jimi played half a number, "Sgt. Pepper", *pcchh*, everything collapsed and he spent the rest of the thing ... you always saw the back of Jimi adjusting things, that was it, no show, the curtains came down.

'That was in the days when they couldn't take his electronics through the system. It blew up. Now, it's huge – Jimi would be able to play ten times more volume. Then you didn't have anything. If you played theatres you had the spotlight and you had the footlights, but if you weren't in a theatre, forget it, you didn't have anything.'

Speaking of theatres, the Stones stepped into boiling water when they appeared at one in January 1967. They performed on the top-rated, geriatrically old-fashioned variety show *Sunday Night at the London Palladium*, playing four songs, including the already eyebrow-raising 'Let's Spend the Night Together'. The Stones' refusal to appear for the finale, where they were expected to uphold the tradition of waving to the audience from the show's famous revolving stage like Eurovision Song Contest rejects, outraged the nation.

What happened on the following week's show had a link back for Charlie to a jazz accomplice of the early 1960s, Dudley Moore, who had become a comedy superstar in the meantime. He and Peter Cook appeared on the show and, when they *did* do the requisite farewell wave, did so with slightly sinister-looking lifesize papier-mâché dummies of the group.

'I didn't want to do [the show], and I don't know why we did,' said Charlie in *Melody Maker*. He made a lifetime's habit of saying he didn't want to do events with the group, from Hyde Park to Glastonbury. 'We thought we had made it clear before we went on we wouldn't go on the turntable.'

Then, one of his piercing put-downs: 'What are you arguing about? Just going round on a bit of cardboard for ten seconds. Yet it's been going on for days in the papers.'

Amid Mick and Keith's infamous drug bust and butterfly-on-a-wheel redemption, the Stones spent much of 1967 struggling to reach a conclusion to the widely slammed, early acid-rock entry *Their Satanic Majesties Request*. The upside for Charlie was more time at home and, before the end of the year, a new address for himself and Shirley.

They stayed close to their home of the previous two years, moving to the village of Halland, seven miles north-east of Lewes, and into Peckhams, a centuries-old manor house that, reported *NME*'s Keith Altham, was once used as a hunting lodge by the first Archbishop of Canterbury. 'It's got some land, not that I want to do any farming,' Charlie told *Melody Maker*.

The Wattses bought the property from the former attorney general for England and Wales, Lord Shawcross, and here they had room to indulge Charlie's almost compulsive tendencies as a collector, which we will explore in detail later. As Altham found when he visited, they also kept three cats, three collies (Jake, Trim and Jess), a donkey and an 18-year-old racehorse called Energy.

'It's a very old town,' said Charlie of Lewes, 'the county seat of Sussex, and it's being overrun. I don't like the houses in suburbia. I wouldn't live in one for free. Surburbia is a state of mind, but no one is really suburban. Everyone has a different mind. I know people who have to go on the train to work every morning, but they are as mad as the next bloke.'

For once warming to the microphone, he went on: 'The amazing thing is, when people make out suburbia to be the ideal way of life, and it isn't – is it? I'm glad I don't live in suburbia. The sad thing is most of the people living there were taken out of an open life in London and put into a house on a building site. When their parents were young, the front door was always open and kids from four streets down were always in. There's never any of that in suburbia.'

In 1966 Keith Richard, still without the 's', had taken possession of Redlands, his longtime estate in West Wittering, West Sussex. As Charlie and Shirley made their next move, Mick Jagger was soon to purchase the Stargroves estate, also known as Stargrove Hall, in Hampshire. Bill recalled that Mick assumed the squire role with some enthusiasm, joining the Country Gentleman's Association.

Bill himself was buying Gedding Hall, his 15th-century moated manor near Bury St Edmonds in Suffolk, and late in 1968 Jones purchased Cotchford Farm in the High Weald of Hartfield, East Sussex, the 1920s home of *Winnie the Pooh* author A. A. Milne, in what inevitably became known as 'Pooh Country'. The Rolling Stones had become the out-of-towners.

Finally free of the ardours of constant touring, Charlie was now able to enjoy the thing he had always craved: extended, quiet time away from the music business. 'Two years ago it was like a nightmare,' he admitted. 'The travelling and the speed of everything. There was no time to live. The English tours were the worst for the travelling, and we had reporters and photographers practically living with us the whole time.'

By now, the wariness that he maintained towards the majority of the media was well in place. 'The ones that really frighten me are the powerful writers on some of the nationals,' he said. 'It's frightening to think that with a few well-chosen quotes or clever angles they are capable of destroying someone like John Lennon.'

Wisely observing those who had come after the Stones as column-inch fodder for these dreaded hacks, he went on: 'Things are much easier now, but it's funny to sit back and read about people like Peter Frampton, who the press are building up like they did Mick. Strange to think that he is only eighteen and he is likely to go through all the things that we had to.'

Then with pop-rock band The Herd, Frampton – deathlessly dubbed 'The Face of '68' – was indeed being 'processed' through the media meat-grinder. As Charlie wisely predicted, Frampton's dubious designation had far-reaching consequences: in the latter's 2020 autobiography *Do You Feel Like I Do?*, he described how his media moniker brought all of the band's jealousies, caused by the press focus on him, to a head. 'I knew it was a sinking ship,' he wrote.

While resident in East Sussex, and ever neighbourly to those who respected his boundaries, Charlie befriended Norman Ashdown, who staged concerts in the area.

Ashdown's son Michael told the *Lewes Musical Express*: 'I don't know how it started, but they were big mates and certainly on first name terms.

'I know dad used to consult him quite a bit and Charlie would give him information about producers, managers and agents – who to avoid as well as who to go with and suggest people that were reliable. He's got a lot of good words to say about Charlie Watts.'

In December 1967 Charlie was at Lewes Town Hall when Ashdown staged a concert by the Alan Price Set. The drummer was seen heading for the dressing room with a bottle of whisky.

'I've got time to do things that I've never been able to do before,' he told the *NME*. 'Before I've just swept in and out of dressing rooms, while with the Rolling Stones. Now I'm able to talk to people like Alan and just listen to the band. He was very good. I really enjoyed that evening.'

Retrospective investigation by that Lewes publication uncovered another example of Charlie's obliging nature. He was often driven around Lewes by the horse-loving father of Doug Sanders, the guitarist/vocalist with late-1970s mod revival band the Lambrettas. 'When I was a kid,' said Doug, 'I used to get taken to one of their houses, either the one by The Swan [Inn] or the bigger one at the end of The Broyle at Halland. I knew he was a pretty big star and thought it weird that he was so very ordinary and was making a cup of tea for us. I've got a shirt which Charlie got from Mick Jagger and which, for some reason, he gave to my dad.'

As the Summer of Love drew to an close, Charlie was on amusing form with *Melody Maker* about its presence in his neighbourhood. 'When Flower Power started, it was probably fantastic,' he mused. 'But now it has become a funny word, like rock 'n' roll. There is even a shop in Lewes which has got "Herrings are Flower Power" written up in that white stuff on the window. I suppose they'll have "Sprats are LSD" next.'

En route to Halland, revered writer Keith Altham (later the Stones' publicist) got talking to Charlie's frequent cab driver. 'Charlie's a decent old stick,' the cabbie said of the 26-year-old. 'He's never miserable and always good to have a drink with. He calls us out quite a lot as he can't drive himself. Never out of bed when we go round, but then that wouldn't be Charlie if he was, would it?'

Back at work in March 1968, the Stones were at Olympic Studios with their new producer Jimmy Miller, the New Yorker with great studio credit already in the bank with the Spencer Davis Group, Traffic and others. 'He was one of the best producers I ever worked with,' Keith told me in 2020. 'Before that, we'd not really worked with a producer that was a musician, and I think the fact that Jimmy was, really tightened us up and brought out the best in us. I loved him dearly.'

Bill Wyman would write in his autobiography *Stone Alone* that, despite the usual Jagger–Richards credit, he came up with the famous riff of 'Jumpin' Jack Flash' when he was noodling on an electronic keyboard, to be joined in the jam by Brian and Charlie. When Mick and Keith turned up at the studio they encouraged the others to keep going, just as the song has, for another half a century. Come the filming of promotional clips for this future classic and its B-side 'Child of the Moon' at Olympic Studios, Charlie came out of a room crammed to capacity with film equipment and delivered another of his priceless bon mots. 'It's like bleedin' Paramount in there,' he said.

Soon they were working on another future linchpin of their catalogue, which had the working title 'Primo Grande'. Keith had brought along a newfangled Philips cassette deck, on which Charlie played a pattern he'd recorded on a 'London Jazz Kit Set', a miniature drum kit from the 1930s that was essentially designed to be used by a street performer. True to his collector's mentality, he had bought it in an antique shop and still owned it decades later. The set came packed in a little suitcase, into which the drums sat in a box one inside the next. The snare was a half-sized tambourine. Even if he had never played it, he could never have resisted the purchase.

Keith played the song to the rest of the band and Mick added streetwise lyrics inspired by the civil unrest then erupting around the world. The crude cassette effects of Charlie's toy drums were transferred to the master for overdubs to be added, in the creation of what became one of the Stones' most penetrating, razor-edged rock tracks of all: 'Street Fighting Man'.

'It was made on rubbish,' said Keith in his *Life* memoir. 'Made in hotel rooms with our little toys.' Peter Frampton,

'The Face' of 1968, wrote in his own autobiography, *Do You Feel Like I Do?*: 'It's such a cool intro to that song, and then Charlie Watts comes in playing on the first beat of the bar instead of beat two where you'd normally play the snare offbeat. Unique.'

It was during those sessions, in March, that Shirley Watts went into labour at a nursing home in Hove and gave birth to their daughter Seraphina, their only child. With fresh perspective, and maintaining his poise amid the spiralling chaos of the Stones' court cases and shambolic finances, the new dad was near his childhood home in May as the group made their first live appearance for more than a year, at the *NME* Poll-Winners' Concert at the Empire Pool, Wembley.

In June, braving the crossfire hurricane of their personal and business affairs, they returned to No. 1 in the UK with 'Jumpin' Jack Flash', produced by new confidant Jimmy Miller, and ended the year, to quote that song, with another one-two: the eccentric TV show *Rock and Roll Circus* and the delayed album that is routinely seen as the first entry in their most brilliant recording sequence, *Beggars Banquet*. Charlie was delighted with it, even as he revealed that during its making, his 'fave rave' as a listener was Miles Davis's *Sorcerer*.

During the making of *Beggars Banquet*, Brian Jones's mental and physical health was palpably sliding, leading – in what seems in retrospect almost slow motion – to his firing from the group in June 1969 and his death a month later at, yes, 27. On the night of Wednesday 2 July, with Bill having left a band session at Olympic Studios slightly early, it was Charlie that called him at 3 a.m. to break the news.

'It wasn't unexpected, to be honest with you,' Charlie told me of his friend, whose fragile equanimity was felt by the group to have been derailed long before. 'You didn't expect him to die, but he wasn't well for a long time, a couple of years, and a year of not being very well at all. So it wasn't as big a shock as if it was Bill, for example, [when] you would have thought "Blimey". Or when Stu died, you know, that was really a shock.' There is something quintessentially of Charlie's world-class unflappability that he might have greeted the news of a death in the group with the word 'Blimey'.

'Brian, you could see him going, or not going but getting very unwell,' he went on. 'He was only young, so you didn't go at that age. He got iller and iller, really. So there was that "knock, boink, pick up again", and we hadn't been on the road for a bit. I guess that's what happened.'

The arrival, the very day after Brian's departure, of 21-year-old Mick Taylor signalled the start of a five-year period of recording and performing that Charlie would look back on as the Stones' zenith. Taylor 'was a good choice,' he said, 'because he lifted the band tremendously. He probably didn't know it at the time, but he did.

'He got lovely songs to play on from Mick and Keith – it was a great writing period. And we were lucky, I always think, because it was the most musical period of ours, which

I think was down to Mick [Taylor], the way he played. He was a very lyrical player. Keith and Ronnie both love saying that they weave together a lot. Mick is a seriously out-and-out virtuosic, beautiful guitar player, like Jeff Beck is. Jeff, you follow him and it's him, whereas Ronnie can go behind Keith and come in front of him, and all that.'

In the midst of all that there was the phenomenal 'Honky Tonk Women'. Not even on an album, it was a superb, raunchy summation of all that the Stones were at that point, and by common consent Charlie was rarely better. 'It's got all that blues and black music from Dartford onwards in it,' wrote Keith, 'and Charlie is unbelievable on that track. It was a groove, no doubt about it, and it's one of those tracks that you knew was a number one before you'd finished the motherfucker.'

To say that Mick Taylor was handed a baptism of fire seems an understatement about the flames of expectation and exposure that licked around his debut gig. As we all know, this was at the free show given by the Stones in Hyde Park – just two days after Jones's death – announced a few weeks earlier when Brian was still, officially, in the band.

Charlie gave a trademark response when Mick put the location of the concert to him. He told *Record Mirror* some weeks afterwards: 'Mick came to me and said, "What do you think about it?" I said, "Ridiculous, but why not."'

Ronnie Wood had first met Charlie some years earlier when the guitarist was a member of the Birds, and the Stones were his favourite band. 'I was crossing Oxford

Street, and a little Mini pulled up, and Charlie was in it, at these traffic lights,' he recalls. 'Being driven, obviously, because he didn't drive. I saw his face and went up to the window and he went, "'Ello, you all right?" "Yeah, nice to see you mate." We felt a kind of kinship.'

Now, Woody was walking around the edge of Hyde Park, watching the gathering of the disciples. 'A car pulled up and Mick and Charlie jumped out, and said hello,' recounts Woody. 'Charlie was like, "How you doing?" and it felt like we knew each other. They were like, "We'll see you soon then," and I said, "Yeah, sooner than you think." My famous quote.' I repeated the story to Charlie, who bowled another killer delivery. 'I don't remember that,' he said.

Talking about the 1969 show just before the Stones returned to play Hyde Park in 2013, Charlie's memories were characteristically prosaic. 'I remember going to pick my trousers up before I went to the Dorchester' – history records it otherwise, as the Londonderry House Hotel on the other side of Park Lane, from which the group were banned in 1973 after Keith set fire to himself – 'and being at the hotel with Allen Klein marching about like a little Napoleon. We had Ginger Johnson's drummers with us, which was chaotic but good fun.' George Folunsho "Ginger" Johnson was the Nigerian leader of his African Messengers, who became part of the London scene at its swingingest and opened the free concert.

There to witness the occasion in what passed for the private guests' area were Paul McCartney and his wife of four months, Linda, alongside Donovan, Mama Cass, unlikely customers such as Chris Barber and Kenny Lynch, and Blind Faith's Eric Clapton, Steve Winwood and Ginger Baker, the latter doubtless there as moral support for Charlie.

Charlie's trousers are also part of a story that Tony King shares about that day of primitive optimism in the park in 1969. 'Shirley came to pick me up with friends of theirs from Sussex,' he says. 'She came with Charlie to my flat in Fulham. I went down to the car, and I was about to get in and Charlie said, "You got an iron in your flat?" I said, "Yeah." He said, "Can I iron my trousers?" He came in and he had these silver trousers that he was going to wear in Hyde Park and he ironed them in my flat.'

And there, preserved in the time capsule of the film documentary about the day, is the silver-trousered sticksman on that rudimentary stage, with long hair, green top and his familiar air of detached dedication. He pounds away on 'Satisfaction' and allows himself the merest hint of a smile while the band take home a closing 'Sympathy for the Devil', as Mick chants 'Really had a good time' and 'We got to go'.

The recurrent symbol of the event today is the white-smocked Mick Jagger reciting Shelley in Brian's honour, and releasing hundreds of cabbage white butterflies, supposedly into the air. But, as Tony King recalled, 'They just about crawled out of the basket.' Said Charlie: 'The butterflies were a bit sad, really. They looked good from the audience, but actually if you were near them, there were an awful lot of casualties. It was like the Somme before they even got off the ground.'

Of the music he added: 'Of course it was Mick Taylor's first gig, so it must have been a bit daunting, in a way. He plays great whatever he's doing, but your first gig with a huge audience ... because normally your first gig would be in a theatre or club or even a big stadium, 50,000. This was whatever it was, 500,000 or something. They always change numbers.'

Free rock shows in Hyde Park had started a year earlier with Pink Floyd, Roy Harper and Jethro Tull. A month before the Stones event, Eric Clapton, Steve Winwood and Ginger Baker chose the setting for their first performance as Blind Faith. 'Did that have Denny Laine in it?' asked Charlie absent-mindedly, adding a compliment to his old friend Baker. 'I wouldn't go to an outdoor thing anyway. I'd go and see Ginger play, but I wouldn't want to see it there.

'When Blind Faith did it, they set up this thing in the middle of the grass, put the drums and amplification on it, and everyone turned up and went round it, and it was free, and it got bigger and bigger. When we did it, we had a Mickey Mouse little stage, a tiny thing on metal scaffolding, drums and things, and a bit of backdrop for Mick with his white dress on. Rock 'n' roll shows were in a very infant stage then.'

On record there was a magisterial end to a tempestuous year with *Let It Bleed*, a full-throttled observance of all the ingredients that had served them thus far: pastoral twang on 'Love in Vain' and 'Country Honk', swaggering rock on 'Live with Me' and 'Monkey Man', dark social commentary on 'Gimme Shelter', episodic blues on 'Midnight Rambler', choral drama on 'You Can't Always Get What You Want'. Their fluency in every tongue was staggering. Away from public view, Mick and Charlie were forming another kind of team.

'We did a lot of the artwork, posters and album covers,' says Mick. 'The *Let It Bleed* cover for instance [the layered cake topped with Stones figurines, if you recall, designed by Robert Brownjohn]. It wasn't Charlie's idea, but we would discuss who we should go to for design. He and I would always discuss that, and what would our ideas be. "Not another photo, we'll do something different." That was quite important in launching a record.'

If the sun came out, metaphorically at least, for Hyde Park as it did for Woodstock in that summer of '69, the sky was positively weeping before the end of the year. For the Stones, the death of teenager Meredith Hunter at their concert at the Altamont speedway track in the last weeks of 1969 – 'an event waiting to go wrong,' as Charlie put it – signalled the darkest hour of an often grim era. For Charlie, the new decade would bring professional pride in the independence the group would soon achieve, and personal happiness with Shirley and little Seraphina in a new location across the Channel.

4

A Family Man in Happy Exile

The 1970s dawned uncertainly for the Rolling Stones, with the decade's first summer cast into considerable acrimony by twin divorces from Allen Klein and Decca Records. Charlie was the Stone alone on the memorable cover of their only LP release that year, *Get Yer Ya-Ya's Out!*. He was depicted by photographer David Bailey jigging in improbable jubilation at Hendon Aerodrome, three miles from his childhood home in Wembley, wielding guitars while a donkey sports another as well as shouldering bass drums. Charlie wears Mick's stripey hat and 'stage clothes', he said, of white trousers and a T-shirt with a photograph of a woman's breasts. You can't do that on stage anymore, as Frank Zappa would put it.

The Stones' second live LP after 1966's *Got Live If You Want It!*, the disc was a document of a band in transition, still nodding to their formative R&B leanings as Messrs Watts and Wyman played steady rhythm on Chuck Berry's 'Carol' and 'Little Queenie', and the robust new rock of 'Live with Me' and 'Street Fighting Man'. And just as Mick said, Charlie *was* good tonight.

With the band's finances in intensive care and the quintet being taxed on what George Harrison had called a 'one for you, 19 for me' basis, the drastic decision was taken for lock, stock and barrel relocation. The March 1971 show back at the Marquee was billed as their farewell to the UK; some observers thought they might never return.

Charlie, who was soon to turn 30, told me later: 'We had a new business manager, thank goodness, who Mick found, Rupert Loewenstein, and he had this obvious plan, which was not very popular at the time. It was a bit drastic, but looking back it was the only thing and the best thing, and it was very exciting. Suddenly, you have to sell the house you live in and leave the country. "Bye bye, Mum, bye bye, Dad." And you think, "I'm not doing that." It went on another six months, and it was the only thing to do. What do they call it, a break in earnings? It worked out, thank goodness. My family were very happy there, and I was, and financially, it was the way to do those things.'

At first, the whole business stuck in Keith's throat too. 'You were very resentful about having to leave your own country, because that's really what it came to,' he said. 'Yeah, you could have stayed and made tuppence out of every pound. Thanks a lot, pals.'

'It was a difficult period for the band,' Mick told me. 'To get different management, get financially on your feet, and at that point we had to get out of England, because taxes were very, very high. We owed the Inland Revenue a lot of money.'

In more than one of our conversations, Charlie pointed the finger of mismanagement directly at Allen Klein. 'We [had] stupidly signed with Allen,' he said in 2009. 'He waved dollar signs at everyone, particularly at Mick and Keith. He had a very tough, American manager way of looking at things, and in a way it was not right for us. He was a stroppy sod. But it taught you a lot.'

Andrew Loog Oldham called the pugilistic mogul a 'killer', but intended it as a compliment. Mick, by contrast, said: 'Klein and his various cohorts claimed they owned a lot of [our] stuff. So we wanted to get out of that contract with him. Also we didn't have any money ... so we had to get ourselves into a position that we could keep alive.'

Keith, who was practically railing against the establishment in his sleep by then, remembered: 'At that time, they wanted us in jail. They couldn't manage that, so the next best thing was put the economic pressure on. In order to leave, you had to rent out all of your property and promise never to go through your own front door. You'd immediately broken the rules if you'd done that. I always imagined hordes of IRS men in the trees – "He's opening the gate! Has he walked inside yet?" They would go that far.'

The Stones left the UK with the brilliant *Sticky Fingers* as a parting gift, an instant No. 1 alongside its fiery 45 'Brown Sugar'. It marked the debut of their Rolling Stones Records label, secured for UK distribution by WEA and in America for Atlantic Records by one of the very few record label executives the band ever trusted, Ahmet Ertegun.

Word had it that 21 companies had been bidding, and the optimistic agreement was for six albums in four years, with solo projects as a possible extra. 'We want to keep our overheads low,' said Mick at the time. 'We want to release the odd blues record and Charlie wants to do some jazz.'

Sticky Fingers also ushered in the immortal tongue and lips logo, created by English art designer John Pasche. This magnificent and enduring visual shorthand impressed Charlie in a visceral way, and he was still enthusing about it decades later. 'I thought it was brilliant,' he said. 'Coming from advertising studios, it was what I would have suggested anyway. It's what you hope for, and we were lucky that John did it. It's one of the most iconic symbols. That and the Chase Manhattan Bank. And a very dear friend of mine, who's also a great designer in New York, put it as one of the top three [logos], Coca-Cola being the first one. It's very adaptable, and it's been able to bend with the various trends over the years.'

Charlie didn't work closely on Andy Warhol's daringly innovative 'zipper' cover for the album, but as Mick says, he was much involved in the overall package. 'You had to have inside pictures, and "Where are we going to put this logo?" You had a lot of components there. So it was nice to have someone to share that with. I didn't have the background in art school that Charlie did, but I was very confident in my ability to recognise something good when I saw it. He was very helpful, because he would know more about things like typefaces than I did. He'd tell me about the history of typeface, and give me books about it.'

The newly exiled band's choice of recording location for what became *Exile on Main St*, at Keith's Nellcôte villa on the Côte d'Azur in the south of France, was a classic Stones decision: significantly inconvenient for the rest of the group and a total headscratcher from a technical point of view. Charlie had to commute from his family's new home in the Cévennes, three or four hours east along the French coast, almost into Italy, heading back west again at weekends. Bill was 'only' an hour away. 'Fortunately my wife spoke French,' said Charlie, 'because I moved miles from anywhere. Our daughter went to school there, and our stuff all came down in a horse lorry, along with the horses.'

He said of the sessions: 'A day would become a week, or a week would be all in a day. That's why you had to be there to play. It used to drive Bill mad. He'd drive down at 10 o'clock in the morning, and no one, including me, would be up till about three in the afternoon, because we didn't go to bed until nine that morning, an hour before Bill arrived. It drove him up the wall. So Bill would go home at 6, and Keith would be getting up,' he laughed. 'That was the kind of timetable. We used to work like that a lot in those days. It was how the band functioned.

'It was very Mediterranean, an Edwardian villa, and very beautiful, on top of this point with its own boat,' said Charlie. 'When Keith rented it, the garden was very over-grown, so it was magical. It was fantastically exotic, with palm trees. We had to saw a couple of them down to get the [Rolling Stones Mobile] truck in to record. We ran the cables down into various rooms that we tried sound in. They were various sizes, which for drums and piano was good. We had a grand piano upstairs.

'I remember doing "I Just Want to See His Face". That's got that very echoey drum, with a mallet. It's very acoustic, a lot of that. Most of them were done live. We still record like that. Mick Taylor's a classic one you have to get like that. He could play forever, but his best takes were usually his first two. He's one of those sort of players.'

Added Keith: 'The basement was the strangest place. It was large, but it was broken up into cubicles, it kind of looked like Hitler's bunker. You could hear the drums playing, for instance, but it would take you a while to find Charlie's cubicle.'

The sessions dragged on, partly because of the recording issues and partly because most of the rumours you've always read about the world-class debauchery in play are true. 'Everyone's life was full of hangers-on,' Mick said. 'Some of them were great fun, they're all good for a bit, but when you really come down to it, you don't want them around, because they just *delay* everything.

'But that was the lifestyle then. It was just another way of living. There's a lot of people with a lot more hangers-on now than we ever had. There was lots of drugs and drinking and carrying on. But, you know, it's not a factory. It's not a mill in the north of England. It's a rock 'n' roll environment.'

What came out of it, miraculously, was a double album that many feel they've never bettered, including Charlie. Much as he always insisted he never listened to Rolling Stones records, he said: 'There are songs on there that are fantastic, [like] "Ventilator Blues". That's Bobby Keys' rhythm. He stood right next to me clapping his hands when I played that.'

Charlie felt that some of his playing on *Exile* was a reflection of the music he was listening to at the time, by such artists as Carlos Santana, John McLaughlin and avant-garde jazz saxophonist Albert Ayler. 'Do I like my playing on it? I like the whole thing, so I suppose that means me as well. But I never like me. It's like, "Oh, I should have done that, it doesn't sound right." I like some of the drum sounds that Andy Johns used to get.

'I've been very lucky with the band, because Mick and Keith's priority always is "Where's the drum sound?" If that sounds fine, they can work off it. I'm going back to Decca days. Always the drum sound. In those days the English could never get a sound like Eddie Cochran or Chuck Berry or Chess Studios, and that was mainly the drums.'

Reflecting further on *Exile*, he added: 'I think it's a peak period for our band. You get periods like that with bands, where you can't do a thing wrong, and you don't know why. Then you do something you think is wonderful, and nobody thinks twice about it. We had everything covered, in retrospect. We had a wonderful producer, Jimmy Miller, and you were playing with Nicky Hopkins, who could play blues as well as the prettiest piano. We had Mick Taylor, who for me was the most lyrical player we had, and we had Mick and Keith writing.'

I once made a BBC Radio 2 documentary titled *Jagger's Jukebox*, in which we played and discussed some of the records he was listening to during the making of *Exile*. Fascinatingly, they included 'Rock 'n' Roll' by their pals Led Zeppelin, the Staple Singers' 'Respect Yourself', Peggy Lee's 'Is That All There Is?' and Jerry Lee Lewis's 'She Even Woke Me Up to Say Goodbye'. There were also Jamaican gems in there: Bob Marley and the Wailers' 'Soul Shakedown Party' and Toots and the Maytals' 'Pressure Drop'. Indeed, it was during this period that Mick and Charlie would share their love for reggae, a genre that has rarely been associated with the drummer.

'[Island Records founder] Chris Blackwell used to send me these boxes of 45s when we were recording *Exile*,' Mick recalls. 'Charlie and I were the only ones who were interested, and we would play these records, mostly from Trojan and some other labels. Some very obscure things, with very odd beats and with dub remixes on the B-sides. Charlie and I were really into that, when everyone else in the band was still listening to old rock from the '50s.

'The beat was so different, and it really intrigued Charlie. Later on when *The Harder They Come* came out, everyone was "Oh yeah, reggae," but that was all very mainstream compared with the stuff we were listening to. Bamboo Man dub and really weird shit. Now you can find it on these dub playlists, but in 1971–72 this was kind of obscure. Charlie loved it, because it was just another beat, and then he learned to play it.'

The Stones were off the road for 15 months until the North American tour of summer 1972, which is most often celebrated as the all-time zenith of rock 'n' roll libertinism. The rest of the year played out to all manner of arrests, each of them in character: Mick and Keith for an altercation with a photographer, Keith and Anita Pallenberg for violating French drug laws, and Bill for speeding.

The moment they could, Charlie and Shirley were back in the Cévennes, living the pastoral life and giving Seraphina what she looks back on as the perfect upbringing. 'I had a lovely childhood, totally normal,' she tells me. 'I grew up in a small village in France. I mean, literally in the middle of nowhere. It was a very rural village, hidden away, and we were the only English people. It was before the south of France and Provence was popular. My father was working on *Exile on Main St* and my mother's brother was driving my dad backwards and forwards from that house [at Nellcôte]. We lived about three hours away into the mountains.'

I ask Seraphina when she first became aware that her father did something unusual for a living. 'Probably very late,' she says, 'and they're not very nice memories, because children will tease at school. I probably knew I was different because we had the biggest car. But not in terms of what he did for a living.'

That changed when the family returned to England in 1976. 'That's when I was made aware, by other children, that there was ever any kind of difference,' says Seraphina. 'That's when I heard the word "rich" in a negative way, and I went home and was upset. I really don't remember anything being that different. I got to meet Olivia Newton-John as a birthday present. My mother was very strict about keeping me away. My parents didn't mingle and I wasn't allowed to go to shows, and we didn't have a nanny. My father wasn't interested in a celebrity lifestyle.'

Meeting one of the stars of *Grease* was an early sign of Seraphina's love of pop. One of the first records she bought, on pink vinyl, no less, was Squeeze's 'Cool for Cats', released when she had just turned 11. She was almost starstruck in later years when she took phone calls for her father from his friend, and the keyboard player on that record and all of their early triumphs, Jools Holland.

When Seraphina was first allowed to go to Stones shows, caution was observed. 'My mother was very sensible, and my dad. They must have talked about it, but I never asked them. I was very protected. So seeing my first show, it was nothing like it became later on. There were no children. It was not an atmosphere for children. It was a rare treat, not somewhere you took a child. It was like a crèche by the time my daughter Charlotte got there. I took a nanny. She was on a really short leash.'

A generation on, Charlotte did indeed join the tour, very aware of what had preceded her and very happy to have missed it. She tells me astutely: 'People are always interested in that time of debauchery and madness, and they ask, "Do you wish you'd been around for that?" Well, no. Why would I want to see people I love like that?'

Charlie was always in demand for extra-curricular bookings, and made some very notable guest appearances over many years. In 1970, for example, he and Bill Wyman played on the brilliant self-titled debut album by Leon Russell, recorded by the Stones' engineer of choice, Glyn Johns. The LP, and tracks like 'Delta Lady' and 'A Song for You', began Russell's transition from revered writer and session player to box-office attraction, and it was a starry affair. There were vocals by Mick Jagger on 'Get a Line on You' and appearances by Messrs Clapton, Harrison, Winwood and Cocker, among many others.

'Glyn Johns asked me,' Charlie remembered. 'He used to get me really good sessions at Olympic. I used to live there at one time, and he said, "Come and play with this guy." I always remember, I said, "Who's doing it, is Bill doing it?" I have to know the bass player, either David Green or Darryl [Jones] or Bill. So I said OK. I'd never heard of Leon. And I remember he sat down and played "Roll Away the Stone", and I thought "What the fuck is he playing?!" It took me a couple of run throughs to realise just how great he was.'

'People used to ask for me and Charlie to play with them, because they liked our rhythm section, I suppose,' says Bill, who also vividly remembers the Russell session. 'Leon said,

"We're going to do this song called 'Roll Away the Stone'; I'll play you my rough demo." He starts playing it, da-da-da, chord change, da-da-da, chord change, go over there, go up, two tones up, come back, change chords …

'I'm looking round, and Stevie Winwood's looking at me and I'm going, "Can you hear this?" and Charlie says to me, "Bill, you've got to help me out on this one." I said, "You're just drumming, you should try having to do the chord changes all the time." We did it, and it was great, and he did the same thing when we played with Howlin' Wolf, he asked me to help him. There's no way I could help him, but he just needed, I don't know, to know that there was someone there. He always seemed to need me to just lean on a bit. Even though he didn't really need it, he always felt that he might.'

Charlie would talk about fellow musicians with the awe of a fan, not only jazzers but soul favourites from Bobby Womack to Stevie Wonder to Prince and others again in the rock fraternity. Leon got his vote, and here you appreciated the lofty studio circles that Charlie moved in. 'I'd actually seen Leon play before that,' he said, 'because he was one of the two piano players when Jack Nitzsche [another Stones studio associate from 1964 onwards] took me to the session to see Hal Blaine. And there was Phil Spector, who I knew, and I'm wandering about. Glen Campbell was one of the four guitar players.

'Then it must have been quite soon after, Glyn asked me if I would do these sessions with Leon. I just remember sitting there thinking, "Where the bloody hell is he going with this intro?" Then he did it again and it was, "OK, I got it." He had a great voice, really good songs and he played everything on a piano.' Typically, Charlie then asked me if I'd ever heard the album he played on, because he hadn't.

Soon afterwards, in May 1970, Glyn Johns was on the telephone again. This time, he was asking Charlie and Bill, as part of an outrageously stellar cast also including Ringo Starr, Eric Clapton, Steve Winwood, Hubert Sumlin, Klaus Voorman and Ian 'Stu' Stewart, to play with a genuine American rhythm and blues pioneer. The result was *The London Howlin' Wolf Sessions*. 'Charlie and Bill were quite comfortable,' says Johns, 'and completely ego-less. No attitude, and pleased to be there, the pair of them.'

Charlie's surprising insecurity was, by now, nothing new to Bill, who says: 'He didn't rate himself at all. We'd get one of the American drummers coming in who was in town and was friends with us, and they'd come over and ask if they could do a bit of percussion or something. We'd just be running through a song, and when Charlie was sitting on the drums and this guy was sitting behind him, he was terrified. He used to be so scared and nervous because there was another drummer behind him, and he didn't think he was good enough.

'I used to be like that as well, because we weren't technically brilliant musicians. We didn't read or anything, we just did our thing, ad libbed, by ear, and it worked of course because we knew what we were doing. But if you were with somebody else, like Leon or someone who was really up there, you really felt quite uptight that you weren't quite good enough.'

There was another ragbag of a collaboration in early 1972, when a rough-and-ready late-night session from the *Let It Bleed* recordings was somewhat indulgently released as *Jamming with Edward*. Bill, Charlie and Mick were joined by compadres Ry Cooder and Nicky Hopkins, but not by Keith. Mick called it a 'hot waxing which we cut one night in London while waiting for our guitar player to get out of bed'.

The cartoon artwork was Hopkins's, but it was very much from Charlie's mildly surrealist school. Mick practically threw away the bleary recordings with the closing sleeve note :'I hope you spend longer listening to this record than we did making it.' But the album did earn Charlie some rare songwriting credits, if 'songs' they can be called, as he only did with the Stones as a member of Nanker Phelge. This was the collective name for the Jagger–Richards–Jones–Wyman–Watts aggregation used (originally, at least) at Brian Jones's suggestion on a dozen or so early songs including 'Play with Fire' and 'The Spider and the Fly'. Jimmy Phelge was an Edith Grove inmate; a nanker was a face that Brian and others pulled by sticking their fingers in their nostrils, when time was on their side.

Still exiled, Charlie and co. were on the run again from late 1972, when they relocated to Kingston, Jamaica. The resulting *Goats Head Soup* was described by Mick on its

2020 reissue as 'a very eclectic bunch of songs', from the sophisticated balladry of 'Angie' to out-and-out rockers such as 'Silver Train' and 'Star Star' (or, let's not be coy, 'Starfucker'), and the elegantly bleak 'Coming Down Again' and 'Winter'. The Watts–Wyman rhythm axis turned smoothly, greased with inspired playing by Stu, Billy Preston, Nicky Hopkins and others.

Charlie provided unwitting comedic value when the time came in 1974 for the Stones to make a video for 'It's Only Rock 'n Roll'. Directed by Michael Lindsay-Hogg, he of the original *Let It Be* film, it required the band to don sailor suits and play in a tent that slowly fills with detergent bubbles. It's as much fun to watch as it was unpleasant to make, according to Mick, and Charlie – lower than the others on his drum seat, which no one had noticed – nearly went down for the third time.

The irony was that he didn't even play on the track. The finished version was based on early takes captured at Ronnie Wood's house, also featuring David Bowie and with Ron's fellow Face Kenney Jones on drums. Said Jones in 2015: 'I called Charlie up and said, "I didn't mean to play drums on your album." He said, "That's OK. It sounds like me anyway." He's a lovely guy, Charlie. A perfect gentleman.'

An odd and collectible piece of audio that survives from that era is yet another connection with Dudley Moore, then appearing again with Peter Cook in the Broadway show *Good Evening*. The pair are heard introducing a promotional show about the new *It's Only Rock 'n Roll* album with Mick and Charlie, and the results are often very funny.

Pete and Dud sometimes conjure their '60s heyday, Mick joins in, and Charlie is ... in the room, raising the occasional chuckle, but otherwise almost entirely silent. 'Stop butting in, Charlie,' advises Cook. He says that he can hear track 1 speeding up because it knows track 2 is coming. 'That's the drummer's fault,' jokes Mick. 'What?' says Charlie.

That summer, with *It's Only Rock 'n Roll* just out, Charlie, ever his own man, opted for a near-skinhead haircut. Before the end of the year it was obvious that the album would be Mick Taylor's swansong. The fact that he was still only 25 when his wanderlust was compounded by a lack of recognition shows exactly how precocious a talent he was. 'The Mick Taylor period was a golden era, really, for the Rolling Stones,' said Charlie. 'He's wonderful live, and he had some good songs to play with.'

The 1976 album *Black and Blue*, with the elegant and soulful 'Fool to Cry' as its ensign, was all about guitar auditions. They included try-outs for Wayne Perkins and Harvey Mandel, who played on it, while there were also jam sessions in Rotterdam with Jeff Beck and Rory Gallagher. It goes without saying that the winning entry was Ronnie Wood, on a temporary basis at first for both the record and the 1975 tours of North and South America. He became the hand in Keith's glove and his fellow guitar exponent of the spot-the-join style they both call 'the ancient art of weav-

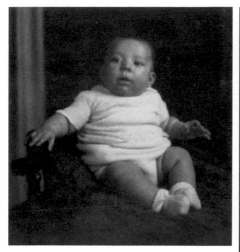

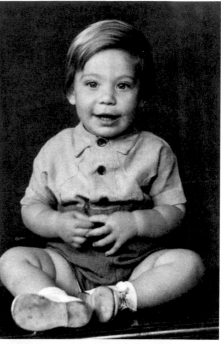

ABOVE: Aged three months, Charles Robert Watts poses for his first publicity photo.

RIGHT: Another image of Charlie from his sister Linda's family album, capturing the war baby at 14 months. 'I remember the mad rush from the house into the air-raid shelters, but I don't think I ever really and truly got frightened.'

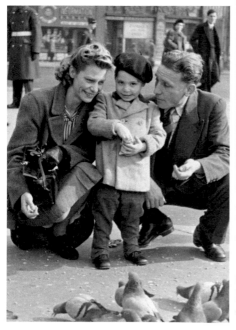

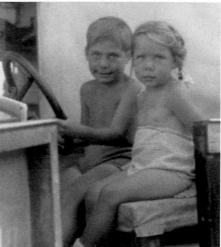

ABOVE: In the driving seat with Linda. 'He was like Mum, and I'm like Dad. Charlie would sit there and not say a word.'

LEFT: Stylish even at two years old, 'Charlie Boy' feeds the pigeons in Trafalgar Square with mother Lillian and father Charles.

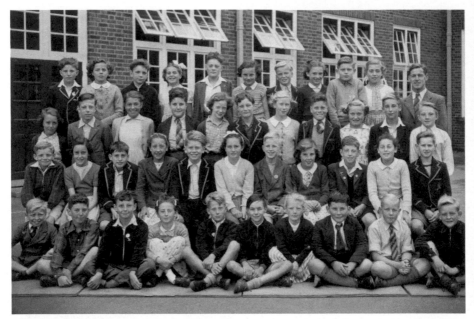

The class of 1952: with his school mates at Fryent Junior in Kingsbury, north-west London. Charlie is third from the left in the back row.

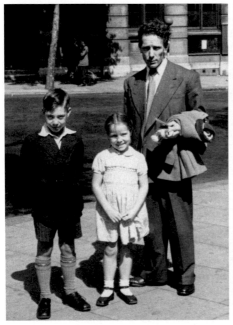

The self-described 'Little Lord Fauntleroy' with Linda and their father.

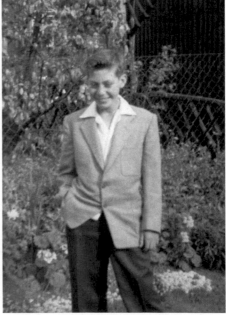

In his early teens, circa 1954, and beginning to hear the siren call of his first jazz heroes.

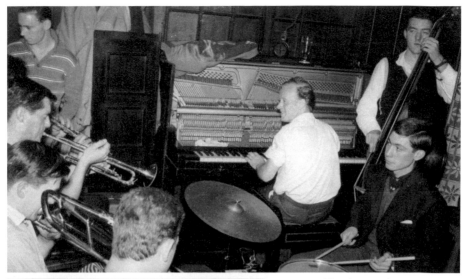

ABOVE: The dapper drummer and, behind him, bassist friend Dave Green, in the Joe Jones Seven, Masons Arms, Edgware, 1959.

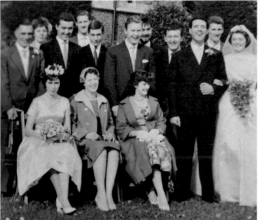

LEFT: Charlie, fifth from left, and Dave, third from left, join bandmates and other friends at the wedding of Brian 'Joe' Jones and wife Ann, 3 September 1960.

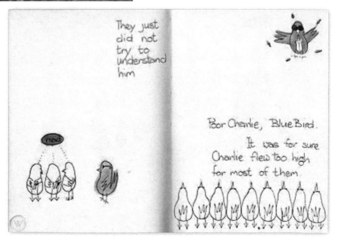

RIGHT: The 1960 art-school project *Ode to a Highflying Bird*, Charlie's beautiful depiction of the rise and fall of Charlie Parker.

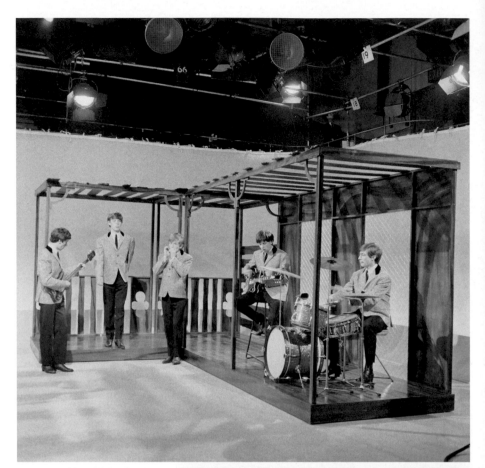

ABOVE: Thankful indeed: on 7 July 1963, the Rolling Stones perform 'Come On' during their first TV appearance, on *Thank Your Lucky Stars*.

RIGHT: When there were six: a 1963 photograph rare for its inclusion of the much-loved Ian 'Stu' Stewart, far left, soon to be removed from the front line to assume the role of road manager and so much more.

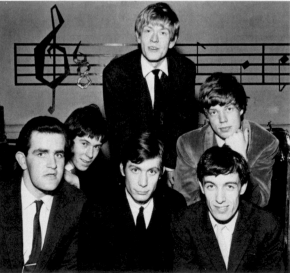

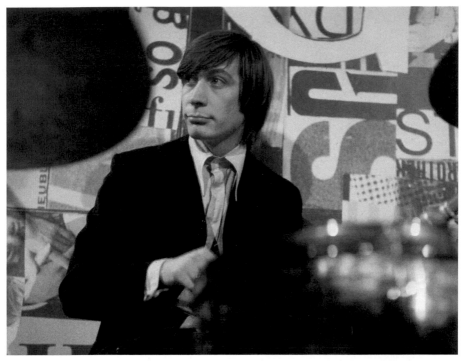

The weekend starts here. In position at *Ready Steady Go!* in London in April 1964, the month in which the Stones released their debut album.

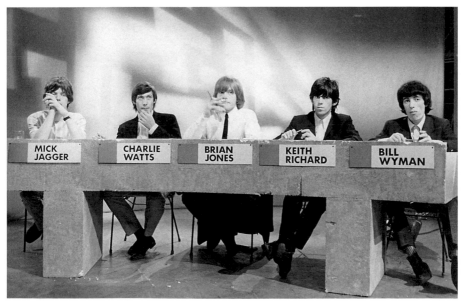

MICK JAGGER   CHARLIE WATTS   BRIAN JONES   KEITH RICHARD   BILL WYMAN

'Scandalising millions of parents': the group enhance their reputation as the bad boys of British pop on *Juke Box Jury*.

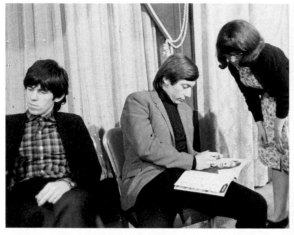

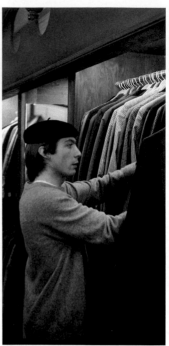

ABOVE: Charlie meets his public at the Astor Hotel, as the group arrive in the Big Apple in 1964. 'New York was the home of what I dreamed I wanted to be,' he said.

RIGHT: Getting down to important business on that US visit, browsing at Beau Gentry on Vine Street in Los Angeles.

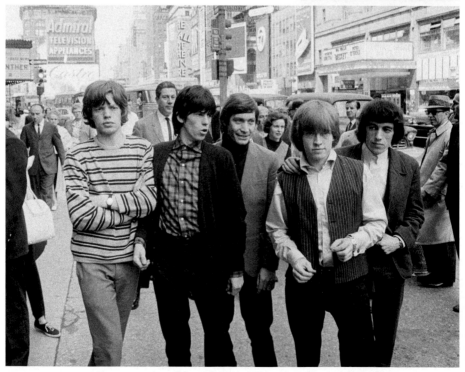

Always magic in the air: Charlie and the boys on Broadway on the same trip.

RIGHT: Another day at the office, unflappable as ever in 1965, a year of countless recording sessions and some 200 gigs.

BELOW: Shirley and Charlie outside Bradford Register Office on the wedding day he tried to keep secret, 14 October 1964.

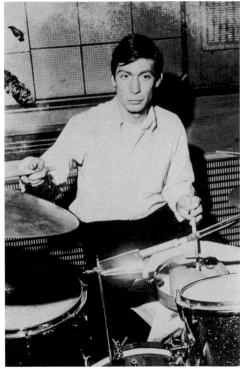

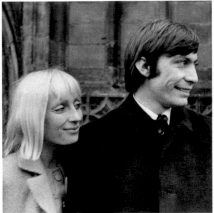

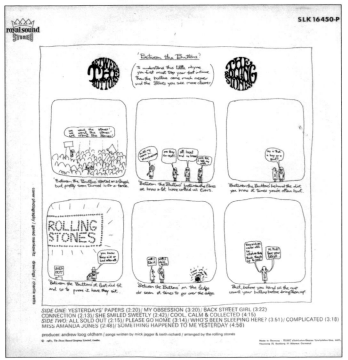

LEFT: 'Then the buttons come much nearer. And the Stones you see much clearer.' Charlie's back-cover artwork for *Between the Buttons*, January 1967.

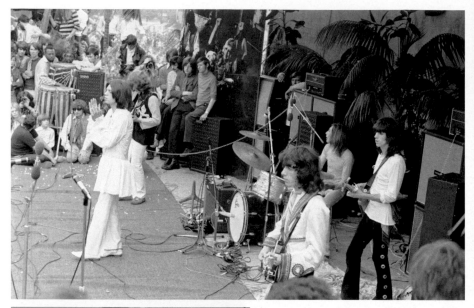

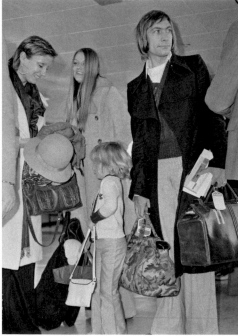

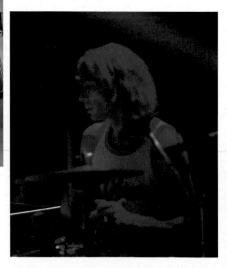

ABOVE: Hyde Park, 5 July 1969, on 'a Mickey Mouse little stage, a tiny thing on metal scaffolding'.

LEFT: Charlie, Shirley and Seraphina Watts, by now living in the Cévennes in the south of France, back at Heathrow Airport, 5 December 1972.

RIGHT: Getting on with the job on 1972's infamous STP US tour, 'the all-time zenith of rock 'n' roll libertinism', at Madison Square Garden in New York, 26 July 1972.

ing'. Less ideally, he fitted the casting from a recreational point of view too: while he was away joining the album sessions in Munich, his house in Richmond was raided for drugs.

The *Tour of the Americas* played to more than a million people, few more special to the band than Howlin' Wolf and his wife, who visited in Chicago. Grosses of $10 million were a preview of the gargantuan touring machine that landed in the late 1980s, even if the American press were, hilariously in retrospect, saying that the band were starting to look haggard. Others were more admiring. 'Mr. Watts is one of the élite rock drummers,' purred John Rockwell in the *New York Times*, reporting from San Antonio, Texas, 'laying down a steady percussive web, letting loose sudden, ornamental flurries and ably augmenting Mr. Richard's rhythmic precision.'

This was the itinerary that magnified all the dimensions of a Stones show and of live rock, period, with its lotus flower stage, conceptualised by Charlie himself, with triangular petals that slowly opened during the opening 'Honky Tonk Women'. No one who saw it would forget the use of a particular giant inflatable. Step forward the 'Tired Grandfather', the nickname earned by the giant phallus that rose up through the stage but often suffered very public dysfunction. And who should be there on one of her very first visits backstage but seven-year-old Seraphina Watts.

'I went to a show, and I remember some balloons on the stage,' she says. 'If I look at books, that was the show with the famous inflatable penis. I just remember chasing balloons on stage. There was lots of confetti. That was a very rude inflatable, but I didn't see that.'

Charlie went home after the tour to La Bourie, the farm in Massiès where he and his family still lived, or at least where he was in between tours and recording. They had still kept their previous residence at Peckhams, the house in Halland near Lewes, and he was soon required there when a burglary saw the loss of antique guns and American Civil War relics that were part of his collection, although some of them were later recovered. But soon the Wattses would be back in England anyway, in a new county.

In 1976 they bought Foscombe House in the village of Ashleworth in Gloucestershire, an imposing 31-acre Victorian Gothic house built in the 1860s by Thomas Fulljames, well known as the architect of several churches in the county. He designed the house in the Gothic Revival style as his retirement home, with a castellated tower, turrets, a carved Gothic conservatory and Gothic windows. Now with room to expand, Shirley was able to establish her first stud farm, the precursor to the Halsdon Arabians.

After *Black and Blue* had spent a month at No. 1 in America, there was the spectacle of their Knebworth Festival headliner, for an audience estimated at anything up to 200,000. Groundless rumours got around, not for the last time, that this could be the last time. Tickets cost £4.25, and backstage admirers included Paul and Linda McCartney and Jack Nicholson, for a bill that also sported Lynyrd Skynyrd,

Hot Tuna, Todd Rundgren's Utopia and 10cc. The Stones started their set four hours late, for technical rather than temperamental reasons, and played until two in the morning. *Melody Maker* said 'they still have power and relevance'; *The Listener* said Charlie looked like Bertrand Russell.

It was nine months before they played live again, by which time the punk infantry were mobilising, supposedly set on consigning the old rock guard to history. In their response, the Stones were fettered somewhat by Keith's *annus horribilis* of 1977, when his drug woes made the Redlands bust of a decade earlier look like a tea party, and seriously threatened his liberty.

But those woes dissolved on the two nights in March that they played two 'secret' but carefully arranged club shows at Toronto's 300-capacity El Mocambo, billed as the Cockroaches. Some tracks made it onto that year's *Love You Live*, but it was 2022 before they earned a full album release of their own. I wrote in its liner notes that the band 'delivered a show that combined at least three Stone ages: early R&B, devilish majesty and a new, lean rock sound that would soon be giving the new wave a run for its money'.

Keith said it was like being back at the Crawdaddy. 'Everybody's going around talking doom and disaster, and we're up on stage at the El Mocambo, and we never felt better,' he marvelled. 'I mean, we sounded *great*.'

'You all know each other?' Mick asked the incredulous crowd. 'This is Charlie. Charlie's a jazz drummer, he's only doing it for the money.'

Charlie may have been keen on club venues for jazz shows, but he was never sold on them for the biggest band in the world. 'I think [they're] usually pretty dire,' he said, 'because there are too many people in them; it becomes really uncomfortable, and we usually play too loud as well.'

The evidence that the Stones had acknowledged the new wave incursion and were ready to mount a trenchant counter-attack was in the grooves of the record they started making later that year. In October, they decamped to Pathé Marconi studios in Paris to create what became *Some Girls*, a masterfully tenacious set of songs that, to this day, is their biggest-selling studio album in America. It out-punked punk on 'Respectable', 'Shattered' and 'When the Whip Comes Down', out-disco'd disco on the anthemic 'Miss You' and included latter-day benchmarks such as the soul-baring 'Beast of Burden' and Keith's autobiographical 'Before They Make Me Run'. Charlie was brilliant on all of them.

'It's very London punk-influenced, which from Mick's point of view, he would probably deny it, but I think it was a conscious thing,' he told me when the album was reissued in expanded form in 2011. 'Certainly Ronnie was playing the guitar very much open rhythm playing, and everything quite fast. But when you say punk, you really mean one band,' he said, nodding to the Sex Pistols.

'I thought they were very good. I hated the punk look, but then I hated bloody Flower Power,' he muttered. 'I lived through it. But [punk] was an interesting movement, from the band's point of view, playing-wise. I can't on my heart say that I preferred it to Chuck Berry and Freddy Below [Chuck's drummer] playing "Roll Over Beethoven", or indeed any of the Motown hits, but it was a very interesting thing do.

'"Miss You" was Mick and me being disco. Keith would laugh at it, but we did like disco records. I did it about four times, maybe more, in different ways in different places with Mick. "Just My Imagination" [the Temptations cover] is done like one would imagine Johnny Rotten doing it. [Punk] was a big influence, I think. People would say, "You were an influence on them." I don't know about that, but that particular period, that was an influence on me.'

Ronnie Wood added: 'On *Some Girls* we had little Mac [keyboardist Ian McLagan], who was lovely because he came as a comfort blanket from the Faces for me. Charlie welcomed him, and Keith did, with open arms.'

They were on the road in support of *Some Girls* in the summer of 1978, from which the eventual release of their gig in Fort Worth shows a band with a transfusion of new energy. Ronnie, by then officially in the fold as a full-timer – you might call it a lifer – said when he watched the performance: 'A new mischievous element had joined the band. I enjoyed playing it and the memories it brought back. There was no brass section, no background singers, just the rawness of the punky style band, and Charlie even liked it.'

Sitting alongside him, Charles had the superb rejoinder as usual. 'Well, I was doing something while it was on. But the bit I saw, I thought the sound was very good. I was pleasantly surprised, because they're usually terribly boring, and the sound is not very good. It's very exciting, actually.'

The Paris sessions gave engineer Chris Kimsey the opportunity to watch Charlie at work at the closest of quarters, and he was fascinated, educated and impressed. As we sit in the members' restaurant at Olympic, the Barnes studio where he has spent so much of his life since starting there in 1967, including so many sessions with the Stones, he says: 'I have such loving memories of Charlie. He was the most grounded, unaffected person by everything that went on in their lives. Mick and Keith needed that to keep them grounded as well. It was like someone they could really trust in every way.

'I think he was one of the most kind musicians I've ever worked with, actually. And considering how his position was in the band, in so much as Mick and Keith as songwriters, getting all the money from that, they're way above him in the business end, but he never, ever complained about that or even saw it as his problem in any way.'

Kimsey had worked on the band's sessions before, but was now in an elevated role, the studio facilitator of the Glimmer Twins' production ideas. 'I think they were really lucky to find me, actually, because I grew up with Glyn Johns, learning and understanding how he worked. I worked with them as an assistant on *Sticky Fingers*, and Glyn by that time had got a bit fed up with it all, so I ended up doing some overdub sessions as the engineer.

'The first time I met Charlie and Bill was on a Glyn session here at Olympic. As you had to do as an assistant, you set up the whole room, everything, so the engineer can just come in and push up the faders. I'd worked with Glyn a couple of times before and I knew you had to be on your mark with him, otherwise you were out. So I'd set the room up. Seven o'clock, no one had arrived. Seven thirty.

'I was in the control room, and the entrance to the studio was quite a way down the big room. So the doors open and these two guys walk in, and I looked and didn't recognise them, so I called security and said, "There's two chaps just walked in to Studio 1, I don't think they're meant to be here." It was Bill and Charlie. They were just so unassuming and did not look like rock stars. Not that I was impressed by rock stars.

'Working with Charlie in Paris was terrific,' Kimsey goes on. 'His drum sound was unique as well. That was down to how and what he played. I've never worked with a drummer that plays like Charlie. I learnt there's this thing where most drummers play the snare and the hi-hat at the same time. Charlie never did that, so he's always got this wonderful space. When he hits the snare drum, there's no other cymbal or drum interfering with the sound, so it was so open. For a recording engineer, that's a dream. I learned that by accident – I suddenly realised what was going on, what he wasn't doing. Also his touch was fantastic. He was a jazz drummer, that's where that touch comes from.'

Johns concurs about the unusual technique. 'Charlie is the only drummer I've ever seen do that,' he says. 'If others did it, they were copying him. Quite obviously, the snare sound is completely different if it's not accompanied with the beat of a hi-hat. But that was very much to do with Charlie's sound. He had a jazz kit and that's all he ever wanted, all he ever needed. He ended up with exactly what he started with. Ringo's the same. He actually had two tom-toms, but he never had a massive kit trying to make a big statement. It was totally unnecessary. But neither of them are particularly brilliant technicians. Their forte is their feel, without any question. You can have great feel with a tambourine.'

Adds Kimsey: 'One of my favourite things about Charlie's drumming, and this is more in the early Paris days – songs were being written in the studio and jammed out, and that's how they came together. They're jamming around the verse chords and nobody really knew when the bridge was going to come up, or the chorus, until Mick would go, "Now! Now!"

'So in doing that, sometimes Charlie's drum fills, instead of a fill leading into a part, they would come after the part. Instead of being on the down beat, they would come *after* the down beat, which actually works just as well, but it's quite unique. Again, it was like genius. I can see his face now, because he would be playing along, and the change would come, and he knew he'd missed the down beat so he still hit the tom fill. Then he'd look at me and smile, like "Again?" This wonderful look on his face.'

'He played a seven-piece kit,' marvels Bill of Charlie's economy. 'Everybody else was playing a 30-piece kit, double bass drums, tons of stuff all over the place, and Charlie just had seven pieces. Because it isn't how much you've got, it's the groove you get. All the great drummers in blues and R&B, they were all very simple. It's just the offbeat, and he did that so well, and it just suited our music perfectly because we were in between jazz and blues in the beginning.'

'That small kit proved a bit of a problem when we were in Montserrat,' says Kimsey, 'because having everyone playing in the room at the same time, which is what we did with the Stones, was a bit difficult, because it was small. We had to build a tunnel for the bass drum to make it sound big, because in that small room, it didn't sound like Charlie's bass drum should sound. I always preferred him to have the front skin on the bass drum, and he did as well. That's definitely the style of a jazz drummer.'

But back on *Some Girls*, he adds: 'When I said they were lucky to find me, I mean in so much as I inherently knew the best way to capture them, and that was to set them up in a semi-circle like they're playing in a club, in a rehearsal, and let them get on with it, and just make sure I was aware that if something sounded good, that the tape was rolling. Because they weren't the type of band that you would go, "OK guys, Take 1." It wasn't like that at all.'

Charlie's typically laid-back attitude and his acceptance by the band made for happy sessions on *Some Girls*. 'When

I started working with them in Paris, for the first week, or maybe two – because we were there for quite a few months – we were in the cheaper room, but for me it wasn't the cheaper room, it was the best-sounding room, because it had the EMI classic console in it,' continues Kimsey. 'The other room had a huge, brand new Neve [desk], which was equally nice, but this room really had a great sound. Fortunately, Keith backed me up and we didn't move. We stayed in that room for everything.

'But I was unnerved, because Charlie never came in the control room, or very rarely, and the same with Bill. Mick and Keith would only come in maybe once every two days to listen to stuff. I thought, "They must like what they're hearing," but I think they'd already second-guessed it. I think there'd been a conversation, with Glyn and Stu telling them, "You should go with Kimsey."

'I had so much fun in those sessions just messing about with stuff,' he goes on. 'You're sitting there for nine or ten hours, and you'd get a feeling of "That sounds like shit." Andy Johns – Glyn's younger brother and himself a Stones studio lieutenant – said something about "They sound like the worst band on earth, until that magic five minutes when it all comes together." So I really enjoyed creating different sounds on the board, and they kind of just left me alone to get on with it. That stood all of us really well for the whole time we worked together.

'I would generally be the first one there, but I'd always check with Alan Dunn or whoever was looking after Keith, when they'd be coming down, when was Mick coming down,' Kimsey recalls. 'I didn't want to be sitting there for three hours. There was a band called Téléphone working in the studio. They were good, and huge Stones fans, and sounded like them.' The likeness was visual, too. Formed in 1976 and huge sellers in France, the Parisian quartet would go on to open for their heroes at several shows, and were later described by one writer as 'the first French band that mattered'.

'One day the Stones were really running late,' Kimsey says, 'and the Téléphone guys said would it be OK if they came in and played Charlie's drums and Keith's guitar. I said to the roadie, "It's all right, isn't it, to let them in for half an hour?" So they did, and Charlie walked in as they were doing it. I can't remember what he said, but he was very, very nice to them; he didn't say, "What the fuck are you doing, get off my drums!" He actually commented on how good they were.'

The Pathé Marconi sessions gave their engineer endless opportunity to observe Charlie's insouciant brilliance at close quarters. 'Another time, I'd got there, and this must have been quite a way into the sessions by now, at least a month,' he says. 'As I was always fiddling around in the control room, I'd extended that to going outside to change the guitar amp sounds. Not a lot, and nobody noticed that.

'But looking at the rim of the snare drum, there was all this confetti still in the rim from Hyde Park [more than nine years earlier] on that snare. Charlie never changed his drum heads at all. That's a jazz drummer. It's not like a rock drummer, who changes their heads definitely each album they make, and more than likely once a month if they're touring.

'I thought, hitting the snare drum, "I'm just going to tune it up just a bit to see what happens." I literally did half a turn on that lug and half a turn on the bottom lug, and then left it. I didn't want to destroy it, obviously, but to my ear, that was cool. An hour later, Charlie comes in, takes his jacket off, folds it up, sits down. He raised the drum and as soon as his stick hit the snare drum, he jumped up and raised his arms in shock. I was in the control room, and he said, "Did someone touch my drums?"

'I said, "Yeah, it was me," and he said, "Oh, OK, that's fine." I couldn't *believe* that he noticed. Half a turn didn't change the tuning. That really alerted me to how that man was so connected to his instrument that just that one hit – obviously it didn't quite bounce back the way that he would expect it to – and he knew immediately. I felt really guilty. But it wasn't a problem, he just put it back. Really amazing. I had respect for him anyway, but that was like, "Wow, that's extraordinary."'

The effortless precision of Charlie's craftsmanship was mesmeric for Kimsey. In 2022, with 300-plus albums and 100 artists under his belt as producer or engineer, he was not only back at Olympic, designing its newly updated studio and overseeing the Dolby Atmos sound for its cinema, but also giving masterclasses on sound at universities. 'I'll only teach if the uni's got analogue as well,' he specifies. 'It's a bit like starting with pen and paper rather than with a laptop, because those restrictions of 16 or 32 track really expand your mind.

'So in teaching that, the students come in and go, "Oh my God, where's the computer, where's the grid, the screen?" I say, "Forget all that, we're here to use our ears, that's what we listen to music with, and our minds." And we talk about timekeeping in particular, and they say that I have to put it all in time. I'd say, "Well if you've got to put it all in time, get another drummer." That's the source thing of the record. Whoever the timekeeper is, is the backbone. Music ebbs and flows. It doesn't have to be perfectly in time.

'I said, "I can give you an instance of a good drummer." When I recorded "Some Girls", the title track, it was essentially a long jam. Mick had so many verses about so many women that he would sing those and then a bridge would be interspersed maybe twice in the 15 minutes. When that track went down, the 15-minute version of it, Mick did come in to listen to it, and pretty much said to me, "That feels really good, can you edit it down to about four minutes?" I went, "Yeah, OK. What verses do you want to use?" He said, "Oh, you can pick 'em."

'So I made a little map of what all the verses were about. I didn't make it too hard for myself – it wasn't like dipping in after four minutes and then going to eight minutes, but I did do about maybe four edits to get it down to four minutes. I had to lose ten minutes, and it wasn't all at one end of the song. I was going to near the end of the song, putting that near the front, and it's only because of Charlie's clockwork precision timekeeping that I could do that.

'It fascinates me now, because I never even thought about it at the time, I just did it. Obviously if everybody slowed down for any reason, you couldn't put that in near the beginning because it would flag and then pick up again. But across the board, Charlie's timekeeping was absolutely constant.'

The 1978 American tour was followed by more recording in California, interrupted by the terrible news of Keith Moon's death at just 32 years old. So much more than just the cartoon loon, he had been a good mate of the whole band's throughout their mutual fame, and both Charlie and Bill flew home for the funeral. As Pete Townshend later recalled, Charlie wept.

'There was a character,' Charlie said of Moon in *Rolling Stone* in 2013. 'Loved him. There's only one of him. I miss him a lot. He was a very charming bloke, a lovely guy, really, but ... he could be a difficult guy. Actually, there wasn't only one of him. He was more like three people in one.'

1979 was a year of no shows but much recording, in Nassau, Paris and New York for *Emotional Rescue*, released in June the following year, with Chris Kimsey now elevated to the title of associate producer as well as engineer. Charlie's performance on the routinely underrated title track, which features Mick's best Barry Gibb impersonation, was scintillating; the song may not have proved as adhesive as its disco-rock forerunner 'Miss You', but it's every bit as innovative, and Charlie is plenty of the reason why.

That was partly because he was attracted by both the beat and the culture of the disco explosion. 'Charlie was a student of the beats of dance, and he liked to dance, he was a very good dancer,' says Mick. 'He danced ballroom, and obviously being a drummer he had an affinity with the grooves and the new versions of them. So first we got straight-ahead four-on-the-floor, then we started having these Latin-influenced dance records. He was always interested in that, and I'd always play him whatever new thing I'd got. Or I'd buy things for him, or he'd tell me about something he'd heard.'

The new decade was starting with fresh imagination for a band already nearly two decades in, but the merciless demands of touring would soon have Charlie looking for an escape clause. He retreated with Shirley and Seraphina to Gloucestershire, and then to Devon, at every possible moment. But the 1980s would also be a time when, to everyone's surprise, he would find a retreat in the worst possible place.

BACKBEAT

Sixty-Eight Inches of Style

Even at the age of two, Charlie Watts had style. The charming photograph that was widely shared on his death, of him in London with his parents in 1943, has him in a short, chic, double-breasted coat, complemented by the courageous but brilliant addition of a beret. His die was cast when his father took him to a Jewish tailor in the East End, and once Charlie started not only listening to jazz but looking at the stunning covers of records by Miles Davis, Charlie Parker, Duke Ellington and all, he was in love.

'His style of dress comes from my dad, who was very smart,' confirms his sister Linda. 'Dad used to buy material and had suits made, and always wore a trilby, never a cap, to go out. Every night, he would polish his shoes, and Charlie was exactly the same – and so am I. We went to see him one day and he was sitting there in a smoking jacket. He *loved* clothes.' Her husband Roy adds: 'He used to be the country squire. He walked from the house to the stud farm with a couple of dogs, and he'd be walking up the road eating an apple. Then he'd have a wander around the stud farm and come back.'

When Charlie died, long-time admirers *GQ* said that his personal style 'should be your blueprint for buying a suit in 2021'. An editorial noted that his suits 'always leant into his rock star roots, with broad lapels, striking structured silhouettes and willowy flared trousers. His styling choices lent him the kind of presence you simply couldn't get from a boring navy or grey business suit, without you quite being able to put your finger on how he was doing it.'

On the road around the turn of the 2000s, Chuck Leavell was backstage with Charlie and Keith Richards. 'We were chatting, the three of us,' says the Rolling Stones' touring music director and keyboard player, 'and this fellow walked up who I didn't know. I guess maybe he knew one of the others. He was pretty well dressed, he had a really nice jacket on. We talked a little bit and Charlie complimented him on the jacket. The guy just lit up, he was really happy. We made small talk and then he turns to go away. As soon as he got out of earshot, Charlie said, "Shame about the shoes."'

From his silver hair to his handmade shoes, Charlie was approximately 68 inches' worth of understated style – a fashion victor, never a victim, with a quiet but essential elegance that many attempt but few can achieve. I recall once visiting him in his hotel suite in Amsterdam during a European tour, everything laid out just so and with a Miles Davis album playing gently, chosen with precision from a travelling CD case. Jeans and trainers were beneath his contempt. He was the elegant uncle you never had.

At the end of a show, when he put his official Stones jacket on to keep warm and take a bow, he did more for official merchandise sales than any marketing campaign. Backstage, he could even carry off the bathrobe with the tongue and lips logo he was so proud of. 'It had to fit a particular way,' remembers vocalist Lisa Fischer.

'He had such a great sense of style. He seemed like he would just be happy designing clothes. Not that I could see him as a model, but I would see him as somebody that would be tailoring clothes. If he wasn't a drummer, design would be his thing. He just loved textures and quality and looks, and he looked so great in his clothes. Very few people can pull off pinks and blues, and he just did with no problem. If anything, it would bring out the pink glow in his cheeks. He'd be kind of shy, but still knowing he looked good.'

One such instance was when Charlie and Shirley rose to the occasion of Royal Ascot in 2010. With his beautifully demure and quietly glamorous wife proudly on his arm, he went to town in top hat, sunglasses and a double-breasted dove-grey morning coat custom-made by Huntsman, his tailor, with diagonally arranged buttons. The waistcoat and tie were both pale pink, the rounded collars of his shirt pinned beneath the knot of the tie. Study the cover of saxophonist Dexter Gordon's Blue Note classic *Our Man in Paris* for the inspiration that Charlie was happy to credit. It was the same when he saw Miles Davis looking cool and relaxed in a green shirt on the sleeve of 1958's *Milestones*: he, and every afficionado of jazz style, had to have one.

At Savile Row tailoring house Huntsman, which has made clothes for the discerning since 1849, Dario Carnera tells me of his family's proud history of having Charlie as a customer and a friend. Such was their relationship, a fabric designed by the drummer himself, the Springfield stripe, remains in their catalogue. 'He was Savile Row, man,' says Keith Richards admiringly. 'He could have lived there. I said, "Why don't you marry a tailor?"'

After Dario has introduced me to the cutters who made Charlie's bespoke suits and jackets – and shown me, with huge poignancy, the last four beautifully cut jackets that he commissioned but never collected – we walk around the corner to the Royal Arcade, Old Bond Street. Here we step even deeper into a world of London craftsmanship that most will assume has been lost.

We are meeting Dario's semi-retired father and master shoemaker John, who made Charlie's beautiful footwear for the better part of 30 years at family business G. J. Cleverley. Its list of clients has included Winston Churchill, Humphrey Bogart and the Prince of Wales. This is a craft far removed from the modern world of instant gratification: Carnera Sr's apprenticeship alone lasted five years.

Soon after John took over the business following the death of founder George, he had a new visitor. 'Charlie comes to the door,' he remembers. 'I said, "How are you, Mr Watts, isn't it?" He said, "Yes," very understated. I said, "Please come in," and he said, "I wondered whether you'd make me some shoes?" I said, "I'd be delighted." He said,

"I have got a shoemaker but they're taking rather a long time to make them. Can you do them faster than two and a half years?"

'I said, "I think we can guarantee that. The first pair would take three to four months." "Oh, that's wonderful," he said. "You've got some nice shoes. Will you measure me?" Almost like, "Will you do me a favour?" That was the way he was. So we measured him, and, beginning in 1993, we went on until 2021.'

John shared Charlie's passion for jazz, and reminisces about hanging at Soho dives in the late 1950s and early '60s, especially the original Ronnie Scott's, now commemorated with a blue plaque. 'I always remember going down to that basement,' says John, echoing a conversation he would certainly have had with his famous client. 'It was next to the post office in Gerrard Street. Pokey old hole, but I always remember the lineup. There was Ronnie Scott, Tubby Hayes, Phil Seamen on drums and I think it was Johnny Hawksworth on double bass. Charlie and I used to have some great discussions.'

A pair of handcrafted shoes from Cleverley's will generally take six months to make, and cost in the region of £4,000. They only make a dozen pairs a week in total. Charlie had at least 80 pairs made there, with the 'Cleverley toe' ('like a chisel toe,' John explains. 'Every time we finished a pair, he'd say, "What haven't I had, John?"').

Adds Dario: 'He had such slim, elegant feet ['The foot that everybody dreams of,' notes chief lastmaker Adam

Law]. He'd come in, if he was collecting something, and say, "What do I need? Well, I don't need anything, what do I want?"'

As Charlie developed his friendship with the family, he would invite them to Stones concerts, and his own, around the world. John Carnera laughs at one particular memory concerning the group's financial guru Prince Rupert Loewenstein. 'He used to have his shoes made by Cleverley's nephew Anthony, who was an even better shoemaker than George, although you would never tell George that,' he chuckles.

'Anyway, Anthony used to go and see his customers privately, he didn't have a shop, and Loewenstein was one of his best customers. He had a flat off Kensington High Street. He went to see him to deliver this pair of shoes, to try them on, and Mick happened to be there. Loewenstein said, "Well, as usual, Mr Cleverley, great pair of shoes, blah blah." And Jagger's looking on and saying, "Lovely pair of shoes, Rupert." He says to Anthony, "Would you make me a pair of shoes like that?" He said, "No, I'm not having you prancing about the stage wrecking my shoes." As far as he was concerned, he could have been John Smith.'

Talk of Prince Rupert reminds John Carnera of another story, about one of Loewenstein's associates. 'The Charlie connection is that when the man died in 2004, Charlie's ears pricked up. He said, "Do you think I can get hold of some of those shoes, John?" I said, "I understand they're having an auction," and he went over to Paris and bought some of them. I think he bought something like a dozen pairs.'

Charlie may have insisted on old-school artisanship, but there was one tradition about hand-made shoes that he didn't agree with. He felt it was the customer's own responsibility to break a new pair in. He said: 'Most of the aristocracy who could afford to have shoes made would have the gardener or butler wear the shoes first, to break them in.'

By contrast, Rolling Stones keyboard player Chuck Leavell remembers a touring story. 'In Madrid my wife Rose Lane and I had got up, and it was fairly early. We were going to go out to a museum or something and Charlie was in the lobby. I was a little surprised, because it was like 8.30 a.m. or something. So I asked him where he'd been, and he said: "Taking my new shoes for a walk." How brilliant is that?'

As the Rolling Stones became the talk of every town in the 1960s, Charlie became a customer of celebrated fashion maverick Tommy Nutter, who practically clothed showbusiness, and rewrote the rules of the Savile Row suit in the process. Charlie then became a customer not just of Huntsman but also Chittleborough & Morgan, co-founded by Roy Chittleborough and Nutter's graduate Joe Morgan. It was there that he bought his friend and work colleague Tony King a suit as an end-of-tour gift.

Charlie would arrive on the Row in his chauffeured limousine, learning to love and respect the nuances of tradition and custom unique to each tailor. His fondness for wide

lapels and statement cuts helped him present a more imposing figure than suggested by his modest frame; indeed he
would say that if a favourite pair of trousers was becoming
a little tight around the waist, he simply wouldn't eat until
they were comfortable again.

On stage was a different matter: he would have loved to
emulate the formal, jacket-and-tie dash of another hero, Art
Blakey. But after wearing jackets as a young man, he later
opted for the sensible work clothes of a T-shirt or short-
sleeved shirt. Even those were custom-made – you somehow
knew without asking that they weren't going to be off-the-
peg. Sunspel, the British clothing manufacturer dating back
to the 1860s, designed a T under the guidance of stylist
William Gilchrist that was easier for Charlie to play in. It
inserted an extra side panel, allowing for two seams down
the side instead of one, and with a shorter cut than the
normal. He was so pleased with the results that the entire
band wore the design at the Glastonbury Festival in 2013.

His fashion knowledge extended far beyond his own
tastes or his own clothes. 'When we first started working,'
says producer Chris Kimsey, 'my wife Kristy was with me a
lot of the time, travelling and working. He turned her on to
Opium, the perfume, which had just come out. Working
with him in Paris was terrific. He used to take me round all
the vintage suitcase shops, because he'd got a collection of
suitcases, and the hat shops as well.

'Every session he walked into, he was always so smart, so
beautifully dressed. Something that he and Glyn Johns

shared – Glyn, my mentor, said to me at a very early age, "Kimsey, make sure you dress sharp for every session." Every evening when we'd start the sessions in Pathé Marconi in Paris, Charlie would be one of the first to arrive. He hardly ever came in the control room. He just walked to his drum kit, took off his jacket, folded it perfectly, hung it over a chair and got himself settled with all his little accoutrements. Really like unpacking everything.'

Adds Lisa Fischer: 'Near Charlie's drum kit, even at rehearsal, there was always this little place where he could hang his jacket. It was like he was going to his office. I loved his little space.'

Dario Carnera tells me, by now unsurprisingly given everything we know about Charlie's acquisitive tendencies, about his collection of old *Tailor & Cutter* pattern books. 'They go for a fortune online now,' notes the tailor. 'He said he had quite a collection of them.

'Sometimes if he wasn't doing anything, if he was in London, he'd call up, or I'd say, "There's some things ready for you, shall I send them round to the house?" he recalls. Charlie by this time had a family residence with Shirley and Seraphina off the Fulham Road. 'His basement in Pelham Crescent was turned into a big walk-in closet. He'd say, "If you're not busy, bring them round yourself and we'll have a cup of tea and a chat, and look at my clothes."

'He'd look at certain cloths,' Carnera continues. 'We made this very special cloth and he was thinking about it. I said, "I know it's a lot of money, and it doesn't wear that well, it's like cashmere." He said, "I'm not worried about that, I'll probably only wear it twice." He used to love wearing them. I'd always try to make a comment about what he was wearing, because he appreciated that it was being appreciated.'

There were times, his family admit, when Charlie's style sense beat his common sense hands down. His granddaughter Charlotte describes such times with huge affection. 'I'd come down and visit them in Devon,' she says. 'We'd be in the middle of nowhere. He's literally not going to see anyone, and he'd be in a three-piece suit at the table. I'm like, "What, to go and walk in the mud?" "Yeah."

'It was quite funny, because he'd wear these very fancy outfits, in his style that he had, in London, in Devon, or wherever he was going. Then we'd get on the plane and he'd be in fancy trousers and some loafers, but with a white T-shirt and a leather jacket. I remember thinking about the contrast. When he was seen the most, he dressed in his tour way, and when he was seen the least he dressed in his own way.

'He came to visit me at boarding school in upstate New York, and we'd had terrible snow, several feet, freezing. But it was May, and it hadn't snowed for weeks, so you're thinking it's springtime. But they had a freak blizzard over the weekend, and he hadn't packed for it. Sometimes in London we'd get unexpected snow. I'd seen this twice – his absolute refusal to buy the right shoes for snow.

'He came out with Tesco bags wrapped around his shoes. And we had to walk him up the hill for breakfast.

Mortifying. He didn't want to wear any other shoes for the weather. He so badly wanted to wear his own shoes that he was quite happy to go out with Tesco bags round them. We'd be in tears of laughter. I don't know if he ever did it on tour, but he did it out in public in London, and when he was walking around the village in New York.'

Broadcaster and musician Jools Holland, who was proud to call Charlie (some 17 years his senior) a good friend and kindred soul, says that Charlie also had a fashion totem from the royal family. 'I do remember he bought some of Edward VIII's suits,' he says. 'He said he thought he was a stylish fellow. Charlie was the best-dressed man I think I've ever met. Immaculately turned out, and his role models had been some of the jazz greats. He'd looked at some of the great blues and jazz artists that always seem to look great, and at historical figures from the 18th century, but also from the 1930s.

'So he bought – and I'm pretty sure without seeing them – two of Edward's suits, just because he thought they were so beautiful. He was going to either get them copied, or at least see what the material was and find it again. That's exactly the sort of thing he'd enjoy doing, going to Savile Row and saying, "Where do I get this material?" "Oh, they don't make it anymore," that sort of thing.

'I was on tour with him, and when he got back I saw him again and said, "How did it go?" And he said, "I can't believe it, they fit me *perfectly*. Like a glove." So he was looking at auctions to see if they were selling any more of his clothes. He was exactly the same size. Many people as they age, if I was to take myself as an example, seem to grow larger around the centre, and change shape. For some reason, whatever the Rolling Stones consumed, they're all the perfect shape they were in 1962. I don't know what it is they're doing.'

Music conversations with those who worked for and with Charlie could be revealing, especially those who had ambitions of their own. Says Dario Carnera: 'I said to him I played guitar. He said, "You don't play all that loud guitar music, do you?" Another time, I remember I told him my band were covering "Honky Tonk Women". I said, "Our drummer's struggling a bit." He said, "What do you mean?" I said, "At the start, you've got a cowbell and then it starts on a really weird offbeat. He's really trying to capture it, he keeps listening." And he said, "Oh no, I just came in wrong."'

Steve Balsamo, a distinguished British vocalist with a wealth of stage musical experience – not only his own recordings but also in such groups as the Storys and Balsamo Deighton – offers a delightful example of Charlie's humour and class. 'I've always loved Charlie, one of the reasons being that he was the sharpest dresser in rock 'n' roll, and I always love someone who dresses sharply,' says Balsamo. 'So I always promised myself that if I ever met him, I was going to tell him.

'I end up doing a gig for Ginger Baker, singing in a band with Keith Carlock, Tony Levin and Ray Russell, some of the best players on planet Earth,' he says, speaking of the 2008 event at which Charlie presented his old friend Ginger with the Zildjian Drummers Lifetime Achievement award. 'We did "White Room" and "Manic Depression", some cool songs. It was at Shepherd's Bush Empire and it was great. Charlie Watts was there, and I came in and video'd the dressing room, which was full of everyone.

'I saw Charlie, and he came up to me and said, "Good singing, mate," and I went, "Thank you, Mr Watts. Listen, I've always promised myself that if I ever met you, I'd say this: you're the smartest-dressed man in rock 'n' roll." He went, "Don't say that!" I was shocked. I went, "I'm sorry," thinking I'd offended him. He said, "I'm the smartest-dressed man in *jazz.*"'

5

Dirty Work and Dangerous Habits

Even if that giant phallus couldn't always perform every night of that mid-1970s tour, it felt as though everything in the business world of the Rolling Stones was getting bigger and bigger. Contractual obligations were now in danger of outpacing creative momentum, and certainly in Charlie's life, thoughts of the world beyond the band were ever more prominent.

In March 1981 his father died at the age of 60, news that had him in reflective mood, especially as he would soon be turning 40 himself. Another North American tour was mooted, and another album was required, at which point Chris Kimsey distinguished himself by pulling together the disparate strands that became the surprisingly muscular *Tattoo You*.

'Rupert Loewenstein [the Stones' long-standing business manager] said, "Kimsey, do you know if anything is left over?" I said, "Yeah, I know a ton of stuff. I know what was recorded when I was on session, so there must be some left over from previous albums." But they weren't very good at keeping their masters, they'd lost a lot of tapes.' He assembled the LP from tracks whose origins traced the Stones' '70s sessions, all the way back to *Goats Head Soup* and *Black and Blue*.

A more fully rounded picture of those scattered sessions emerged when the expanded deluxe edition of *Tattoo You* was released in 2021. It contained the working version of 'Start Me Up', from the *Some Girls* tapes, which showed Charlie thriving in a somewhat reggae-flavoured discipline. There was also a homage to 'Brown Sugar' on 'Living in the Heart of Love' and more examples of the Stones' diversions into soul covers, notably of the Chi-Lites' 'Troubles a' Comin'' and one that Kimsey remembered with particular fondness, of Dobie Gray's 'Drift Away'.

Charlie's was an important opinion as an unpictured observer for the album cover sessions, for which photographer Hubert Kretzschmar, illustrator Christian Piper and designer Peter Corriston won a Grammy Award for Best Album Package. The Glimmer Twins were memorably captured by Kretzschmar at his New York loft studio in Tribeca on West Broadway against striking red and green backgrounds, with Piper bedecking them in tattoos.

'Charlie was there too, though he wasn't meant to be photographed,' said Kretzschmar in the accompanying book for the deluxe *Tattoo You* edition. 'We were all set up and ready to go, but Charlie hadn't arrived. I got a call that he was stuck in some bar in SoHo – he'd stopped in for a drink, been recognised and had gotten cornered. I had to send an assistant down to save him.

'I loved having Charlie there. We shared a love of jazz. We'd listen to records and talk about them while we worked, though he was really there because Mick and Keith really respected his artistic sensibility. He had a designer's way of looking at things.'

As the album began a heady nine weeks atop the American charts, the band started a 50-date North American tour, again marshalled by heavyweight American promoter Bill Graham, who had overseen several previous itineraries. The new outing allowed Charlie's viewpoint to be even more invaluable. This from a man who, in the lead-up to the tour, was sounding more uneasy than ever about hitting the road at all, insisting on several occasions that he wasn't going. They talked him around, as they always would. 'I have resigned at the end of every tour since 1969,' he said.

These were afternoon shows, with stages 65 feet wide and wings that were each a further 80 feet wide, coloured panels designed from original paintings by the Japanese artist Kazuhide Yamazaki. Said Mick: 'We had the bright, bright primary colours, which were designed by Kazuhide, and we had these enormous images of a guitar, a car and a record – very Americana – which worked very well in the afternoon.'

Charlie was all over it, drawing on his instinctive flair for design and the far-off experience of the only other day job he ever had. 'That [tour] was when Mick and I started getting seriously into stages, because we were playing in football stadiums, so we had to think big,' he said. 'When you're out there in this vast stadium, you are physically tiny up on stage, so that's why, on the 1981–82 tour, we made the stage something to look at. When the show gets that big, you need a little extra help. You need a couple of gimmicks, as we call them, like the coloured panels we had around the stage, and lighting, and fireworks. You need a bit of theatre.'

At the opening show in Philadelphia, the *New York Times* marvelled that 'men approaching 40' could pull a crowd of 90,000, an estimated 12,000 of them having slept in the parking lot the night before. The effects were equally mesmerising for Charlie's own daughter. 'My first actual show I was allowed to go to was when I was about 13, and my cousin came,' Seraphina told me with a smile. 'It would have been 1981–82, and that was it, I was off. I wanted to be in that world, and my mother was, "Oh, no." Pony club was over. I wanted to go on the road.

'My father had his career, he went off and did his thing, and that was separate. I always got the feeling that work was work and home was home. We did have someone that helped out at home with the horses and the dogs, and my uncle lived with us for a while. Mum did used to go out and join him, but I didn't go, because I had school.

'Then I went to boarding school as a teenager, and I was always begging to go and see him, but you didn't get to leave school to go on tour, it was a no. But it was not for lack of trying on my behalf. The same way, it was homework or "Do the horse." My mother was very strict, much more so than my father. Looking back, it was probably very good.'

This was also the tour on which the Los Angeles show featured the unintended extra stage accoutrement of a lead balloon. 'The first performer, a new wave-funk singer called Prince, proved the only sour note to the mainstream-rock-oriented audience,' reported Californian newspaper the *Oxnard Press-Courier*. 'Prince lasted only three songs and 25 minutes before being chased by an audience throwing objects onto the stage at him.' The other openers, George Thorogood and the Destroyers, and the J. Geils Band, were far safer bets. Stones fans *can* always get what they want.

Mention of Prince is prompted by the memory that Charlie was always a fan, just as he was of Motown, James Brown and other soul and funk rulers. He especially admired the Four Tops, playing their records at home and, with Mick and other notables such as Georgie Fame and Eric Burdon, attending their celebrated UK debut show in November 1966 at London's Saville Theatre.

At a certain point in 1998, when Prince was in something of a non-purple patch – although perhaps not to the extent that Charlie imagined – he told me: 'Someone I thought is fabulous on stage is Prince, or the man who used to be called Prince. He doesn't kind of mean a great deal anymore, and I wonder why. You need to be able to project what you're doing, and from what I've seen there are very few bands who can do that. Michael Jackson and Prince can, but you need a Mick Jagger.'

With potential further touring in Australia and the Far East failing to get beyond the discussion stage, it wouldn't be long before work started on what became the *Undercover* album, a mixed bag with a scintillating and inventive near-title track in 'Undercover (of the Night)'. But with the room temperature between Mick and Keith cooling tangibly, stock needed to be taken, often from the distance of extra-curricular activities. For Charlie and Bill (who had by now taken a turn as a pop star, with the UK hit '(Si Si) Je Suis un Rock Star'), it led them to accept Glyn Johns' invitation to take part in the ARMS concerts of 1983.

Raising money for research into multiple sclerosis and in support of their old friend Ronnie 'Plonk' Lane, who had been diagnosed with MS in 1977, the band of old mates including Eric Clapton, Jeff Beck and Ray Cooper delivered a night of archetypal benevolence at the Albert Hall. The company then did a series of US concerts with various appearances by Ronnie Wood, Joe Cocker and Paul Rodgers. It was like a hall of fame before its time, and one with the best charitable intentions, which would soon be abused.

'When we did the tour with Beck, Page and Eric and all that lot, all the money got stolen,' says Bill. 'The million dollars we raised just vanished. Someone walked off with it, which was disgusting. So we formed Willie and the Poor Boys with Andy Fairweather Low and all that, to make some money for Ronnie. Lots of people came in and joined us, and Charlie came in and worked with us as well.'

That led to an album and a London show. 'We filmed a special at Fulham Town Hall over two days,' Bill remembers. 'We were expecting a plumber in the dressing room when we were doing the shoot, because the taps weren't working or something. Chris Rea came in, who was another guest. He came in, and Charlie thought he was the plumber. Typical Charlie. Chris emailed me last week and just signed it "Chris, the singing plumber".

'We used to record at The Mill, in Cookham, which was Gus Dudgeon's, and later Jimmy Page's, then Chris's. Charlie would fall asleep on the floor in one of the rooms. All the other musicians used to be amazed. "He's gone to sleep, shall we wake him up?" "No, that's the way he is, just leave him, he's all right."'

The Stones' 1981 American tour and its European continuation would be followed by the longest stasis in the band's entire history as a live act. Between their last show at Roundhay Park in Leeds in July 1982 and the latter-day Stones behemoth hoving into view in Philadelphia as the *Steel Wheels* spectacular arrived in September 1989, the only time they played live as a group was at the February 1986 memorial for their beloved Ian 'Stu' Stewart at the 100 Club in London.

For one night only it was back to the rhythm and blues clubs of their youth, with so many friends joining in on stage (Beck, Bruce, Clapton, Townshend) and many more in the audience (Glyn Johns, P. P. Arnold, Kenney Jones, Bill Graham et al.). The set list was appropriately nostalgic, reheating such chestnuts as 'Route 66' and 'Little Red Rooster', along with a couple that hadn't seen daylight since the 1960s, Jay McShann's 'Confessin' the Blues' and Howlin' Wolf's 'Down in the Bottom'.

The stalwart early keyboard player and road manager whose face didn't fit the front line was the contemporary who herded his mates around for nearly 25 years, would rather play golf than rock 'n' roll, and could still get away with calling them 'my little shower of shit'. 'He was the one who organised the Stones,' reflected Keith. 'In a way, it's still his band.'

When Charlie first met Stewart, the drummer's sartorial standards were gravely offended by the fact that Stu was wearing shorts. 'He never changed from the day I first knew him,' said Charlie. 'He never made any attempt to acknowledge the '70s – nor did I really, but I had a go at it and looked stupid. The first time I met him in the early '60s, he looked exactly the same as when I said goodbye to him on the steps of Fulham Town Hall, which was a day or so before he died. He was wearing jeans, loafers and a cardigan with the crocodile on, exactly the same as ever, and he was going to a golf game – just like he always did. Stu used to dump us off and leave us, and he'd be out at some golf course while we had to sit around waiting because he was finishing a round.'

* * *

The nadir of the Rolling Stones usually centres on the *Dirty Work* album of 1986, and Ronnie Wood says that you can measure how unharmonious the Jagger–Richards marriage was at that stage by the fact that he achieved four co-writes on it. Mick is routinely held up as the baddie of that time because by then he'd signed his own deal with CBS and released *She's the Boss*, the first of two solo albums in two and a half years, and toured with his own band.

An alternative point of view, one recounted by Tony King, is that Mick felt the Stones were in no shape to tour, and the new casualty, starting an unfashionably late habit in his mid-40s, was Charlie. His surprising decline into thankfully brief but serious overindulgence came to a head in Paris during the sessions for *Dirty Work*. It's an often unloved album that nevertheless has its moments, overseen by co-producer Steve Lillywhite, such as the slinky 'Harlem Shuffle' cover and Keith's thoughtful 'Sleep Tonight'.

Two nights after the Stu tribute, all the Stones were at the Kensington Roof Gardens for a live insert into the 1986 Grammy Awards, in which Eric Clapton presented them with a Lifetime Achievement Award. Two things stood out: one, the absurdity of the fact that the Stones had not only never won a Grammy before, but weren't even nominated for one until 1978; the other, how skeletally unhealthy Charlie looked.

Herein lies a story that has assumed almost mythological status, and, having already been widely repeated and embroidered over the decades, underwent a new round of embellishment on Charlie's death. The circumstances and details may have been doctored and touched up, but it has basis in truth that Charlie himself owned up to.

The deafening chorus of Chinese whispers makes a definitive version of the yarn impossible to establish. The incident took place in either Amsterdam or New York. Mick either was, or wasn't, wearing Keith's dinner jacket. Charlie either laid a blow on Mick, or he didn't. Mick fell into a plate of smoked salmon and almost went out of the window, or he didn't.

'Keith has invented a new idea of that,' says Bill without rancour, appearing here in his role as the Stones' eternal archivist. 'He says it was in Amsterdam, and he saved Mick from going out the window. Complete invention! Keith does that. It was in New York, and Mick was entertaining all these celebrities in his hotel suite. I was told this by Paul Wasserman, who was our publicity guy, because he was there [heavyweight PR 'Wasso' had other clients such as the Who, Bob Dylan and Neil Diamond]. None of the rest of us were there. Keith was asleep.

'Charlie came down, like he was bored, again, looking for somewhere with someone still up and awake. So he comes down, he walks in and Mick goes [to his friends], "Oh, it's Charlie, this is my drummer." And Charlie just lost it. He went, "I'm not your fucking drummer, you're my fucking vocalist," and he went *whack*, and knocked him right across the room. Of course all these celebs were in total shock, and Charlie just walked out and [went] upstairs.'

Bill continues his received version of events: 'Mick said, "He must be drunk," and the phone rang and they said, "Oh, it's Charlie. I think he wants to come down and apologise." So there was a knock on the door again. Mick went there and Charlie said, "And don't you forget it!" and hit him again, and he went flying across the room again, and Charlie went off to bed. I was awake, so Paul Wasserman called me and told me the whole story, and I called Keith, but he was asleep, so I told him in the morning. Luckily, I always keep diaries, so I always know exactly what happened that day, and who was involved.'

To my surprise, Mick doesn't dismiss the subject when we speak in the lead-up to 2022's *SIXTY* tour. 'I might have said that, but it's not really the worst thing in the world you can say about anybody, is it? It was sort of a friendly thing. And he didn't knock me out or even hit me. Someone stopped him before he got anywhere near me. I remember I was near a balcony, then the security people said, "That's enough." It never got to any blows or anything. My memory is, it was an incident, but it never got to that. And it was very out of character for Charlie.'

Quoted in *According to the Rolling Stones*, Charlie mixed embarrassment and justification: 'The bottom line is, don't annoy me,' he said. 'It's not something I'm proud of doing, and if I hadn't been drinking I would never have done it.'

Keith does have another memory of Charlie losing control, and 'even that was in a very retiring way,' he says. 'Some loudmouth had said something, we were in a restaurant somewhere, I think in America. I don't know about what, but Charlie copped it. We sat down in this booth together – I think a couple of the other guys were there as well, I'm not sure – and Charlie gave his order, then he stood up and walked around to this guy. He said, "I heard what you said" and *bang*, this guy was on the fucking floor.'

Tony King was alarmed at how drugs changed Charlie as a person, but thankfully, and still in time, Charlie looked in the literal and metaphorical mirror. 'I was personally in a hell of a mess, and as a result I wasn't really aware of the problems between Mick and Keith, and the danger these posed to the band's existence,' he said. 'I was in pretty bad shape, taking drugs and drinking a lot. I don't know what made me do it that late in life, although in retrospect I think I must have been going through some kind of mid-life crisis. I had never done any serious drugs when I was younger, but at this point in my life I went, "Sod it, I'll do it now," and I was totally reckless.

'What scared me was that I became a totally different person by going down that path, to the one that everybody had known for over twenty years. Some people are able to function like that, but for me it was very dangerous, because I'm the sort of person that could become a casualty quite easily. I just don't have the constitution. This phase lasted a couple of years, but it took a long time for me, and my family, to get over it.'

On our first meeting, Charlie refuted the idea of him as the sensible one, either in the Stones or the wider music community. These remarkably confessional comments to me have remained unpublished until now. 'I'm not that sensible,' he said. 'But I never used to indulge in anything to excess until about [the age of] 45, so the male menopause, you might say, and I tried everything then. And I very nearly killed myself. I don't mean overdosing or anything like that, I mean I nearly killed myself spiritually, I nearly ruined my life.

'I did everything totally out of character, because that's what drugs do to you, they make you wonky in more ways than one. And drinking a lot. Now, luckily, thanks to my wife, I've stopped everything. I'd never broken anything in my life, and I broke my ankle, going down to the cellar to get *yet another* bottle of wine at my home. I was playing at Ronnie's in about three months' time, I'd booked the orchestra in there. And I thought, "This is it. It's ridiculous. What have you done?" And I stopped virtually from there, I eased off everything.

'Looking back, it's silly what I used to do, just over that little period. It's quite easy to mess yourself up, and accidents happen easily that way, when you're very tired and drunk. You're liable to fall down and break your neck, quite easily. That's what happens a lot, isn't it? You bash your 'ead on things. There is a safety net that you don't feel it. And when you get to 50, you can't carry it so well.'

Charlie continued to bare his soul, and this at our first encounter. 'I used to drink, and I'd smoke a lot,' he said of his younger years, 'but I [was] only a part-time alcoholic junkie, two days a week, that sort of thing. But a few years ago, I started to do it a lot. I went right off the rails. So now I can see how Keith Moon, for example, if you're that temperament, it's quite easy to see how you mess yourself up. And a lovely bloke, Keith was. Very kind. Barmy, but in the nicest possible way. You need characters like that, otherwise it would be bloody boring, wouldn't it? But I'm not saying it was the drugs that made him like that. Keith was like that on a glass of milk.'

Says Chris Kimsey: 'It's not like Charlie. He wasn't a drug fiend, I think he just experimented for a while.' Charlie's oldest friend, Dave Green, was aware at the time of some of their fellow musicians being severely over-medicated, but never Charlie himself. Tony King did notice him being rude to his wife, which was all the more noticeable in a man with pristine manners. 'He wasn't too healthy in those days. But he got through it,' he says, tactfully. The hard-drug spiral certainly endangered Charlie's marriage, but eventually he had the strength to recognise what he was doing to himself and his family, and to come out the other side.

'My father wasn't this wonderful person 100 per cent of the time,' says Seraphina. 'He was a man with his own demons, like every musician. Obviously he got sober, and he was sober a very long time, and there was no fuss and fanfare, no story about that. He got clean, and there was no rehab, he just did it.' Adds Chuck Leavell: 'When he decided to clean up, he did it in a big way. He became vegetarian, didn't touch a drop or anything else. He really made a complete 180 degree turnaround. That's a lot of willpower.' The chief downside, by Charlie's own admission, is that he also cut out eating, living for six months, as he said, on 'water, sultanas and nuts'.

Of all the people to compliment his recovery and understand what it took, Charlie received rich posthumous praise from Keith. Years before, talking about the collective misbehaviour of the *Exile* era, he admitted readily that 'drugs were the tool, and I was the laboratory'. But he also pointed out that in that early '70s period, Charlie 'did a good dent in the Cognac industry'.

Fifty years on from that record, Keith reflects: 'Charlie could drink, and hold it. What he hated about it was that it blew him up. He started to get chubby on it, and that is unforgivable for him. A few years later, he was dabbling once or twice, in Paris. But Charlie certainly doesn't need anything to change the vibes around him. He would make the world's worst junkie.' On his friend getting clean, he adds with admiration: 'I think he realised, "I've been through this period," and said, "Done it, finished, never again." Well done. It took me ten years!'

For Dave Green it was a time of predominantly happy memories, as he was invited to work again with his old neighbour and jazz countryman. 'He rang me up and said, "I'm going to get the big band together and do a week at Ronnie's," as a thank-you gift to the club. Fantastic. The band was unbelievable. Too big, really – two or three drummers, two bass players, two vibraphone players, 12 trumpets. Outrageous.' *Variety*'s word was 'elephantine'.

'Nobody could have done it except Charlie, and he funded it,' marvels Dave. 'He paid us all £1,000 each for the week, which in 1985 was very good money. The band was, I say 40, but maybe it was "only" 35. That cost. Ronnie and Pete [King] and the club took the entire proceeds. And then he took the band to the States.' Charlie told friends he was having the time of his life.

With the Stones pointedly out of action, those big band shows crossed the Atlantic in 1986 and into 1987, and yielded the first album ever to carry the drummer's own name. The Charlie Watts Orchestra's *Live at Fulham Town Hall* stands as an elegant memorial to an expansive outfit, as refined as one of his finely cut suits and with some distinguished squad members, including Courtney Pine, Stan Tracey and, tracing Charlie's lineage back to Blues Incorporated days, Jack Bruce.

Together they gave modern-day transfusions to swing-era standards such as Benny Goodman's 'Stompin' at the Savoy' and Lionel Hampton's 'Flying Home'. The *New York Times* enthused that on 'Lester Leaps In', 'seven tenor saxophonists spit fire and brimstone. When the seven trumpets and four trombones hit their stride, you can almost feel the rafters shake.'

The choice of setting – perhaps his beloved Ronnie's was booked – was also just right. 'I'm lucky that I don't need to play to 90,000 people in a jazz festival, because I do that with the Stones,' he said. 'So I can say I want to play in the King's Head and Eight Bells for 20 people, just turning up when they want. It's that sort of cushion I have with it.'

1987 and 1988 were focused largely on individual priorities. There were solo records for Mick and now, reluctantly, for Keith; Ronnie pursued his art and Bill some charity projects, also developing his idea for the restaurant that became Sticky Fingers. Charlie was coming back to life in the warm glow of his big band as they made two visits to the US. Then it was home to Devon to work diligently on restoring family equilibrium.

His period of self-help had, by the time he got home, produced happy results, leading him to a clear vision of how he had been, and how he was now. One particular piece of analysis in *According to the Rolling Stones* showed a man of rare self-awareness.

'While the Stones weren't on the road,' he said, 'I got together an orchestra that consisted of all the musicians I liked, but who I'd never played with, as well as people that I had played with, and I ended up with this huge band. It's something I could never have done if I hadn't been in that state, but I'm very pleased I did, because I was able to work with some of the great people I had loved since I was a kid.

'So my bad period had its downside and its good side. I just wish that I had been more together when I did it because it would have been better than it was but, on the other hand, without the drugs I would never have had the courage to ask these guys to play with me. During the period we were playing I had cleaned up, so the first phase was completely barmy and the second phase was totally straight.'

There was another benefit to Charlie's new sense of clarity, as Tony King describes from his many years of superintending promotion for the band. 'I remember when he wanted me to work on the orchestra stuff, I said, "If you want me to work on it, you're going to have to do a lot of interviews." He said, "I'll do what you ask." Mick said to me one day in the studio, "What are you going to be doing with Charlie?" I said, "A lot of interviews" and he said, "Are you sure?" But once Charlie had done those jazz interviews, he then became much more open to doing Rolling Stones stuff. He realised that the world of interviews wasn't necessarily a bear pit. It depended on who you were talking to.'

As Seraphina moved through her teens in Devon, and in later times when she came back and visited her parents while living abroad, she describes a home life for her dad that was delightfully removed from the micro-scrutiny of being in a world-famous group. 'Just a good man, but not a perfect man,' she muses. 'A fair man, but impossible to live with at times. The washing-up, oh my God. I have a photo of him by the sink. He liked things put away a certain way, and he made the most incredible cup of tea. So it's the everyday stuff. When I'm doing the washing-up now, I talk to him.

'There isn't enough time,' she says softly. 'You wish you'd asked more, or known more. Certainly [for me] living in

America for so long, I asked him, from all his travelling, "Don't you think it's changed?" and he felt it had. But it was very hard to draw him on things, to draw him out, to have opinions. He often answered, "I don't know" or "Don't care." But I tried.'

His granddaughter Charlotte remembers one time when her godfather Tony King came to spend Christmas with the family. 'He bought Pa an apron, like a tuxedo apron, because Pa was really funny about tidying and turning lights off. He was very, very tidy. So you couldn't open a present, the paper would never hit the floor. He'd be around with the bag tidying it up. So Tony bought him a butler's apron because he was always tidying around the Christmas tree. Always doing the washing-up.'

Another mega-group who lived in each other's pockets for aeons, the Eagles, famously came to declare that they would work together again only when hell froze over. With shadowy humour, they then used that phrase as the title of their reunion album. For the Stones, something of an unseasonal thaw came about in the winter of early 1989. Mick and Keith had done some tiptoe-talking the previous summer to explore middle ground, but with both about to tour their solo records, this was never likely to be a United Nations breakthrough moment.

Nevertheless, with those tours complete, the band once again became the centrepiece, as the twins rediscovered some glimmer at a meeting in Barbados that combined rapprochement and songwriting. 'We got on quite well when we just got down to work,' Mick said. Their arrival in New York for the band's induction into the Rock and Roll Hall of Fame was hardly an exercise in band unity, as neither Charlie nor Bill made the trip, but soon afterwards they were a full five for rehearsals in Barbados and then recording sessions in Montserrat. The modern era of the Rolling Stones was about to begin, and Charlie's role would be more important than ever.

Chris Kimsey, back in the fold, was raring to go. 'When I was asked to do *Steel Wheels* I already had an image in my mind of what that album should sound like,' he says. 'I'd heard the songs, because it was agreed that Mick and Keith go somewhere and write together, rather than all turn up and it all gets written in the studio, which would take a year. They were in Barbados doing that, so I got to hear the songs at an early point. I had [imagined] this sound, that the album should be very almost like technicolour, quite lush, not raw like *Exile*, not polished but really quite rich sounding, and I think I achieved that as well. It's a really interesting sound, different to what they'd ever had before. It was great fun doing it.'

In some quarters the group were now being accused of making identikit music like a tribute act to themselves. But *Steel Wheels* is a record of undervalued delights, including a later contender among classic Stones singles in 'Mixed Emotions', the soul-drenched 'Almost Hear You Sigh', a terrific throwback to Richmond in 'Break the Spell' (complete with Mick's always nimble harmonica playing, which Keith always praised to the hilt), and Keith's emotional closer, 'Slipping Away'. For Kimsey, it was a track that Charlie *didn't* play on that brought a telling moment.

'Continental Drift' was a highly unusual, percussively thrilling semi-instrumental with a mystical air of Morocco, heightened by the presence of the Master Musicians of Jajouka. Memorably, it played as the band took the stage on the *Urban Jungle* European leg of the *Steel Wheels* tour in the summer of 1990.

Late in the album mixing at Olympic, Kimsey remembers of 'Continental Drift': 'Charlie wasn't on that track – it had the African drummers and Keith playing bicycle. He borrowed the assistant's bike, put the seat on the floor and moved the pedals so the wheels were going round, and he's tapping it with a drumstick. So we tried to put Charlie on it. We had a click [track], and we set him up downstairs and he put the headphones on, and after about three minutes, he just took his headphones off and said, "Fuck it, I can't do this. I don't overdub, I play live." And he was quite right. Charlie just reacted to all the musicians around him. He didn't have a particular part in mind, he would just react to everyone.'

The album also prompted the release of a documentary video called *25 x 5*, marking the 25th anniversary of the Stones' conquering year of 1964 (rather than the first-gig 1962 landmark, which has since become their year zero). In it, Charlie uttered one of his true classics, apparently with no forethought or preparation. To record it precisely, the question was: 'You must have done a great deal of hanging around in 25 years with the Stones?'

And the effortless reply: 'Worked for five years, and 20 years hanging around.' Says Bill, laughing as he remembers it: 'That's what he could do. He could always encapsulate things in a one-liner.'

'Any interviewer that was in the jet stream got kind of blown out of the way,' chuckles Ronnie. 'I remember we did Geraldo Rivera's show in America, and they made a big deal of it. Charlie was put in the room, and Geraldo was like, "OK, roll the cameras. Now Charlie …" and Charlie went, "Hang on a minute. I don't know you, you don't know me, so what am I doing here?" And he got up and walked out. That was Charlie's range of interviews.'

Steel Wheels also saw the arrival of some vocalists who would play a huge part in the Stones' tours for decades to come. Lisa Fischer and Bernard Fowler became linchpins of the live band, joined in the studio this time by Sarah Dash, formerly of LaBelle, who had duetted sublimely with Keith on the sumptuous 'Make No Mistake' from his first solo record *Talk Is Cheap* the year before. Fischer, one of the most soul-steeped vocalists ever to cross the band's path and a dynamite stage foil for Mick, formed a special bond with Charlie.

'We call each other husband and wife,' says Tony King. 'She was a show-stealer. When she did "Gimme Shelter" with Mick, it was amazing.' Adds Charlie's daughter Seraphina, referring to the December 2021 tribute to him at Ronnie Scott's: 'My dad adored her, that's why she sang at the memorial. We asked her specifically to do it for us. On tour, he dreaded it when she'd call his name and run up and give him a hug, and he'd go "Oooh, go away." It was a great thing between them.'

'I met Mick first,' says Fischer, 'then they flew myself and Bernard and Sarah Dash to a studio for the *Steel Wheels* recording, somewhere in London, and Ronnie and Keith were there. I don't remember Charlie being at that session. I remember meeting him more once the job was slightly more secure, because I think that was like my testing ground.

'I remember him more backstage or during rehearsals, just kind of slipping in and out, almost like an apparition. He was always so quiet on his feet, and you would never hear him, he would just appear. Or, if you finally noticed him, he'd be in the corner watching you, or standing almost blending into the walls, with that look, "What's she doing over there?" Or talking to Tony King, who was a dear friend. They had a similar sense of energy, very classy. They just seemed to get on so well, and you saw the two of them huddled and you knew not to go over by the looks on their face when they were deep in conversation.

'Sometimes Charlie would kind of tease people, like if maybe I was eating something I shouldn't have been eating. "What are you doing with that?" "Charlie, get out of here."

He'd always catch you in the middle of something you didn't want to be caught in. But he would never judge, he would just be a mirror in an interesting way.

'After that I would always try to pick on him, in a sweet way, but like a game. So he's behind the kit on stage and he can't go anywhere, right, so it's not like he can run from me. Usually when I would start teasing him, going, "Ooh, Charlie, you're so cute," he'd run. He would get so shy and just run. He didn't want any of it. He didn't want anything to do with any of the teasing stuff, because it wasn't who he was.'

The *Steel Wheels* tour was entertainment of stadium dimensions, an 80-truck flatpack monster roaring from one city to the next, by a band refocused on proving that they still had no rivals. They would take the stage to fireworks and towers of flame, in their first road trip with the Fischer–Fowler vocal buttress, with keyboard maven Chuck Leavell and their last excursion with Bill.

Tony King remembers one date where another of his close personal superstars was in awe. 'Elton came to a show [near] Chicago and was on his feet throughout the whole show,' he says. 'Shirley was looking at me and she said, "Elton's really loving it, isn't he?" He was punching the air. We had the best back-up singers, Lisa, Bernard and Cindi Mizelle too, on that tour. The three of them together, I never heard the back-ups better than that. I loved it when Cindi was there too. And the band knew they had something to prove, so they came out blasting.'

More than 25 years in, the future had begun. Mindspinningly, Charlie Watts was to be an indispensable part of it for almost another 30 years.

6

Around the World
and Back to the Farm

The 1990s began with Charlie's uncredited role as design consultant with the Rolling Stones becoming more significant than ever. Now reaping the dividends of their peerless fame as they never did on their first go-round, they may have been en route to the status later disdainfully described by the *New York Times* as 'an organization with long off-seasons and unending profits'. But vast sums from their empire were poured back into the business to make sure that they remained bigger, better and more spectacular than any of their largely benign competition.

Charlie was no stadium afficionado, but he understood the basic economics. Otherwise, he mused in a 1998 conversation, 'You'd be playing a month in a town to play to 30,000 people. Where would you play, in a 3,000-seater hall? So it's to accommodate that, and hopefully you can fill it up. And that's what we've become. It's our own fault, or pleasure, or whatever you call it. That's how we've directed what we do. That's how the world of doing what we do has gone.

'And you're in the world of following yourself, really,' he went on. 'You get the occasional band like U2, "How did they do in Denver?" and you think, "Blimey, we'd better do as well as them." It's like friendly rivalry, in a way. And often, it's just you that's been there, so it's, "Why aren't we doing as well as last time?" and a worry goes out.'

Charlie and Mick worked closely on the *Steel Wheels* tour with the late set designer Mark Fisher and lighting director Patrick Woodroffe. It won one of trade magazine *Pollstar*'s first awards for most creative stage production, in an itinerary that went on so long, the European leg had a different name, *Urban Jungle*, and a look all its own.

Fisher was the founder of Stufish, the set designers whose relationship with the Stones continued all the way to 2022's *SIXTY* festivities. As the company prepared for the launch of that European itinerary – sadly without Charlie's new input – modern-day chief executive Ray Winkler told the *Guardian* about *Steel Wheels*.

'The tour was, at the time, the biggest in terms of sheer volume of different elements used to construct the stage. It took over 100 men to build it. The stage stretched over 300ft and was flanked by 80ft high towers on each side that Mick Jagger appeared on for "Sympathy for the Devil". This is when the modern-day touring industry was born – when architecture and music came together to create these rock spectaculars.'

Mick Taylor, as a once and future collaborator but also as an admirer, agreed wholeheartedly. Talking to me in 2013, during his temporary reintroduction to the fold for the Stones' 50th-anniversary celebrations and beyond into the

14 on Fire tour, he mused: 'I'd say the beginning of the modern-day Stones in terms of theatre presentation was … well, it was always very theatrical and musical as well, but in terms of big presentation and stage lighting, there was such a huge development between '69 and the '80s. Their really big, massive tours all started with *Steel Wheels*, really. I saw them in 1999, at Wembley Stadium, and they were fantastic.'

Charlie's daughter Seraphina glows when she talks about her father's huge importance in those uncredited visual decisions. 'He was behind the creative process, that mega-touring, those stages, before U2, before any of those guys,' she says. 'Because of his design history, he did merchandising, designing of stages. Art direction, really. He was involved with the lighting, all the behind-the-scenes stuff. They have a really fantastic team and the same people [each time], and I don't think people know quite how involved he was.'

Charlie downplayed it, naturally. 'That's Mick, really, and I'm with 'im. That's us. Then when we get on the road I tend to leave it, but he's very aware of a lot more. He works very hard. Also people go to him more. Thank goodness they've learned not to come to me,' he laughed. '"Grumpy old sod, don't go to him."'

After a year and 115 shows, the combined *Steel Wheels/ Urban Jungle* pageant bowed out with two more concerts in August 1990 at Wembley Stadium, for an awe-inducing total of five there. At one, I distinctly remember Ronnie playing a solo and milking the applause a little more than usual – only to be told that we were cheering news of England scoring a goal in the World Cup. 'I went "Wow, I didn't know I was playing that well,"' said Woody.

For all the absurdity of a man yearning to be performing in a jazz club playing to a combined total on the two legs of the tour of 5.5 million people, Charlie told me soon afterwards that doing those gigantic shows was painless. 'The Stones are very easy to play with. In this day and age it's very easy to play, because ...' Here came another of his unexpected pauses and changes of direction. 'Let's see ... I blame Led Zeppelin for the two-hour-long show. Now, you see, we jumped in a few years from doing 20 minutes, all the hits and off – the Apollo Revue, we'll call it – we went from doing club dates which are two sets a night, which was great fun, to doing two minutes, because you got pulled off the stage, to doing 20-minute Apollo-type shows to doing, thanks to Led Zeppelin, this two-hour long show.

'If you're Jimmy Page, you can do that, and [with] Bonham's 20-minute drum solo. It wasn't about that with us, it was a different thing. I don't like doing drum solos, period. I don't hear things like that. When Zep, we call 'em, used to do that – what are we, early '70s, I suppose – that was hard work physically, because the monitors weren't so good, and the volume you played at. As a drummer, I'm talking about. But now the sound equipment is so sophisticated. The hardest thing with a drummer on those big stages is to be heard. Now, it's done for you, virtually. The amplification is there, so I just play naturally, at the volume I feel like playing, in this little cage I live in, and they adjust the volume of it.'

Chuck Leavell's arrival in the Stones' touring company had begun with the 1982 European tour and continued through the next two albums, so he was a no-brainer of a choice when the *Steel Wheels* circus hit the road. A Southern rock bastion, previously admired as a member of the Allman Brothers Band, he was another important component in the future of a group that had no intention of retreating into posterity. In time he was elevated to the role of music director of the Stones' shows, with an especially vital channel of communication with Charlie.

Leavell had seen the Stones as a 14-year-old, paying his $3 to see their package show with the Beach Boys and the Righteous Brothers at Legion Field in his home town of Birmingham, Alabama in 1965. He was in the crowd again for the 1969 US tour, then met Charlie for the first time when the Allmans made their debut performances in Europe, their second show being as Knebworth headliners in July 1974. Unusually, Charlie was present at the record company party, where Chuck asked him in small talk 'How's it going, man?' The drummer's answer was as inscrutable as ever. "Do you mean for me, or for the others?" Leavell remembers: 'He was very cordial, except for the short answers.'

Charlie, like all the Stones, made everything seem instinctive. But a great deal of rehearsal and symbiosis goes into mastering a two-and-a-half-hour set containing people's cherished musical memories, and Leavell has been instrumental in that process. 'Charlie played on some of the most iconic records ever made, obviously,' he says. 'But when we would go to present those things live, he couldn't always remember all the exact things he did, or where the changes would come.

'That's largely where my role as musical director came into play, to help Charlie when section B was going to come up. He would always look over to me for that, and it was very special for me to be able to give him those cues. It wasn't just Charlie, I did it for Mick – sometimes he's out there trying to work the crowd and he would look at me and I could say "verse" or "chorus". But Charlie especially, we had that kind of a bond and that was very endearing for me. It meant a lot to me to be able to do that.' The Stones' investiture of long-standing friend and collaborator Steve Jordan as Charlie's locum and then successor brought admirable continuity, but also an inevitable change in the stage dynamics. 'Quite frankly on the [2021] tour [the resumption of North American *No Filter* dates] I missed it, because Steve Jordan has a great musical mind and he doesn't really require that.'

Charlie had immense pride in the Stones' dedication to their work, but knew that it was somewhat at odds with the unjust idea that their collective hedonism somehow undermined their commitment to their craft. 'Unbeknown to a lot of people, the Rolling Stones are theatrical and terribly professional,' he said. 'They always have been, about whatever large or small facet of talent they have. The band has only ever not turned up once, and I only ever missed a show because I got the wrong date,' he said, referring to the 1964 diary malfunction we heard about earlier. 'Even as young tearaways, which we never really were … a lot of that was bullshit. I know people who were much more … whatever the word is. Newspapers are dreadful things, bless 'em. I can't read them. I flick through the cricket page, and that's it.'

Now Charlie could go home and concentrate on his next jazz venture: the reissue of his art-school homework project *Ode to a Highflying Bird* of 30-some years earlier. In the spring of 1991 the book was reprinted by UFO Records and newly accompanied by the mini-album *From One Charlie* …, on which he was joined at Lansdowne Studio in London by Dave Green on acoustic bass; bandleader Peter King, Charlie's longtime friend as manager of Ronnie Scott's Soho jazz idyll, on saxophone; Brian Lemon on piano; and teenage discovery Gerard Presencer on trumpet. Together they made the perfect complement to the book, combining five new King compositions with two Bird originals, 'Bluebird' and 'Relaxing at Camarillo'.

Charlie's instincts as a designer had led him to reject many previous offers to reissue the book because, on seeing the proofs, he was unhappy with the print colours. 'The book was an exercise in drawing, and we interpreted it musically,' he told me the first time we met, in August 1991. 'Peter King wrote the music for me – I chose sections of the book to illustrate and Peter wrote around that period. It's pretty closely observed. There's only one thing that I missed in the book, and that was mentioning the string section, but we do that musically.'

His explanation of how he heard the record was typical of how meticulously informed and voraciously enthusiastic he was for the music. 'My instructions to Peter, as far as the writing went, was that I wanted the band to sound like the scratch band that [Charlie] Parker got together in the studio, and they made four tracks. It's the one with Red Rodney, who happened to be in London and New York, when we played there recently, and he sat in with us.

'So there's an amazing tie-up with Parker. It went from the book 30 years ago to doing this record, and the group I wanted to sound like was the Red Rodney group, which had Kenny Clarke on drums, one of my favourite drummers, and John Lewis the piano player and Ray Brown the bass player. The next greatest thing is if Parker could have been alive and got up there with us. There's no nearer you can get to it.'

As Charlie turned 50, *From One Charlie* ... came to life in shows that included a one-night stand straight out of his dreams, at the Blue Note in New York, with Bernard Fowler, now very much aboard the Stones' ship, narrating from the book. Keith was in the audience. There was also a visit by the quintet to Tokyo, and a little later in the year, the illustrated volume formed part of their week of shows that opened Scott's new Birmingham club, this time with Ronnie among the visitors.

'I consider it a great honour to be asked to do that,' Charlie said in advance of the event, with entirely needless modesty, 'because I'm not very well known in that world. I would have thought there were a thousand other people they could have asked. But it'll be nice to do.' That performance yielded the Charlie Watts Quintet's live album, *A Tribute to Charlie Parker with Strings*.

The momentum stretched into the spring of 1992 in South America, including no fewer than 11 shows in Brazil, before a slip at home and an elbow fracture caused the cancellation of German dates. But then came more American shows, including more bookings at the Blue Note, again with Keith in the crowd. At the Hollywood Palace, *Variety* enthused that this 'may well be the most artistically successful solo project by any Rolling Stone, regardless of category'.

Charlie's conclusion about the book-plus-album Parker tribute was straightforward. 'What would be nice is if people heard it and thought, "Well, now I'd like to hear the real thing," and they bought the LP *Parker with Strings* or all the great Verve stuff.'

Home life in Devon continued with the usual priorities and diversions. The *Antiques Trade Gazette* reported, for example, that Charlie was spotted at the Irish Antiques Dealers'

Fair in Dublin. With Mick and Keith's fighting in abeyance and civility restored (some future explosions notwithstanding), there was confirmation that the Stones would forge ahead into the 1990s with their November 1991 signing of a hugely lucrative new deal with Virgin Records.

They would do so without Bill Wyman, whose agonisingly drawn-out departure was finally confirmed in January 1993. The bassist had been through his extremely messy marriage to Mandy Smith and was soon to be wed to long-time girlfriend Suzanne Accosta. He now wanted to spend time developing his many other interests besides music. Charlie got it, but observed: 'It was a shame he left because (a) it was great having him and (b) I think he missed out on a very lucrative period in our existence. There were very sparse periods you went through building the band, and he didn't really reap the rewards that we do now.'

Bill once said that, some years after his departure, Charlie telephoned him from South America and told him: 'Tonight in the middle of the show, I looked over to say something to you, and you weren't there.' He even admitted to some rare and revelatory reviewing of his and the band's work. 'When we were in Toronto rehearsing for the *Forty Licks* tour I was listening back to a lot of the songs that Bill and I had played together,' he said, 'and I found myself thinking that he was a lot better than I had remembered. I suppose I'd never really thought about it before. Bill had been a bass player who I worked with, and a friend, and I had never sat down and considered his actual bass playing.'

Such analysis of their recorded catalogue was rare. If you'd asked Charlie for his favourite Stones tracks he would have told you that he never listened to them, except perhaps in some unconventional context. As he shared with me: 'I was lying in bed last night, and I heard this ad for the RAC and I thought, "I recognise that intro," and it was a copy of the intro of "Street Fighting Man". It sounded very good. That's how I like to hear the Stones.

'There's nothing nicer, and this is a bit of egotism now, than driving down Mulholland Drive in Los Angeles, the sun shining, the roof down, a pink Cadillac, and your record's playing, No. 1. Now that is a silly schoolboy thing, but it's a wonderful feeling. I've heard some of our records at parties, and they sound a bit weak. But occasionally, you'll get one that is really a lot stronger than you remember it. Usually our records sound amazing when Chris Kimsey or whoever runs a tape off at the end of the day, after you've done two tracks or whatever. Nothing's on them except us. The actual five of us make very good ditties.'

Charlie's next recording obligation was self-imposed, as his quintet with Dave Green, Peter King, Brian Lemon and Gerard Presencer reconvened for sessions in March and April 1993 to make *Warm and Tender*. The album was a masterful showcase for the songs of the Gershwins, Rodgers & Hart, Cahn & Styne and more, and for the supple vocals of Bernard Fowler.

The New York vocalist entered the Stones' orbit via his backing vocals on Mick's first solo album *She's the Boss*. He became an adroit and enduring part of the band's shows and records, but Charlie was also entirely sold on him as the voice of his jazz ensemble. 'Bernard Fowler is a fantastic singer, as good as Bobby Womack,' he told me. 'He did fantastic on my records. I'm not talking about whether you like them or not, because they're all old songs that make you cry, but he sang them so beautifully, all of them. I always thought, if someone had come to you and said, "Would you manage [him]," you'd have to say yes.'

The album was released in October, touchingly with a close-up of Seraphina on the cover; another photograph of them inside showed dad holding daughter as a baby, and looking beatifically joyful. If you didn't know this was music that made him happy, you could tell by the fact that he even agreed to be interviewed about it on the sort of shows that would normally have him heading for the hills, such as *Late Night with Conan O'Brien*. His and Shirley's reward soon afterwards was to fly to Albuquerque, New Mexico, to buy horses. 'He has to pay for all those Arab stallions,' Ronnie told me with a laugh. 'He's got to tour, otherwise he'll be broke!'

'He did take us out to see horses one time,' says Lisa Fischer, 'myself and Bernard [Fowler], to see an Arabian stallion. I think we were in Australia. He was thinking about buying it, and we had lunch. He knew the horses, and it was another peaceful, beautiful side of him that I hadn't seen before.'

* * *

The Stones were indeed starting another run around the sun, with initial sessions for a new album at Ronnie's home studio in Kildare, south-west of Dublin. They had spent an intense week auditioning new bass players until, as Charlie said, they were 'bassed out'. *Everyone* applied, from new kids to old soldiers like Noel Redding of the Jimi Hendrix Experience. The drummer called it 'bloody hard work'. Mick called it 'torture'.

'Eventually,' remembered Keith, 'I said to Charlie, "You decide." And he said, "You bastard, you put me in the hot seat!" And I said, "Yeah, for *once*, Charlie, once in 30 years, you're going to be the supreme judge on this. Mick and I will say what we think."' In the end, a unanimous decision was made, taking temperament and compatibility into consideration as well as chops, on Chicago native Darryl Jones, whose years working with Miles Davis would hardly have harmed his chances in Charlie's eyes.

Mixing sessions for *Voodoo Lounge* took place in Los Angeles early in 1994. On a night off, this time it was Charlie in the audience with Keith, Ronnie and Darryl to see Bernard Fowler playing at the Viper Room. Soon, another giant tour coalesced behind the album. 'You miss the road when you're not on it,' said Charlie. 'Then you get back, and you're fed up right away.'

The schedule was as demanding as ever: North America from August until Christmas, South America in the new year, Africa, Asia, Down Under, and Europe from May until the *next* August. Parole was not available. Even with a turnover of hundreds of millions of dollars, breakeven on such a tour would not be targeted until about halfway through the run, in or around February.

On opening night at the RFK Stadium in Washington, DC, I watched them move through the gears to a comfortable fourth, if not fifth, from Charlie's opening salvo on 'Not Fade Away' to 'Jumpin' Jack Flash' 26 songs later. An admittedly veteran band was collectively and understandably tired of this-could-be-the-last-time clichés. 'I haven't heard so much about health care for the elderly since Bill left the band,' Mick griped. But new songs like 'You Got Me Rocking' and 'Love Is Strong' stood their ground against their much older brothers. Charlie played indefatigably and smiled plenty.

Three weeks short of a year later, as the tour arrived at Wembley Stadium, I wrote in *The Times*: 'As most men their age contemplate light gardening chores, the Rolling Stones are still in the office until 10.30 at night ... the songs that link Washington to Wembley sounded brighter and bolder as only a year's repetition could achieve ... the old devils are doing more than just seeing this tour out, they're chasing it home.'

Charlie had his road routine, and woe betide anyone who messed with it. 'Don't let him fool you, he kind of loved the adulation,' says close friend Tony King. 'He didn't like himself for liking it sometimes. He didn't like travelling, but his wardrobe was immaculate, all laid out. I remember once I said, "Can I look at your wardrobe?" And he had all his socks lined up in perfect colour range.

'I saw one sock that I thought should have been in front of one of the others, so I said, "I'm not sure about that sock" and he looked at me like, "How dare you?" Later on in the evening, backstage at the show, he came up to me and said, "You know what you said earlier about the socks? You were right." It bothered him tremendously that I noticed that one sock wasn't right.' Seraphina took great pleasure in moving his footwear out of order when he wasn't looking. 'Shirley would do it at home as well,' says King. 'She would disturb his sock drawer.'

'Charlie would do all this stuff like when he arrived in a hotel room,' says Bill. 'He'd unpack his suitcases, which were absolutely perfectly packed, as mine were, and take everything out one by one. He always used to have a two-bed room or a small suite, and the other bed he wasn't sleeping on, he'd just lay out all his clothes, like a military inspection. I did military, so I know the way you had to do it for the officers in the morning. Everything had to be precise. Charlie used to do that, and he was never in the military. But he'd lay his shirts out, all neatly squared, and ties, and socks, then he'd have all his shoes in a row,' he laughs. 'It was like a shop or something. But he did it all the time.'

'On the road, Charlie was two suitcases, and that was it,' says Keith. 'Me, I'm dragging around sound systems and trunks of crap. All my crap travelled with me, but he left his crap at home. To watch Charlie pack was like watching a Buddhist ceremony.'

Says King: 'Most people on the tour knew that he and I were tight and we would do things together. We'd go to museums, to lunch. I remember one time we went for dinner in Rome and there was this fella sitting there with his lady friend, and he leaned across to Charlie and said, "Are you in show business?" and Charlie said to him, "I think you could say that." He said, "I'm in show business, my name's Harold Davison." Charlie said, "I've got 23 of your [concert] programmes."'

Davison was the American impresario who brought Frank Sinatra, Judy Garland and other exotic attractions to Europe and indeed, in reverse, helped the Stones and other British invaders mount their first transatlantic sorties. Charlie clearly had not known him personally at that time, but was excited now to talk to the man who put Ella Fitzgerald on British stages. 'Harold looked at him in shock,' says King, 'and we ended up having a fantastic conversation about Ella and Sinatra and all the people that Harold Davison had worked with. It was a big thrill for Charlie.'

Keith's end-of-tour report after the *Voodoo Lounge* itinerary was glowing. He and Mick were getting along just fine, and the drummer was all the better for his own touring. 'I've never seen Charlie Watts so happy on the road,' he said. 'He's a happy guy, normally, but the road can get to anybody. He's brought his old lady with him more, and I think he's enjoying playing with Darryl, playing with the Stones. I think part of that comes from taking his own thing around, the jazz band. He took it around the world, and he learned a lot, found a lot more enjoyment and possibilities of playing.'

It had become de rigueur for a Stones tour to be followed by a live album, but in 1995 they excelled themselves in original thinking. *Stripped* was a combination of back-to-basics, live-in-the-studio workouts in Tokyo and Lisbon, and smaller club performances at Amsterdam's Paradiso, the Olympia in Paris and Brixton Academy back home. It was their take on *MTV Unplugged* but on their own terms, rather than the pipe and slippers acoustics of that series. No stools required, if you like, and the Stones hadn't sounded so spontaneous in years.

Charlie could get the brushes out, for one thing, notably on a glorious remake of 'Spider and the Fly', an early, half-forgotten Mick and Keith co-write from 1965's *Out of Our Heads*. But he and the boys were still rocking too, with a terrific salvo of 'Street Fighting Man' and Dylan's 'Like a Rolling Stone'. 'Thank you, Bob,' said Keith at its conclusion. *Stripped* was and remains greatly underrated. Charlie called it 'one of the most interesting records we've done'.

Everyone had earned some downtime. Except that, after a certain amount of R&R, none of the Rolling Stones has ever been any good at knocking around the house for long. Charlie, as he always admitted, would only be getting under Shirley's feet in any case. In the new year of 1996 he had all the more reason to focus on work, with the death of his mother Lillian at the age of 74. She had been ill for some time, in Milton Keynes Hospital, where both Linda and Charlie visited every day.

So it was that he and his jazz compadres stepped into extremely familiar ground, both geographically at Olympic Studios in Barnes, and musically, leafing through the song-book pages of Porter, the Gershwins and Hoagy Carmichael. The resulting *Long Ago & Far Away* was promptly released in June, with Bernard Fowler taking one more turn as featured vocalist.

Charlie cut perhaps his most debonair figure ever on the cover, besuited and in a gaberdine raincoat by a lamppost. By now he was almost the media maven, appearing on the *David Letterman Show* during a run of North American shows that included one at Carnegie Hall. Keith, ever loyal, was there again, and there was a London date for the quintet at the Shepherd's Bush Empire.

The next Stones album, *Bridges to Babylon*, fell pregnant later that year in productive Jagger–Richards songwriting sessions. Mick was keen to work with Los Angeles producers and sampling wizards the Dust Brothers, which meant a different and potentially difficult role for Charlie, playing along to loops. But Mick said the timekeeper rose admirably to the challenge of combining technology and tradition.

'He loved doing it,' said Mick, 'and he was able to do both things – be traditional, play with the band, and do loops and experiment. He likes jazz a lot, and jazz is very experimental music. It's much more experimental than rock music, and rock can be very hybrid.' Along with the flagship single 'Anybody Seen My Baby', Charlie was rock-solid on archetypal but exciting tracks such as 'Flip the Switch' and 'Low Down', and sparkled on the outstanding electro-blues 'Might as Well Get Juiced'.

There was a memorable final flourish, too, as the album concluded with Keith's beautifully vulnerable 'How Can I Stop', described by producer Don Was as 'the most radical thing on the album'. Its jazz-drenched bravery, also incorporating some extraordinary saxophone detail by the great Wayne Shorter, harnesses one of Charlie's finest performances, and certainly one of the most attuned to his musical passion.

'It was the last thing recorded for the album,' said Was. 'There was a car waiting for Charlie outside the studio and it took him to the airport immediately after we finished that take. Charlie did this really intense flourish with Wayne at the end that was almost like his farewell to the record. Then he got up and left and went back to England. It was maybe 5.30 in the morning and it was a really poignant moment that got captured.'

That summer I flew to Toronto for the next round of interviews with the band, which took place one by one (and one *to* one) throughout the day in a former Masonic temple that – over six floors – they'd converted to their every need. It ended, after a delightful late-night chinwag with Keith, with the outrageous privilege of being invited to join a handful of people watching them rehearse into the small hours. 'We have as good a time rehearsing up there with no one in the room at 2 o'clock in the morning as when you're doing a big show,' said Charlie.

These were not just cursory passes at, say, 'Satisfaction', despite its constant presence in their lives for more than 30 years, but a full run-through. Just the four of them, as I recall, although perhaps Chuck Leavell was on keyboard duty too; certainly not the full live band. Each song was played, not in the direction of a largely absent audience, but facing Charlie, awaiting his approval, his eye contact, his verdict.

Ever the expert at dispelling the sense of awe that such an experience brought – and if it didn't, you would have no business being there – Charlie had the perfect matter-of-fact aside. 'Here, in rehearsals, is the only time I ever know the Rolling Stones catalogue,' he said. 'Other than that, I've forgotten it.'

Musing on that specific physical shape the band made in rehearsal, he added: 'That's what we do. I always play with Keith's amplifier right by my left foot. I never wanted to go on risers, because I couldn't hear him.'

The ensuing tour ('They've talked me into it again') started in September, and went around both the globe and the year. It embraced 97 shows and the superbly audacious innovation of a cantilever bridge that telescoped out into the audience, leading to the 'B' stage that allowed the Stones to re-create Richmond R&B in corporate stadia, 'Little Queenie' and all. Charlie was much involved in its design along with Mick, Mark Fisher and Patrick Woodroffe, and the potency of the production was overwhelming.

'He watched old Busby Berkeley films and took in the sets,' says his friend Jools Holland. 'He was very much involved in the aesthetics, so anybody that went to see a Rolling Stones show over the years, he was very much part of that.' Holland was the keyboard player with Squeeze in their first run of hits, including 'Cool for Cats', one of the first records bought by Charlie's daughter Seraphina. Much later the two men became friends. 'My dad used to laugh at me,' she says, 'because I was always starstruck. "Oh my God, Jools Holland called, Pa."' One time she was embarrassed to have to tell Holland that her father had gone to bed at 8 p.m.

Holland was an established music TV presenter on *The Tube* and *Later …* and a bandleader in his own right when he and Charlie recognised their kindred spirits. He joined the *Bridges* entourage to interview them for the book *The Rolling Stones: A Life on the Road*, but that wasn't their first meeting.

'I think I played at Mick's 50th birthday with my band,' he says, 'and I spent some time talking to Charlie there, because he liked the boogie-woogie nature of the Big Band. He had it at Strawberry Hill, the big Gothic house in Twickenham. It was quite surreal because you were in this weird, 18th-century Gothic fantasy room talking drums, so I think we realised we quite liked one another.'

Hardly one to be awestruck around world-famous artists, the keyboard player nevertheless understood the magnitude of mixing with someone he had admired on disc from afar. 'I'd always loved their records, of course, and I really loved his drumming, because it was special, it was the feel of it,' says Holland. 'Not that we want comparisons, but Ringo had the same thing.

'Earl Palmer was a person they both admired, the drummer who played on all the rock 'n' roll records, and he had that same feel. If you were to try to define it, it almost goes across the beat, and because of that, it fits it perfectly. It's not *against* everything, but it's a contrast, where he's almost slightly swinging when they're straight, and straight when they're swinging. It's a minuscule thing of feel, and it's a hard thing to define, but when you've got it, you've got the world, and not many people have it.

'So I went on tour with them for maybe three weeks, which was great, and they were fantastic socially. They looked after me so well. So it was great fun, but the person I probably saw the most of was Charlie, so that's when I started to get to know him more. You're in this bubble with everybody and you've got a certain sense of camaraderie. We went round Japan as well.

'I think we shared the same humour. He was very dry. He'd sit there, and there'd be quite long silences. I have a couple of friends like this. One of you would say something, then one would say something else, then there'd be quite a long pause. Then someone would say something that was so funny you'd be unable to speak, having had a very long, dry conversation before that. Very gentlemanly.

'I realised that Charlie had a lot of the same interests as me. Also, Ronnie and everybody else had their families with them, so Charlie was a bit more available for dinner. So I had dinner with him quite often, and if we were in a town, he'd always want to find the jazz clubs. I got to like him very much then, and I got to learn things about him that were very endearing. He showed me some of the sketches of the hotel rooms he'd been in, and they were really great. You thought, "What an incredible idea to sketch each bed, to take the moment, it's such a Zen thing."'

After his love of jazz, probably featuring next in the rather short list of Things People Know about Charlie is what you might call the Daily Sketch, and the completely true story of how he drew the bed in every hotel room he had been in since 1967. 'When we were recording in Paris,' says producer Chris Kimsey, 'we stayed in the same hotel as Charlie, the Château Frontenac, and after a session one morning – because we didn't finish until 4, 5 in the morning – he said, "Chris, I want to show you something." And they were books of drawings of every hotel room he's ever been in. It's remarkable, it was so cool. Really nice little etchings, too. We know that all bands when they're on tour, all they see is the hotel and the gig. They never see the city they're in, really. Maybe that's why he drew all the hotel rooms.'

'When we were in America,' remembers Holland, 'he liked to go out. But he didn't drink, so he got up in the morning, he sketched the room, he liked to go shopping, for socks or whatever his necessities were. Never bothered with security or anything, just had a hat of invisibility. He was so laconic, and he had this incredible aura that spread to everybody else. He was one of the calmest people that you'd ever met, and because he was laid back, people around him immediately became laid back.'

'With that level of fame, people generally were pretty good, they left him alone,' says Seraphina. 'But when you're touring like that, day after day … I'm not saying he didn't love the fans, that would be disingenuous, of course he did, but he wasn't particularly interested in going to a nightclub.'

Bill Wyman remembers Charlie's meticulous approach to passing the hours and the days on the road. 'He used to sit and draw the telephone, in one room, or in another room he'd do the television, then he'd do a chair or something. He drew everywhere he went. These books, they're absolutely invaluable. They would be amazing for the British Museum or something, they should be saved.' The drummer just swatted away the fuss, as ever. 'It's a fantastic nonbook,' he once said.

In 1996 he had even more reason to want to stay home, as Seraphina gave birth to her only child, Charlotte (*not* named after him, as many assumed). He couldn't have been more happy or proud. 'Charlie was this wonderful doting grandfather,' observed Chris Kimsey.

Back on the road, Holland recalls one particular moment of relaxation with Charlie. 'I think we had one afternoon of sketchcraft, where I sketched his television. I tried to sketch him, but that didn't work, and I thought he'd sketch me, but he wasn't interested. He was sketching his room again.

'Then I went to Mick's château in France and, rather embarrassingly, I stupidly didn't have any money. I'd got a later flight, got a taxi and had to borrow the money off Mick for the taxi. Anyway, Charlie was nearby, so Mick had a little party. He's very inclusive, he invited me and Charlie, and Tom Stoppard, the playwright, was there. Mick was doing a film with him [2001's *Enigma*, written by Stoppard and produced by Mick's Jagged Films]. Maybe three other people, a handful.

'Mick had a little thing around a camp fire and made us food. It was lovely. I remember Charlie saying to me [about Mick]: "He is amazing, isn't he? Wherever he goes, he gathers these amazing people. I've never known anybody like him." He loved Mick. In a band, people annoy one another, that's family for you, that happens. But he genuinely had great respect for Mick.'

Tony King says: 'He was very proud of the Rolling Stones, and he always said to me that Mick was the best lead singer in the business. He admired Mick like crazy and they were great friends.' Adds Lisa Fischer: 'I loved the way Mick and Charlie huddled. They loved each other. They all loved him.'

'He's a huge worrier,' Charlie confided to me about Mick, the man whose bum he had watched wiggling in front of him for half a century. 'He's not like me and Keith, and thank goodness he [isn't], at times. Sometimes I wonder if he worries too much. For me, it's a question of whether my hands hurt. With him, if his throat hurts, he can't sing, can't perform. You have to be very strict like that, and he's a very bright man, he's very aware.'

While gleaning that opinion about Mick for one of the many BBC Radio 2 documentaries I made on the Stones, I went further and pinned Charlie down about his other bandmates. He was expectedly unexpected. 'Ronnie? He's a lovely man,' he said, this in 2006 before the guitarist's dramatic new-dad clean-up. 'He has demons, but he's the most gregarious one in the band, and he has the biggest head. People love him. My granddaughter thinks he's wonderful. He's a very loving guy.

'Mick is the one I speak to more than anybody. Keith is the one you never hear from, from one month to the next, because he hates telephones. He's the most eccentric of all of us, that man. He loves touring. Whenever I say I'm going to retire, he says, "What are you going to do?" He reads these tomes. I don't think he reads anything under three inches thick. The thicker they are, the happier he is. He doesn't watch television.'

The point was rather well emphasised in 1998, when the band's European tour was delayed by nearly a month after Keith fell off a library ladder at home in Connecticut and cracked two ribs, reaching for a book on Leonardo da Vinci. 'I was looking for da Vinci's book on anatomy,' he said. 'I learned a lot about anatomy, but I didn't find the book.'

When Mick's laryngitis caused a shorter interruption to that schedule, with the European tour under way, there was no time for Charlie to travel home. But he made the best of it, travelling to Spain for two or three days off and visiting – by now you might guess – the Guggenheim Museum in Bilbao. Mick would sometimes join him on his culture trips; in 2015 the pair visited the Darwin D. Martin House, designed by Frank Lloyd Wright in his Prairie School style, in Buffalo, New York.

When dates resumed, another milestone arrived as a sociological triumph. After many years of trying to part the Iron Curtain, the Stones played in Russia for the first time, at the Luzhniki Stadium in Moscow. Charlie's response to the idea was amusingly familiar. 'I didn't want to go there. I had no interest in going there. Mick kept saying, "It'll be great when we get there." When we finally did, it was fantastic, actually. I thought they were going to be a really miserable lot, 'cos when you've come up through the Cold War and Khrushchev, you thought, "Oh God." But they were so nice to us. We were like this thing that they never had.

'It was like 95 degrees there the week before we got there, and by the time we played it had dropped to about ten,' he said. 'It was freezing and raining, and when we got there it was night, and I thought, "Oh bloody hell, Moscow, snow," and everything. I opened the window of the hotel, which was just across the river, and you could see Red Square and the cathedral, and it was like fairyland. It was a real magical thing to see, every time I looked at it. Fantastic. And I went out with Mick a couple of times, which was hilarious, some of the places we went. Felt like an elder statesman.'

The irony is that if Charlie had ever carried out his threat not to tour again, he might never have experienced any of that culture, or indeed much social interaction at all. 'I'm what you would call a loner,' he once said. 'I can get along just fine without people around me. We live on a farm, you know. Even worse, we have two – one in England and one in France. My wife runs the farms and I live there, so to speak. The only people about the house are men and women who are in agriculture.

'Occasionally we go out and dine with friends, but not too often. I'm not like Ronnie Wood, who needs to have people around him all day. If I'm honest, I enjoy the company of dogs more than that of humans. Not that I loathe my species, but I'm of no good to them. They would find me a miserable little man after a while.

'Keith doesn't go out at all either. He lives with his wife in Connecticut and his life isn't all that different from mine. Mick is the only one who, through the years, has succeeded in dragging me out of the house, time and again.'

It would be easy to interpret these comments as some sort of self-critical confessional, but not a bit of it. Charlie was simply someone who knew that he was wired up differently to most other people, and wasn't bothered about it at all.

Touring with him for more than 25 years, Bill got to see his foibles and eccentricities at close quarters. 'Sometimes he didn't sleep, he'd just walk,' he says. 'A typical Charlie day would be, you finished the concert, you come back to the hotel and you kind of unwind a bit, then he'd go into Keith's room, where music was being played at full blast – usually what we'd just recorded, which was the last thing I wanted to hear, having just done a concert.

'He'd hang around there and he'd go to Mick's room, then he'd come to my room and hang out there, and we'd watch TV for a while or something. Then I'd say, "I'm going to bed now, Charlie." It'd be two in the morning or something. He'd say, "All right, I'll see you tomorrow." He'd go to his room, put his coat on and he'd go out to the town, and just wander about for two hours, then come back. Then he'd be walking the hotel corridors looking to see if anybody was awake before he went to bed.

'He did it so many times, and there are some hilarious stories. I've got one, in Canada. He came back from a walk and told me the whole story, so I told everybody else. He was walking, and saw this clothes shop with this George Raft-type suit in the window of a shop. They said the trousers were a bit big, so they said come back in a couple of hours, they'll be ready. So he went to this Indian restaurant. He went in there and ordered some food. It took forever and he fell asleep at the table, and the Indian people thought he was a druggie or something, so they called the police.

'They came and shook him up, and said, "Who are you and what are you doing here?" He said, "Where am I?" and they said Toronto. He said, "What the fuck am I doing in Toronto?" So the guy says, "It's three in the afternoon" and he said, "Oh great, my suit will be ready." That bottom line, he did it all the time. He'd take a whole situation and break it down to one sentence.'

BACKBEAT

A Man of Wealth and Taste

Charlie's appetite for collecting was voracious. There was a place for everything, and everything was at *his* place. Cars, first edition books, silverware, flatware, records, photographs, memorabilia on the American Civil War and Horatio Nelson. And vintage drum kits. They all surely deserve the attention of the National Trust.

'He collected all kinds of things. He was worse than me in some ways,' says Bill Wyman, the group's archivist-in-chief. 'I collected all the [Stones] memorabilia and small bits and pieces, he collected American war stuff. He used to have 14 bloody guns and all kinds of things, all the hats and uniforms. You'd go in his house and they were all displayed, like a museum.'

For Charlie's daughter Seraphina, every artefact is a page from her life, just as likely to bring sadness as laughter, and a certain bewilderment as she and her husband Barry Catmur attempted to log it all after her father's passing. As she shared with me: 'I opened this cupboard the other night, a piece of furniture with drawers, and I found all these things, Edwardian glasses and carved pipes.' She adds in mock indignation: 'I was like, "He's forgotten about this stuff, hasn't he, totally forgotten about it!"

'I just felt like saying, "More bloody stuff!" I really wanted to speak to him. "What is *this*? This could be Roman and incredibly valuable, or it could be a piece of junk." Another thing was a tin. Just some tin! And it's clearly a 1940s football thing, all a bit rusty. You know, am I going on the *Antiques Roadshow* with this, or is it just a piece of crap?'

Seraphina recognises and remembers the stages where her father would have a particular attack of the obsessive-compulsives. 'He's had phases where I can see he's gone completely OCD-collecting mad, throughout his life. There's been the Nelson phase, which my mother said was her thing and he nicked it from her, so she stopped collecting.' She feels gratitude towards über-fans who have helped catalogue items of what we might call Wattstuff, and have helped her to identify things she remembers from childhood, like a sweatshirt he wore in Brazil one time. Trivial and yet paramount, all at once.

'He had refined tastes,' notes another long-haul comrade, Seraphina's godfather Tony King. 'He liked Stuart silver. He liked autographed pictures of famous people from way back. He loved making collections of things, and he had some beautiful first edition books.' Charlie loved to rummage for bargains in junk shops, once delighting in finding an Edison phonograph and 30 cylinders, £30 all in. He collected Georgian silverware, and his war memorabilia included bullets that were reputedly fired at the Battle of Little Bighorn in the Great Sioux War of 1876. It may have been Custer's Last Stand, but Charlie was just getting started.

It wasn't enough for him simply to own the records on which his drumming heroes played. He wanted to own their actual instruments. He bought a drum kit given by Kenny Clarke to Max Roach from Clarke's widow. He owned the Sonny Greer kit from Duke Ellington's band, and that of 1930s swing drummer Big Sid Catlett, the man whom Art Blakey said could 'make a drum sound like a butterfly'. *Every* Agatha Christie first edition, every one by Greene, Wodehouse, Waugh, all signed.

'He was a collector,' says Mick. 'When I was a kid I used to collect stamps, but I don't collect anything now.' He describes his friend's immense aggregation of drum kits as 'crackers', but agrees that all of his collections deserve to be in a museum. His drum technician and friend Don McAulay, who curates them, says confidently that they will be.

At Charlie's London residence in Pelham Crescent, what else would he have next to his collection of first editions, says McAulay, but Napoleon's sword. 'I'd go and find him cool drums by tons of jazz artists. We'd find their kits and other people would help him collect and he said, "You need to look after this thing we've created here."

'I found these Gene Krupa items from Gene's widow, which were a huge part of musical history. He had original acctates by Krupa and Billie Holiday, which he was never going to play. He also gave me a gift that shocked the hell out of me. He said, "I only need this. You take that," and he gave me a handful of Gene Krupa items. He had watches from Benny Goodman, suits, jewellery, awards. We packed his room. It's a museum that's out of control.'

During the Stones' 1976 European tour, Lord Lichfield invited Charlie and Mick to stay at his home at Shugborough Hall in Staffordshire. They had visited the society photographer, first cousin once removed of the Queen, in the 1960s, and the man sometimes called the 'rock 'n' roll aristocrat' had taken a famous picture at Mick and Bianca's wedding. During the later stay he took Charlie and Mick for a walk around the estate and its farm, and snapped Mick when he picked up a cockerel, an image later displayed with the inevitable caption 'Little Red Rooster'.

He also gave the pair a private viewing of the house, and when Charlie saw the collection of Paul de Lamerie silverware, he politely pointed out that the date on its caption was incorrect. It was disputed, but checked. He was, of course, proved right. In a television interview, Lichfield recalled asking his butler who was the nicest house guest he'd looked after. 'Without doubt, Charlie Watts,' he said.

Even from when Charlie and Shirley moved into their first apartment in Ivor Court, they set about filling it with objets d'art. Danish photographer Bent Rej, who travelled with the Stones as part of their trusted cabal for most of 1965, wrote: 'The most important room of the apartment ... is locked. It is a small room – three by four metres –

which is filled with treasures. Here, in cupboards with glass doors, Charlie keeps his precious collection of fine, antique weapons, caps, uniforms, banners and newspapers. Charlie's newspaper collection is a rarity that many a museum would pay a small fortune to get hold of. Here you will find some of the oldest examples of newspapers in the world.'

He developed his curiosity about fine art on early tours. 'Modern art is like modern jazz – it's just people you like,' he told *Melody Maker*, with his customary pretentiousness bypass. 'Obviously anybody who lives in 1967 should be aware of art. What you mean is Picasso, I suppose, and that's not modern art. Really I can't talk on the subject. You should ask my wife.'

When the Wattses bought Peckhams in Halland, outside Lewes, the *NME*'s Keith Altham was invited to view its antiques and ornaments among the oak beams and open fireplaces. The living room contained a green marble bust of the Greek god Hypnos and a library stocked with Dylan Thomas and Wilde; the study had American Civil War rifles and revolvers and, in a glass case, a muster roll for a US cavalry troop listing each man's pay in 1880. A bedroom had a sword rack at its head, a small side room housed Shirley's collection of Victorian dolls.

'He amassed a great collection of American Civil War stuff,' says Keith Richards, 'and I knew a little bit about that, so now and again he would show me a trophy he'd got. I think because he never expected to get to America, and then suddenly we did, it opened up that passion. He got what he wanted out of it, then I said, "Are you still getting any more stuff?" "No. Collection's finished. I got what I wanted."'

The cars that he never learned to drive, nor needed to, were another obsession. He would put on one of his best suits just to sit in these beautiful vintage vehicles and bask in their craftsmanship. 'I just love the shape of old cars,' he told the *NME* in 2018. 'I can't drive, so I just sit in them and listen to the engine. I suppose you could call it a rich man's indulgence.'

The pride of the fleet was a stunning 1937 Lagonda Rapide Cabriolet with a V12 engine, one of only 25 ever produced, which Charlie bought in 1983. He also reclined in a Bugatti Atlantic from the late 1930s, a yellow Citroën 2CV as driven by Roger Moore's James Bond in *For Your Eyes Only*, a Citroën Méhari, a Lamborghini Miura and several Rolls-Royces. He didn't feel the need to augment the collection, as his friend Keith Moon did with his, by adding an ice cream van or a hovercraft.

Jools Holland recalls a conversation while touring in Europe with Charlie and his later jazz quartet the ABC&D of Boogie-Woogie. 'He was talking about some of the cars he had at the moment. If people are a success and they like cars, they will buy the cars they looked at as a child, or had a Dinky toy of. I've observed that a lot. At the same time, because you've got to get from A to B in the modern world, you'll try and get whatever the snazzy car of the day is.

'Charlie had some old American cars, because he loved those, and he'd also 1930s ones. He was also talking about how he got the material from one of Edward VIII's suits and had the car trimmed in the same material, because he had some spare and he thought it was so lovely. Then we were talking about old Rollses and Bentleys and I had some of those, the '60s continental ones, and he did too, what they called the "Chinese Eye" Rolls-Royce.

'He said, "We used to drive down to Devon, the hood leaked slightly but all cars were like that in the '60s. But it went along, it had a certain momentum." Then I was asking him about this 1930s car that was beautifully trimmed and I said, "I'd love to see it. Do you ever drive up to London?" He said, "No, no." I said, "It's good exercise for an old car, a journey like that." He said, "No, I can't drive." I said, "What?" We'd been speaking literally for an hour about cars but he never had a driving licence. I assume it was because it took people a while to do that, and the Rolling Stones were such a success, and it gets to a point where it gets a bit late. It was so Charlie-esque not to mention that until the very end.'

Lisa Fischer remembers, on joining the Stones' extended family, hearing about that particular eccentricity for the first time. 'It was hilarious,' she says. '"Charlie, you don't drive? What do you do?!" I say, if you can, and you want to, go ahead. Life's too short. Enjoy just looking at them.'

This was a man who truly knew how to enjoy life, whose purchases would deserve the invention of a new award for

Best Use of Rockstar Millions. 'One time I saw him in the back of his limousine in Soho,' says Dave Green, who was doubtless carrying his double bass to a gig at Ronnie's or Pizza Express. 'I'm walking down the street and Charlie's in the back, he probably didn't even see me. When we played with the ABC&D, we used to fly home together. We'd meet his guy there with a Bentley at Heathrow, and Charlie would drop me off at Ruislip.'

Says producer Chris Kimsey: 'I think Charlie was the type of person that liked to sit and be driven, to really get the full enjoyment of the car. As you know, it's different when you're driving yourself. When you're a passenger, it's a bit different.' And on one occasion, he insisted on sharing the luxury.

'The last time I saw him socially was at Ronnie's house in Holland Park with Seraphina and Charlotte,' Kimsey goes on. 'We were talking about different art, music and clothes. Then we were going to leave, so he said to me, "Do you want a lift?" I said that was very kind, but I was parked the other end of Holland Park Road, about half a mile away. I said, "I'm not far away at all, Charlie." He said, "No, I'll give you a lift." I thought, "Wow, why is he ..." So we got outside and he'd rented a Rolls-Royce Phantom, a big new one with a chauffeur, because he was taking the family out. So he gave me a lift in the Phantom, just down the road.'

Holland saw at close quarters that Charlie had refined the art of savouring his financial stability to an enviable degree. 'At that time, people would get art catalogues. I think it's all online now, but he'd have catalogues of paintings and things.

You'd say, "You can't see it in the auction, are you still going to buy it?" and he'd say, "Yeah, I'll get a few things. I won't go mad, but I may get half a dozen things, and if I'm on tour for a few months I'll have treated myself. When I get home it's like Christmas, because I'll have forgotten what I've got. So I'll get in, and there'll be a painting, a suit, a watch and some 78 records." I thought, "What a great thing. Everybody works and has their rewards, and they were his." He was a man of simple, old-fashioned tastes."

Albert Einstein used to claim that he had no particular talent, just an enquiring mind. Charlie had both. 'We'd go round Christie's in South Kensington and look at anything,' says Holland, 'whether it was clocks or picture frames. We weren't going to buy anything, just have a look. He seemed to be one of those people that had the view that he didn't really judge things, he was just trying to understand them.'

Chuck Leavell, the Stones' musical director and keyboard player on tour, would often see Charlie out and about on days off. 'And most of the time with no security. It wasn't until the very later years that the band insisted he had security,' he says. 'He frequented museums all the time, and my wife Rose Lane and I would run into him on occasion, because we like to go out as well to those kind of things. He was constantly interested in art of all kinds. Antique furniture, paintings, flatware, anything. He just had this brilliant knowledge of and interest in all things artistic.'

Often, Charlie's combination of inquisitive and acquisitive got the better of him. Holland remembers: 'He bought a copy of the Bayeux Tapestry, made in the late 19th century. It was maybe three feet high, whereas the original is perhaps eight or ten feet tall. It had these winding barrels at each end, beautifully made in mahogany with brass handles. You'd wind it and the tapestry would come past you, and it had a little description. I said, "What are you going to do with that, then?" And he said, "Dunno. It's great, though, isn't it?"'

Charlie shared Mick and Bill's passion for cricket: one of the eight pieces of audio he selected on *Desert Island Discs* was the BBC Radio archive recording of John Arlott and Michael Charlton's commentary on the 1956 Test match between England and Australia. 'He used to watch the cricket on the television but listen to it on the radio,' says his sister Linda.

'He had collections of cricket stuff, and I used to give him signed photos of Bradman and all kinds of stuff like that,' says Bill. 'He used to go to all the auctions. He was mad about cricket, as Mick is, and he used to go and watch all the time. He used to watch, I used to play – I did eight years of charity cricket with Eric [Clapton, for the Bunbury Cricket Club] and played with every international player in the world, batting with David Gower, and facing the bowling of Viv Richards, Wayne Daniel and all those people.

'Charlie never came to any of the charity things because they were always on weekends, and they were in Hove or up in Birmingham,' says Bill. 'We did all the international places. But when I took my hat-trick at the Oval against an Old England team, I had my idol Denis Compton and his mate Keith Miller, and Gower was umpiring. Charlie heard about it and I got this phone call at three o'clock in the morning.

'I picked the phone up. "'Ello?" "It's Charlie." "It's three o'clock in the morning, Charlie, where are you?" "I dunno, wait a minute." And it was like the Goons, you heard these footsteps. "Er, somewhere called, I think it's called Boonus Airies." I said, "You're in Argentina." He said, "Oh yeah, that's right." I said, "Why are you calling at three o'clock in the morning?"

'He said, "I just found out that you took a hat-trick at the Oval? They said you were smoking a cigarette when you were bowling?" And I said, "Yeah, I always do." There's pictures of me with the cigarette, bowling my leg breaks and googlies, getting a hat-trick. And he said, "And you were treading your cigarette ends on the hallowed turf?" He was more interested in what I was doing with my cigarette ends than the fact that I'd taken this hat-trick against an Old England team.'

Charlie and Mick often visited Lord's or The Oval together, sometimes as guests of Sir Tim Rice. Writer Jim White recounted the story of Australian broadcaster James Brayshaw turning around in the commentary box at the Melbourne Cricket Ground during a Test match and seeing an older gentleman, impeccably dressed and sitting on his own. No minder, no entourage, no fuss. He had been invited by Shane Warne. Every time Brayshaw plied him for rock 'n' roll war stories, Charlie answered politely, but was far more keen to talk cricket. He and Mick were also friends with Australian fast bowler Dennis Lillee, who they first met during the Ashes tour of 1972.

'We mostly watched cricket but we were great football fans too,' says Mick, who follows Arsenal while Charlie was a Tottenham Hotspur fan. 'We loved talking about cricket and we'd go to a lot of games, mostly Test matches, and one-days. Most English people who normally wear a black suit, they go to Lord's and dress in this ridiculous 1920s striped blazer, those Marylebone Cricket Club [MCC] colours. Lurid, to say the least. Charlie used to sometimes dress up in those blazers. He would be very sociable at these games, he wouldn't be the quiet Charlie that we all talk about. Yakety-yak, all day long.'

In 2014, after the Stones played the Adelaide Oval on the *14 on Fire* tour, Charlie and Mick met Sir Don Bradman's son John and took a tour of the Bradman Museum. The day after the band performed at Murrayfield Stadium in 2018, Charlie caused many to whisper behind their hands – 'Look! It's Charlie Watts!' – when he turned up at the Grange Cricket Club in Edinburgh to watch the one-day international between Scotland and England.

Linda remembers that often, when he would phone her while he was on tour, Charlie would spend a cursory moment asking how she and her daughters were, then ask to speak to her husband Roy, and spend 45 minutes talking about the cricket. 'I'd do a running commentary while he was in America,' says Roy. 'Then he's linked up with Mick in another room, so I've got both of them on the phone while I'm doing a ball-by-ball commentary.'

The other passion, of course, was records. Not just jazz, because he loved classical, soul and beyond too – but it was in pursuit of his oldest musical love that Charlie took Jools Holland into his confidence about one of his favourite places. From Holland's description, you can almost see either him or Charlie rummaging for England in the sort of shop that Charlie would have dreamed of. On tour with the ABC&D of Boogie-Woogie, he and Dave Green stepped into Teuchtler Schallplattenhandlung und Antiquariat in Vienna. Charlie left having signed a record crate, and many euros lighter.

'He told me about this record shop, which, again, only he would know about, in a bit of Vienna that's out of the centre,' says Holland. 'The grandfather had a shop and ran it at the end of the war, and had all these 78s. He specialised in blues and jazz, and it was the go-to place to get this music that everybody was wild about. When vinyl came in, or when the 78s stopped and it became LPs, everybody else sold theirs cheap. He said, "I'm not selling mine off cheap because one day these are going to be worth a lot." The shop continued, as it does today and it's one of the best blues, jazz and classical music shops in the world. The daughter ran it, and her two sons run it now.

The shop advertises second-hand classical, jazz, Viennese songs, rock, pop and dance records for sale. No mention of 78s, but Charlie knew they were there. 'He said to me, "They never open the upstairs room. Go there and you'll find what I found. Tell them Charlie sent you, and they'll show you." So you go in, they were pleased to see me, and you go through the back of the shop. There are these alleyways and back stairs, and it's like something out of a 1940s European film. You go past a smoking woman who might have been an informant, looking disdainfully at you as you go past her doorway. Somebody's got their washing out, it's down these corridors, round the back, in this unchanged kind of world.

'You go up, into these rooms and they open these shredded, motheaten curtains, which are falling apart, like Miss Havisham's in *Great Expectations*, and light comes in the room. Charlie said for him, one of the loveliest things he could imagine finding would be a new Victorian or 18th-century shirt, in its box, or its packet, that had never been opened. This was like that, because some of the 78 records had never been played, in their original wrappers. I said, "Did you play them?" He said "No, I couldn't, not knowing they'd never been played. If I played them, then it's all over."

'So I got some records, and as Charlie said, you mustn't play them on a wind-up gramophone. That will ruin them with a big needle. You have to play them with a proper needle through big speakers with an amp. And they sound fan-*tastic*. What Charlie said was, with a record, you're getting something that was made at the same time the music was being made. He was very sensitive to that, and loved it. So I was very pleased he introduced me to that, and whenever I'm in Vienna, I go there. But of course it's one of those things that only Charlie would know. Who else? He was in contact with these lost worlds.'

7

Born with Grandpa Energy

At a certain point in the clockwork precision of a modern-day Rolling Stones show, some ten songs in and before Keith's two-song frontman spot, Mick introduces the entire company. Working his way through the live band, he arrives at his fellow core members, and at one part of the event that I will miss the most.

As Charlie grew older, first grey, then silver, adoration of him among scores of thousands of stadium fans grew ever more palpable. He simply didn't know where to put such adulation, other than to sit at his drum stool looking like he was praying for it to finish. Mick would routinely announce him as the 'Wembley Whammer', sometimes adding a 'Boom Boom!' in the middle of his name as an extra term of endearment. The crowd went as wild as at any other point in two hours-plus of an honour roll of megahits. One time, as the cheering continued, with Charlie uncomfortably magnified on giant screens, Mick commanded: 'Say something.' After a pause and a bewildered look, Charlie offered a token 'Hello.' 'He speaks!' retorted Mick.

'I loved that,' says vocalist Lisa Fischer, who would be watching from very close quarters, 'and because he hated it so much, the more we loved it. It was so cute. We loved watching him squirm, because he deserved the love that was coming to him. It was too much for his heart to bear.'

At the end of a show, says friend and drum technician Don McAulay, 'he'd grab the hi-hat clutch that holds the top hi-hat and the bottom hi-hat. Show's over, don't worry about it! But he would just be making sure it was tight for the next time. Then it was, "Put your jacket on, got to look good, you don't want to show any sweat." Very self-conscious about it. He'd say, "Here we go. This is showbusiness," and he'd go out there and look his very best.'

His granddaughter Charlotte also got in on the action. 'They were very funny when the introductions would go on,' she says. 'Right before they'd start doing that, at a lot of shows I would run behind the stage and say hi to him, just go and check in halfway through, and say, "You're doing great." But they would start joking among themselves, Keith shit-stirring with Mick. He started a rumour that Mick had forgotten to announce so-and-so and panic him, but he hadn't forgotten. Pa would be like Muttley laughing in the corner. I'd see them giggling to each other and be like, "What's going on up there? Up to no good." But with the bow, they would find new ways to mess with Pa. I felt so bad, but I couldn't help laughing.'

'You know Charlie,' says Keith. 'He was the most reticent, modest man in the world. It's enough to get him out on stage when he's called out by Mick. Beloved Charlie, man. And God, did he hate showbusiness. Or at least the trappings. I mean, *I'm* pretty reticent, but Charlie's reserve is infamous. As you say, later on it was, "I love Uncle Charlie," every show.'

Charlotte remembers what Shirley used to say to her husband. 'My grandmother used to joke, "Oh, why do you want to be an old man before your time?" I think he was just born to be an old man and a grandpa figure. Ever since he was young, he had grandpa energy. It suited him very well.'

The Stones rolled into the 21st century with no sign yet of a new album, but with an increasing awareness of their limitless bankability as a touring attraction, especially as big anniversaries came around. The $300 million-grossing *Licks* tour of 2002–03 went around the world in support of the *Forty Licks* compilation, which duly mined platinum as the era of the multi-million-selling album began to wind down for everyone. Charlie, as ever, moaned about the months away from home, but he was never really going to say no. 'You're almost nailed to the job,' says Keith. 'How are you gonna get out of it?' Meanwhile, Charlie and Darryl Jones honed a truly formidable rhythm section.

'I think he was really conflicted about it,' says Chuck Leavell. 'Of course he loved his home, but he loved to play the drums. He knew there was a trade-off there, and he would make the best of it in his mind, to be comfortable and to do it. But I could never see him quitting. There was always one more session, one more tour.'

Arenas and stadiums had long been the Stones' office, but by now the supreme efficiency of this massive touring operation allowed the key cast the chance to cut loose, have fun and to observe each other. 'He was funny to be with on stage,' Fischer smiles. 'He had this way of breathing, it was almost meditative. The way he would suck in air, the way his nose and face would [she breathes out] and then he would just play, but he was giving off a lot of energy. You would almost think it was circular breathing, but it's not. But the way he would just pull in air and energy from what was going on on stage was magic to watch.

'Every once in a while I would really try to mess with him, just because I could. You know, I'd kiss the baffling [the plexiglass cage that surrounded the drums for sound-proofing purposes] and leave lipstick stains, and he would just look over and go, "Ugh, just go on." He couldn't snap me away because he was sort of trapped. So when he would give me the evil eye, I'd go, "I think he's had enough now." I would definitely get a rise out of him. Once he smiled, I left him alone.'

Charlie had begun the new millennium with easily the most surprising and adventurous record in his own name. The *Charlie Watts Jim Keltner Project* was a set of recordings made with his old friend, contemporary and fellow rock stalwart, who had traversed a similar path from early jazz leanings to rock ubiquity. Recordings had begun in 1997, when Keltner was drafted in for percussive contributions to *Bridges to Babylon*.

Keltner told mixonline.com that the Stones 'wanted to know if I wanted to play double drums, and Charlie was into it. But I refused. First, it's not something I like to do, and secondly, it would be a crime to interfere with somebody like Charlie's groove. It would almost be sacrilegious. So basically, I'd sit back and play around his stuff on part of a drum-set without a bass drum or snare.'

The instrumental album was distinctly avant-garde by comparison with Charlie's earlier songbook offerings. For an old-school drummer, Keltner was an inveterate sampler, not from records, but by his own description of every sound from that of a metal shelf to a fish steamer. We weren't at Ronnie Scott's now.

Thus, with Charlie's and Keltner's minds wide open, the *Project* became a sample-driven step into the electro world, with tracks named after the two players' mutual exemplars, such as 'Art Blakey', 'Kenny Clarke' and 'Roy Haines'. 'I used the drummers' names because Tony Williams had just died that week, and his was the first cut,' said Charlie. 'That gave me the idea to call all the rest after drummers.

'It started with Jim and myself, just the two of us playing around, really. Jim had some sampled sequences that he wanted me to play along with, and so I did. I didn't approach it like I would normally do in a band, where I'd just hire five guys to play the music with me. The overtones

253

of the rhythm make a melody in themselves. So I wanted to keep the drums as sparse and as simple as possible. At the same time, we did it very electronically. And that was kind of the interest because I'm normally not very into that.'

Tammy D. Moon's review of the album for the *Folk & Acoustic Music Exchange* emphasised its reach beyond his regular constituency by saying: 'No one likes jazz less than me and I LOVED this disc!' *Inside* the often surprisingly buttoned-down jazz world, by contrast, the *All About Jazz* review called it a 'mess'.

Either way, approaching 60, Charlie was unshackled. 'I did all sort of remixes of various tracks from it,' said Tony King, who oversaw its promotion, 'and Charlie loved working on remixes, he thought that was really cool. I loved that album, I thought it was really adventurous. We got some great write-ups, too.'

When he did get home to Shirley, he cherished, at least briefly, the insulation of the quiet life, ensconced with their horses and dogs (18 of the latter, by an early 2000s count), his cars and collections, and always his jazz and classical records. Such simple passivity is the prize that so many musicians fantasise about when they're away. When they're home, of course, it can swiftly turn the other way around. For Charlie, the thrill of playing and the familiar embrace of the Stones' touring family would always draw him back, coupled with Shirley saying decisively: 'It's time to go to work.'

'Keith loves touring,' Charlie said. 'Whenever I say I'm going to retire, he says, "What are you going to do?" And

I'm speechless, because I actually don't do anything except play the bloody drums. So it's a very difficult one to answer.'

Speaking to *Record Mirror* back in 1969, he showed how well he knew himself. 'I'm basically lazy,' he said. 'I've never found something I really wanted to do outside the Stones. I know it must sound boring, but it's not. I do waste a lot of time, but I would if I was working in a bank too.

'I never really wanted to learn the guitar and there are two in the Stones already, so it would be pointless,' he went on. 'Mick Jagger is a very good guitarist as well. He took to it and practised with conviction. I'd like to play the trumpet or maybe the sax. A trombone, maybe. The trouble is that I've never sat down and decided to learn it, because it means going back to the very beginning again. I've blown on one before, but that's about all. I suppose you could toot a tune with a little work, but it's a case of putting yourself out, which I suppose I don't do enough.'

When he wasn't travelling to Poland to buy horses, Charlie made use of Stones downtime in other ways. In December 2000, for example, he was back at Olympic Studios to play on a session out of a childhood fantasy, with the great Chico Hamilton, who was the drummer on one of the very records that had paved the footpath Charlie had trod ever since, Gerry Mulligan's 'Walking Shoes'. When Hamilton named the resulting track 'Here Comes Charlie Now', on the 2001 album named for his late son, *Foreststorn*, Charlie was reduced to boyish fan-worship.

Some years later, when the ABC&D of Boogie-Woogie quartet played in New York, Hamilton was in the audience. 'He was one of Charlie's first idols,' says Dave Green. 'Eventually he came to see Charlie. He was so humbled. In quite a few places, big-name drummers would come to see him, because he didn't have that whole rock drummer ego. He admired jazz musicians, and they adhered themselves to him. Steve Gadd came in to say hello. *Steve Gadd*. A giant. Charlie called himself a charlatan, but he was a lovely drummer. He had great time, great swing.'

At that Blue Note show in New York, there was a friendly heckle from another regular member of the audience. Charlie introduced Dave as his oldest friend. 'You have one?' shouted Keith Richards. In London there was the mutual appreciation of Charlie attending Bill Wyman's Rhythm Kings gig and, three nights later, Bill coming to see Charlie's band, expanded into a tentet, at Ronnie Scott's. Later in the same residency, Mick attended; the following night, Keith and Ronnie.

Throughout his career, Charlie was not only generous with his gifts to friends, but with the time he gave to other musicians. As well as earlier sessions with Leon Russell and Howlin' Wolf, it led him to credits on projects by Pete Townshend, Peter Frampton, Brian May and many others. Another highlight was his playing on a fizzing rendition, cut in Paris, of the Stones' 'Hey Negrita' for their touring sax man Tim Ries's 2008 album *Stones World*, also featuring

Bernard Fowler, Chuck Leavell and Ronnie, with a brilliant harmonica cameo by Mick.

In Porto they taped an equally imaginative, entirely reshaped 'No Expectations', with Charlie on brushes, Ries adding saxophone and Portuguese fado singer Ana Moura an equally refined lead vocal. Charlie and Ries would sometimes visit jazz clubs together, and Dave Green got to play with Ries at Ronnie Scott's. Like-minded souls, all of them.

'Any excuse to play, for Charlie, he was in there with both feet,' says Glyn Johns. Charlie even played at Glyn's second wedding. 'Very few people ever asked him to play on sessions, that I'm aware of, and I can understand that. If you don't know him, you would think it was a bit of a liberty to call him up. He did a couple of things for me, including Pete [Townshend]'s *Rough Mix* album [on 'My Baby Gives It Away' and 'Catmelody']. Every time I've ever used him, of course, he's been absolutely brilliant.'

Chuck Leavell noticed those same instincts in Stones rehearsals or soundchecks. 'Sometimes when we would be waiting on Mick or Keith, or both,' he recalls, 'I might start some little piece, whether it be something close to jazz … I'm not a jazz player, really, but Charlie would always just jump right on it. He was ready, willing and able to play just about anything. It always made me feel good that he wanted to join in and contribute.'

Charlie's subtle but inexorable passage into 'beloved' status was validated by his March 2001 appearance on *Desert Island Discs*. The presenter at the time, Sue Lawley, was palpably rather thrown and even politely exasperated by his trademark combination of diffidence, hesitancy and refusal to conform to the principles of 'celebrity' small talk. The programme confirmed certain expectations, in his selection of recordings by Parker, Ellington, and, as we've seen, Arlott and Charlton's 1956 Ashes Test match commentary.

But his choices sprang surprises for many, as he ran the gamut from Tony Hancock to Ralph Vaughan Williams, and revealed a book choice of Dylan Thomas poems. His 'castaway's favourite' was Stravinsky's 'Dance of the Coachmen and Grooms' from *Petrushka*, which Shirley had chosen for one of her stallion shows, and he remembered Charlotte 'galloping around the room' to it. Another touching memory was of dancing with Seraphina at a wedding to Fred Astaire's 'The Way You Look Tonight'. His luxury, what else, was drumsticks.

Charlie was a keen listener to classical music, and whenever Linda telephoned for a chat, she would hear Radio 3 playing in the background. 'My wife goes "Eurgh, boring," said Charlie. I asked him if he had favourite classical composers. "Yeah, but I forget 'em all. The usual ones, really. Vaughan Williams, people like that."

Soon the Stones were ensconced, for the third time running, in Toronto, their favourite town for rehearsals. I visited them there for interviews on all three occasions, marvelling at how they turned that old six-storey Masonic temple into their office for several weeks: large stage on one floor, relaxation level with individual dressing rooms, communal dining area on another, all beautifully decorated. Their rehearsals were better dressed than most people's tours.

The eating area was particularly memorable in the fact that it was effectively a works canteen, with band and crew alike lining up to fill their plates from the generous victuals on offer. Mick came by at one point, while Charlie waited dutifully for his grub. Ronnie was enjoying his new, hard-won sobriety. Keith may have been tucking into his beloved steak and kidney pie elsewhere.

The other tradition of their stays in Toronto was the secret rehearsal gig. In 2002 it was at the Palais Royale for about 800 lucky souls, who would largely have missed the nervousness in the ranks that Mick detected. Charlie's reaction when we spoke soon afterwards was also less than enthusiastic. 'It's very uncomfortable, loud and hot,' he said. 'But as long as people enjoy themselves, it's fine.' Was it not a chance for the band to let off steam? 'Probably,' he said. 'I don't feel like that, but I think Mick and Keith do. We don't play enough clubs to do them properly. I prefer to play Wembley Stadium with the Stones.'

The *Licks* tour began in September, this time cleverly combining every scale of Stones show, with a mixture of stadia, arenas and theatres. Keith memorably called it the Underwear Tour, or sometimes the Y-front Tour, because the shows came in small, medium and large.

Said Charlie: 'We've done 'em all before. Some tours have been all theatres, I mean years ago. Some have been all arenas. This time we put the three together. I think it was Mick's idea as a way to make it a bit different, which I suppose is all right. It actually means more work, because we'll be doing three different sets, instead of one all the way through. It's very difficult to translate subtle things into a stadium, because you've got to be very direct and right across the footlights, as they say. Fortunately we have the best guy in the world at it, Mick.

'Playing football stadiums is ridiculous, but that's just the nature of it now. I mean, I play in clubs, and I know it's another sort of music, but it's very pleasant. To play Ronnie Scott's is wonderful.'

Charlie was playing his cards extremely close to his chest when I asked him for clues of the new look for the show ('I'm not going to, you'll have to see it'), but when we arrived for the opening arena date at the Fleet Center in Boston we saw a stage that had been transformed into a giant billboard with a custom-made collage by Jeff Koons, 200 feet wide and 80 feet tall. Protecting the band from the elements was an 80-foot-wide transparent cantilever roof; the now de rigueur B-stage took its usual disguised place mid-crowd.

'We settled on a very stripped-down stage apart from the huge screen overhead, which was all very nice, but we had to decide what was going to be shown on this bloody great big screen,' said Charlie. 'It's an idea I would like to develop more. If you use the screen as a stage set, it could create a totally different environment for each song. It could become a ballroom in Versailles or a black screen with doors and windows opening for another mood.'

'Behind the scenes, him and Mark Fisher and Patrick Woodroffe, that's where a whole load of work was done,' says Keith. 'I'm, "Where's the stage? Put it up and let's go." But Charlie got very well versed. He surprised me, starting to talk about lights – "The super troupers here and the arcs there ..." Jesus Christ! He picked up a lot about it and he enjoyed that. He was a designer by heart.'

There was the usual opening-night rust that evening in Boston, not least because as Charlie pointed out, the band rarely do a full dress rehearsal including the lights, the videos et al., so there is always a hit-and-hope element. 'People all love going to the first night,' he said, 'but it's usually chaos. The best time to see anybody's show is usually three weeks in.' His playing, said *Rolling Stone*, was 'a study in deft restraint', in a band playing 'as if they had both nothing, and everything, to prove'.

Not only was the tour a $300 million-grossing smash, its innovative configuration was a godsend for the band, and for Mick in particular. 'This new format really did break it up,' he said. 'I was surprised and delighted. It worked for the audience, and it kept us awake. Routine kills spontaneity.'

In the spring of 2004 Charlie got the band back together, but it was the other one – his tentet – who hadn't had a window in which to work for some three years. They climbed back into their London office, Ronnie Scott's, for a new residency, although when the album *Watts at Scott's* was released in the summer, it was from recordings made there over three nights in 2001.

Amid the nods to heroes like Duke Ellington and Billy Strayhorn, the record contained what must be one of the most imaginative readings of 'Satisfaction' ever attempted, as Gerard Presencer played lead trumpet on his self-styled, Latin-flavoured 'Faction'. But by the time the album emerged in June, Charlie had had the shock of his life. Ten days before its release, aged 63, he was diagnosed with cancer.

He'd had a lump in his neck for two or three years, which was initially identified as benign, but when it was removed it was found to be cancerous. Then cancer was also discovered in his left tonsil. 'When I first found out about it, I literally went to bed and cried,' he admitted to me. 'I thought that was it, that I'd only have another three months. You go in there and you're terrified. All the machines, it's like space-age stuff. The surgeons and nurses literally have your life in their hands.' Said Keith: 'As Charlie put it, "One minute I'm standing at Ronnie Scott's getting a standing ovation and the next minute I'm on a marble slab."'

Doctors told Charlie that a six-week course of radiotherapy would give him a 90 per cent chance of a full recovery, and so it happily proved. He was able to walk to the Marsden for his appointments, miraculously spared the media glare, although a short press release in August confirmed that he was four weeks into his medical care. In early October Mick said in a press statement that the treatment had indeed been successful. By that month, Charlie and Shirley celebrated a rarely seen phenomenon in rock: a 40th wedding anniversary.

Charlie later talked about his initial absence from the writing and demo sessions for the album that became 2005's *A Bigger Bang*. The group's touring plans hung on his treatment, but ironically, a frightening situation necessitated the closest songwriting relationship that Mick and Keith had had for years. That summer they enjoyed the unusual experience in the band's latter-day history of composing songs in the same room, at the Château de Fourchette, Mick's opulent residence on the banks of the Loire in Pocé-sur-Cisse.

'We spent a lot of time writing at Mick's house,' said Keith. 'We worked very closely together, mainly because we did it in such a small area, and because we were reduced in ranks. All the basic stuff was done very much around the room, on a couple of couches. Then I put him on drums. We had a lot of fun doing that. For the first time in many years, we were just together, just Mick and me, and "Hey, we've got to come up with something." And it was, "I'll try the bass on this, you do the piano." "No, *you* do the piano."'

Mick said: 'When Charlie got sick, it set us back a bit but what it meant was we [both] got to play guitar and drums and bass for a bit, just the two of us together. So when Charlie did turn up, I had a lot of the beats ready already. We changed 'em but we had a solid basis, and we used elements of the demos I'd done.' When he joined the sessions, Keith said he looked the same, as if he had simply combed his hair and put a suit on.

Under the wise sonic counsel of Don Was, who had produced its 1990s predecessors, *A Bigger Bang* was an improbable victory. Its lean, knowing songs befitted a band of sixty-somethings (Ronnie was only 58), but it still rocked with unique élan, from Mick's playful 'She Saw Me Coming' and 'Oh No, Not You Again', to his moody 'Streets of Love' and 'Laugh, I Nearly Died', to Keith's boisterous 'Infamy' and vulnerable 'This Place Is Empty'. And anyone who expected Charlie to be diminished by his health ordeal only needed to hear him fill the room with the exhilarating back-beat of 'Rough Justice' to be proved wrong.

I asked if his undiminished playing was a subconscious message to his bandmates that they shouldn't write him off. 'I didn't want to show them, I wanted to show myself,' he answered. 'That's about the extent of my ego, really.'

By now, Don Was knew the script as well as the band, but he was energised to see their refreshed interaction. 'To say there's love and affection between these guys, I don't think that begins to talk about how profound a relationship this is, that spans generations and marriages,' he told me. 'It's complicated, but so are all profound relationships.'

The suitably huge accompanying tour began in the summer of 2005, and even under the watchful eye of his bandmates, the drummer was back to full Wattage. Mick joked: 'I always say to him, "Charlie, this is how to do

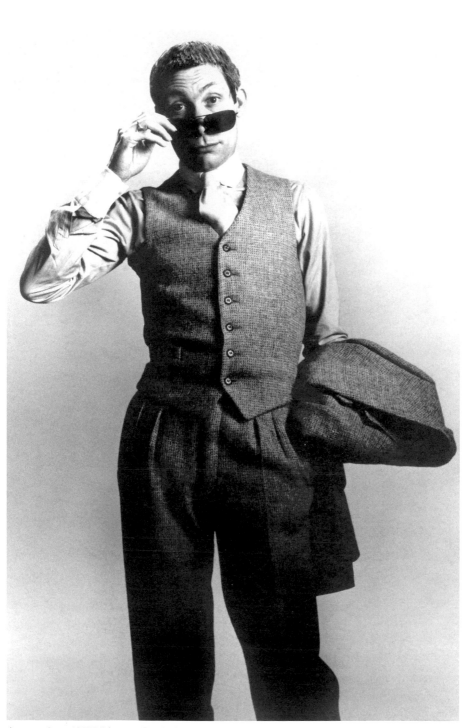

Amsterdam, 1977. 'He was Savile Row man,' said Keith Richards. 'He could have lived there. I said, "Why don't you marry a tailor?"'

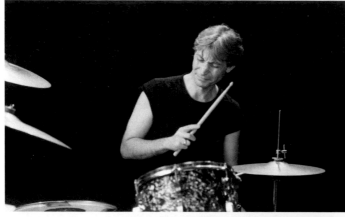

LEFT: Economy of style: at S.I.R. Studios in New York, 30 June 1981, as the Stones tape videos for 'Start Me Up' and other tracks from the *Tattoo You* album.

RIGHT: Michael Philip and Charles Robert captured on stage for the 1981 live documentary *Let's Spend the Night Together*, directed by Hal Ashby.

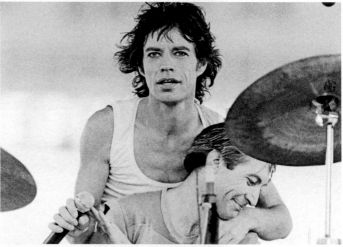

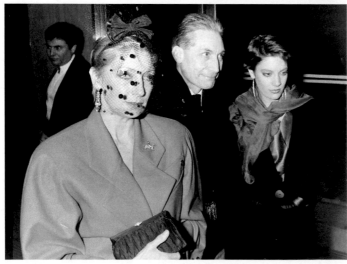

LEFT: With his beloved Shirley and Seraphina at the Kensington Roof Gardens, February 1986. 'The one regret I have of this life is that I was never home enough.'

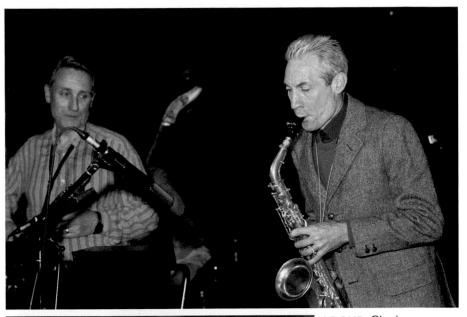

ABOVE: Charlie cuts an unusual figure as he and his jazz group play the opening night at Ronnie Scott's club in Birmingham, England, October 1991. 'I consider it a great honour to be asked to do that,' he said.

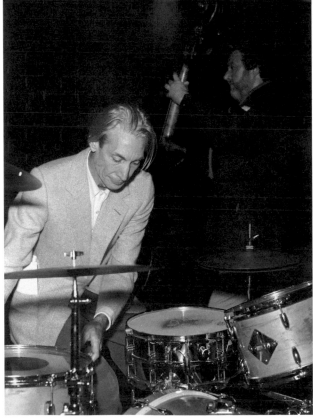

LEFT: Charlie and his favourite double bassist and oldest friend Dave Green set up for the first night of the group's *Tribute to Charlie Parker with Strings* show at one of their dream venues, the Blue Note in New York, 14 July 1992.

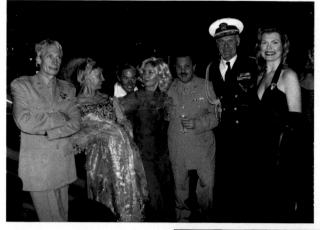

LEFT: Charlie and Billy Joel survive a costume clash at Elton John's 50th birthday fancy-dress party at Hammersmith Palais, 1997. Also pictured (l-r): Shirley Watts, Lulu's son Jordan, Lulu, Tony King and Billy's companion.

RIGHT: Christmas in New York for Charlie, daughter Seraphina and granddaughter Charlotte, on Madison Avenue, 15 December 1997.

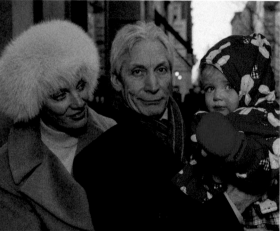

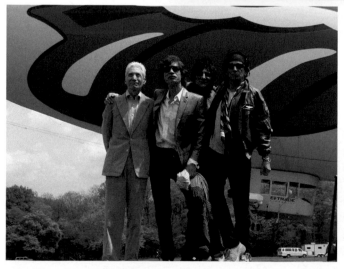

LEFT: 'They've talked me into it again': arriving by blimp at Van Cortland Park in the Bronx to announce the 40th anniversary *Licks* world tour, May 2002.

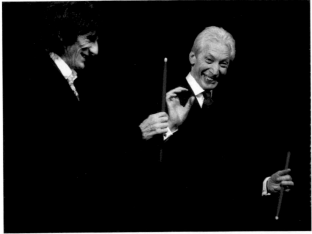

LEFT: Fellow Geminis Charlie Watts and Ronnie Wood at the Berlin International Film Festival, as Martin Scorsese's *Shine a Light* gets its world premiere on 7 February 2008.

RIGHT: Jools Holland's tribute to his friend: the models in his train set are of the prefabs in which Charlie and Dave Green grew up.

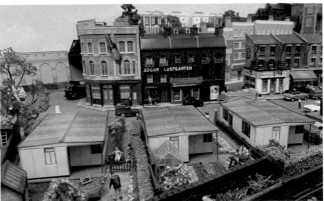

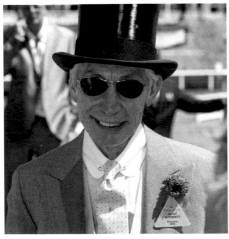

To the nines, at Royal Ascot's Ladies Day, 17 June 2010.

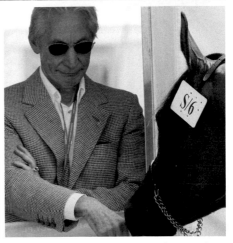

Not so wild horses: on his annual visit to the Arabian Horse Days, an exclusive fair in Jadow Podlaski in eastern Poland.

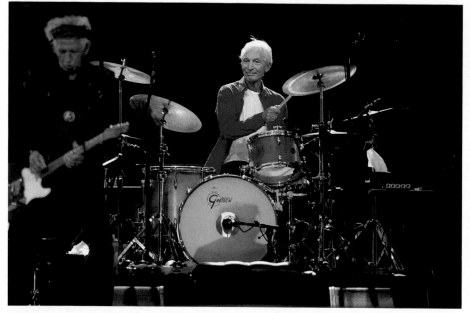

Making Manchester united: a beaming Charlie as the Stones pack out Old Trafford during the UK leg of the *No Filter* tour, 5 June 2018.

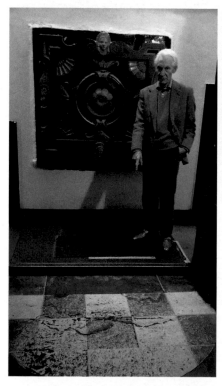

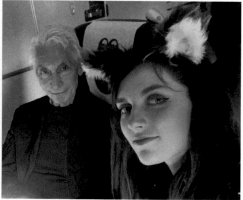

ABOVE: On the private plane (note the logo on the seat back) with granddaughter Charlotte, who travelled with Charlie on later tours and provided a welcome reminder of family.

LEFT: A return visit, on 2 October 2018, to the Troubadour in Earl's Court, where Charlie played with Alexis Korner and where he first met Ginger Baker.

Charlotte on the road. 'A lot of people told me that it made a really big difference that I was there,' she said, 'because it meant a bit of home was there.'

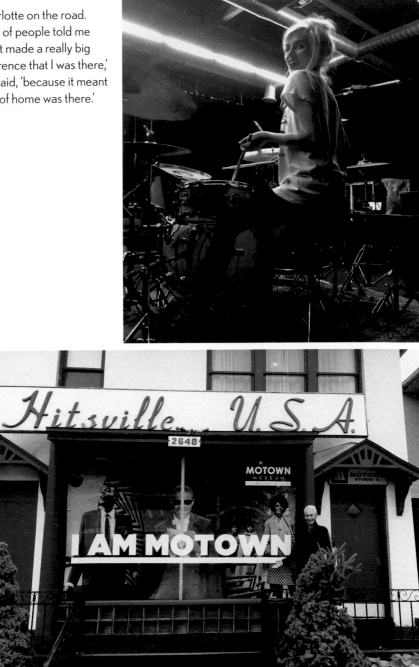

On later tours, Charlie and drum tech Don McAulay would visit such landmarks as the Louis Armstrong House Museum in New York City and the Motown Museum in Detroit.

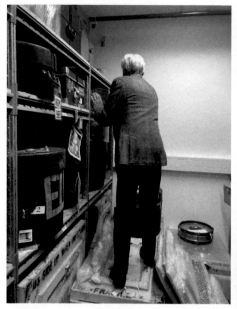

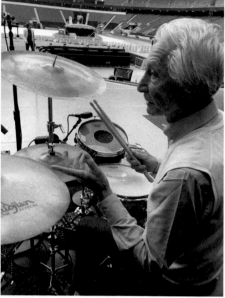

A craftsman among his tools: a true student of his instrument, Charlie takes a rummage in his drum room.

Soundchecking before what turned out to be his last Rolling Stones concert, at the Hard Rock Stadium in Miami Gardens, Florida, 30 August 2019.

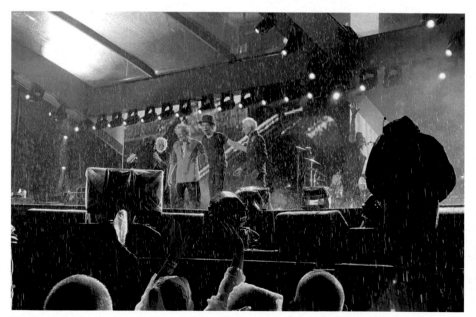

The final bow: at the end of the rain-soaked show, brought forward a day to avoid a (crossfire) hurricane, Charlie joins his mates stage front for the last time.

interviews." You know, I'll say, "Tell 'em about your illness." Because he always gets asked about it, so I always take the piss. But no, he seemed to play really well, he hasn't had any problems. I didn't notice any let-up in him.

'It's very physical playing the drums for that long on stage. I will really notice it if he gets a little bit behind or if there's a little tendency not to hit things. But it was none of that. I really noticed when we started recording that he was really playing really well and loud and with lots of verve. So it's not been a problem.'

Six months and 55 dates in – and this after playing Super Bowl XL a couple of weeks earlier for a US TV audience alone of 140 million – the Stones undertook one of the biggest shows in rock's entire history, on Copacabana Beach in Rio. The turnout, impossible to judge accurately, is regularly esti-mated at 1.5 million people, equivalent to 20 Live Aids at Wembley Stadium or 75 Madison Square Garden sellouts.

Months in the planning, the show required the construc-tion of a different sort of bridge, to take the band from their hotel to the stage, overlooking an audience stretching all the way down the famous beach's two and a half miles. Seventy trucks of gear, 500 security guards, 6,000 military police: it was like the mammoth scale of any Stones stadium show supersized as never before.

Charlie no doubt sat backstage wondering what to make of it all, but even he got caught up in the excitement of the day. Within reason. 'It was fun,' he said. 'To be honest, it doesn't matter if there's two million or what, because you only see a certain area. For Mick, it's different, working an audience. But I could see the boats in the sea. It was a wonderful setting, and the whole day was fantastic. It was like the Cup Final, but it went on all day.'

Added Ronnie: 'That was just insurmountable, inconceivable and very ... what's the word, surreal. I kept thinking, "They're coming by land, sea and air!" Surrounded. But the great thing about that Rio one was nobody got injured or hurt. I think somebody had a baby, but that's about it.'

Then came the Fiji incident, and an unexpected holiday for Charlie. Conspiracy theories abounded about Keith's accident while on holiday in the South Pacific with wife Patti and Ronnie and Jo Wood, but he really did slip and fall, not from a tree as reported, but what he called a 'gnarled shrub', requiring urgent surgery to remove a blood clot behind his brain. His explanation was typical. 'I couldn't get a grip, and I went back, and kissed the tree. Nearly kissed me goodbye,' he said. 'Now people keep giving me rubber palm trees. OK, I guess I've got to live with this. Several coconuts being delivered to my door.

'Charlie was telling me about all his CAT scans and I thought, "At least I don't have to do that." Then suddenly, there I am going through the very same tunnels that he'd described to me. I have six titanium pins in my head now. And they do not ring at airports, I can assure you. I've tested it.'

Charlie made the most of the downtime before the European tour could commence. 'I got the call that it was indefinitely postponed, so I thought, "*Now* what do I do?"' he said. 'As far as me personally, it couldn't have been better because I had to be out of England for tax reasons, so I literally did the Grand Tour of Europe, under my own steam. I went to Turin, Rome, Florence and Paris for a month. I went to lots of places that I'd never been, Pompeii and all that. I had a very cultural time, it was like an 18th-century Grand Tour.

'I had a pair of jeans [*jeans?* This was the extent of the emergency] and a pair of shoes. It was like, for me, disaster. I went straight off to Rome and bought another suit. So for me, it was wonderful. It must have been hell for Keith, but I actually had a very nice time.'

I reminded Keith about it. 'Yeah, he told me that,' he laughed. 'He said, "Do that again. I had a great time."'

Jools Holland observes: 'Charlie was this remarkable cross between an 18th-century gentleman that you'd meet somewhere on your travels, who like magic would appear into your life, and this laconic London bloke who was also a very cultivated man. When I say 18th-century gent, I mean like the posh young men who went on the Grand Tour, sketching wherever they went. That was him.'

Keith reaches the same conclusion. 'I'll tell you what he was: he was a bloody gentleman,' he says. 'I'd take it to the 18th century.' Charlie recognised it himself. 'I should have been born in 1810,' he told *Esquire*. 'I live like a Victorian landowner. I get up, decide what to wear, have breakfast, and stroll about like the lord of the manor. I walk around the stud and look at the horses. We have a horse farm. It's my wife's, really – it's her passion. We've had horses ever since we were married but I've never ridden. I do have the most wonderful outfits to go riding in: britches and three pairs of boots. I have some lovely old carriages.'

Holland travelled with the band in America and Japan when he was gathering interviews with them for the book *The Rolling Stones: A Life on the Road*. These were collated for the 1998 publication by Dora Loewenstein, daughter of their longtime financial manager Prince Rupert Loewenstein. Here, there was time for Charlie and Holland to get to know each other better, and for Charlie to exhibit his studied rejection of the supposedly required lifestyle of the rock generation.

'He was this impeccable gent, in these huge hotels,' says Holland. 'They'd have a suite each, and when they were doing those huge shows they'd have three nights off, because it takes so long to take the thing down and reset it. It's not like four shows on and one night off, like the rest of us.

'So you'd sometimes be invited to what was called the Cage, which was Keith's suite, where he played the most beautiful music. It was like in *The Lord of the Rings*, where the elves were playing music that you couldn't quite know what it was, but it was so beautiful that you wept, and you just wanted to hear it again. I said, "Keith's invited us up to the Cage this evening." But he wouldn't go there, he didn't fancy that.

'But I liked that he had his routine, and you'd go to his room to have a cup of coffee with him. Everything perfectly laid out. He said he would have been perfectly happy as a gent, but he would have been just as happy as a butler, which all the best gents would be. Unless you can understand what needs to be done yourself, you can't expect somebody else to do it.'

As new technological developments emerged both inside and outside the Stones' world, Charlie was either uninterested or completely oblivious. I recall mentioning to him that their 1991 concert film *Live at the Max* was being released in the cutting-edge, high-resolution IMAX format of the day. 'Is it?' he said, with a heavy-lidded lack of interest.

On the *Bridges to Babylon* tour, the 97-date excursion that straddled four continents in 1997 and 1998, a nightly 'web vote' song was performed, chosen from audience requests online. I referred back to it with Charlie at our next meeting, to trademark insouciance, which as usual was so unintentionally amusing that you were frequently stifling a chuckle.

'It's not something I object to, but it's not something I was particularly interested in,' he said. 'I'm not interested in computers or the internet, but Mick is very interested in that, so from his point of view he thought it was great. I'm not that enamoured of it, but I'm not that enamoured of the whole technology world. I never have been.'

Touring business resumed at the San Siro in Milan in July 2006, and when I caught the Amsterdam Arena show eight dates in, you could never have guessed the life-threatening travails that had preceded it. The drummer was now afforded the crowd's full attention as an avuncular elder. One fan sported a T-shirt with the legend 'Charlie Watts and his fabulous Rolling Stones'.

'The thing about going on stage,' said Mick before that show, 'is it must be like playing sport big-time. It's all to do with your confidence and the bottle you've got. You've got to prove to yourself you can do it. I think for Charlie and Keith the initial shows must have been quite difficult. Everyone's looking at you going, "Is he all right?" There must be that element in it.'

Summer brought the Stones almost full circle, magnified to the nth degree, for two shows at Twickenham Stadium. 'We used to play right next door in the Richmond Athletic Ground, and then we used to play in the Station Hotel,' said Mick. 'So it feels really like home, playing in Twickenham. Except for Charlie. He comes from Wembley, so Wembley Stadium is more like home for him.'

Any homecoming show brought another challenge to Charlie's organisational instincts. 'There are always loads of people that you know and like, and they're just all there, so it gets a bit panicky,' he said. 'A bit, "Oh crikey, another lot." You always lie in bed thinking, "Have I asked so and so?"'

Charlie and Ronnie were back in London in November 2006 to give moral support to Mick at the funeral of his father Joe, who had died at the age of 93. It was a few days after the death of Ronnie's older brother and musical forerunner Art, known to Charlie since the Blues Incorporated days with Alexis Korner. Keith's beloved mum Doris departed at 91 the following spring.

In June '07, as the *Bigger Bang* tour reverberated around Europe, the Stones headlined the Isle of Wight Festival. There were guest appearances by not one but two of the hottest turns Britain had to offer, Paolo Nutini on 'Love in Vain' and Amy Winehouse on 'Ain't Too Proud to Beg'. Sadly, and speaking as an eyewitness, she was, shall we say, debilitated by intemperance, and Charlie agreed.

'She was bloody awful with us, but she was great the day before with her own band,' he said. 'I thought, "God, is that the same girl." It's a lovely band, on the record [*Back to Black*] they're great, and she was fantastic on that. I've listened to her properly since, but with us I thought she was pretty ...' He paused, and I pointed out that she didn't know the words of the Temptations song she was duetting with Mick. 'No, she didn't. She wasn't really Amy Winehouse that one knows and loves. But it was a great thing to have her sing with us, in a way, wasn't it?'

Not for the first time or the last, he proceeded to tell me why he disliked such grand-scale events, but enjoyed this one. 'I don't like doing those festival things, I hate going on with 80 other bands,' he said. 'Isle of Wight was very good. I was very surprised how nice that was to do. I've been there as a punter, looking at people play, but to play there I thought it was really good. Going over on the boat was great, too. We're very lucky in that way, we have good fun.

'Having said that, I've done a few jazz [festivals]. Stu used to get you going around Europe, and I used to hate them. I love going to them to see other people, but I hate doing them. They never have the sense of occasion. They're very well paid, but ... I remember going from playing in Paris, Stu drove me, I fell asleep, woke up in The Hague [for the North Sea Jazz Festival]. Alexis Korner was with us, bless him. As the stool for the drummer was getting cold, my one was whipped underneath it, and he was shoved off to the side. We got out, got given a key, went to my room and the bed was still warm from Dizzy Gillespie's band leaving. That's what it's like. But it's great if you meet people you haven't seen for years, and there's always something going on, when there's some great bands playing.'

By August it was three O2 Arenas and out. The *Bigger Bang* tour was their biggest bang ever, a $558 million-grossing epic of 147 shows over two years. Downtime was long overdue, and for Charlie it was back to the farm in Dolton. But he did venture into London in late 2008 to celebrate one of his oldest mates in music, presenting the Zildjian Drummers Lifetime Achievement award at the Shepherd's Bush Empire to Ginger Baker. The photographs of two apparent curmudgeons beaming their heads off were gorgeous.

'They maintained a friendship,' says Baker's daughter Nettie. 'When Charlie was in America, he turned up at Dad's ranch and said, "You can come and see the Stones, but I know you won't, because you hate 'em." When he saw

him at the awards and Charlie presented his lifetime achievement, they were just so pleased to see each other. And all my
dad was talking about was, "Do you remember when we
were on the Bakerloo Line together?"'

John DeChristopher, former VP of Zildjian, developed a
warm relationship with Charlie, and remembers the two
friends talking backstage for an hour before that show.
'Charlie was one of the few drummers that Ginger spoke
highly of and respected,' he says, 'and I think it goes back to
the fact that they'd known each other so long. He saw what
Charlie was. Charlie would always talk about him very
respectfully. That night when he came up to present the
award, he said to me later he had this whole thing worked
out that he was going to say about Ginger. He froze in the
moment and just said, "The best."'

The jazz world was about to offer Charlie one more great
adventure, and possibly his favourite. He began to play
some shows with not one but two boogie-woogie pianists,
Ben Waters and Axel Zwingenberger, including one at the
noted jazz hub the Bull's Head in Barnes, west London, and
another at the 100 Club. Soon, the fun got serious, and it
turned into a tour, complete with European dates, as the
ABC of Boogie-Woogie, styled after their first names.

Before long, there was an album, *The Magic of Boogie
Woogie*, and another initial, with the welcome addition to
complete the rhythm section of Charlie's old comrade Dave
Green. The ABC&D of Boogie-Woogie was complete. 'It's
two acoustic grand pianos, which is very unusual,' said

Charlie. 'That's why I like the band. It's fantastic to look at. Not a guitar in sight.'

'I bumped into Axel in Vienna,' Waters told me when the *Live in Paris* album appeared in 2012 as a memento of their touring. 'I was doing a gig over there and we went to his house and we were playing piano. He said, "I'd love to do some gigs with you in England." So I set up a show with the two of us playing, then I cheekily wrote to Charlie because I knew he'd played with Axel. Ian Stewart was a friend of my aunt and uncle's, they knew Charlie as well. I said, "Could you come and drum?" and he did. It was amazing. We hadn't sold many tickets, just the two of us, and then on the day Charlie said he'd do it we sold out in two hours. Fantastic.'

'When Ben asked me,' said Charlie, 'I had nothing to do and it was time I got out of the house, according to my wife. And Axel is on a mission to turn the world on to boogie-woogie and he's halfway there at the moment. We're hoping this will make it three-quarters. He's phenomenal. This band is a lot of fun to play in, and David is perfect in it. He's one of the lead instruments, funnily enough. I play a bit more drums now, but not much.'

Charlie's whole demeanour in that 2012 interview was different from the usual do-I-have-to stance of his day job. 'This band is the nearest thing to a 1939 night at the Café Society, for me,' he beamed, imagining the group in Greenwich Village. 'That's my ideal of what it should be like. Axel gave me a copy of Benny Goodman with Albert

Ammons, Pete Johnson and Meade "Lux" Lewis playing with Benny's Orchestra in a radio thing. It's fantastic. It's unbelievable. Talk about swing, my God.

'But people love this music when you get going. They probably don't like the look of the old farts playing it, but it's fun music. It's not at all pretentious and it's straight ahead. It's wonderful to play. We've never been in a world where we're competing, you know what I mean? It's like a pickup thing we play in clubs, and I like it like that.'

The live album included an irresistible version of a song that reached back to the Stones' early recordings, the Bobby Troup chestnut '(Get Your Kicks On) Route 66', the first track on their first LP. I asked how the interpretations differed, as a player. 'It's difficult to say that,' said Charlie astutely. 'What you play fits that particular set of players. The Stones one was Chuck Berry guitar-based, with Stu trilling over the top or rumbling underneath.

'This is piano-based, totally, and a jazz swinging bass, which gives a whole difference in feel. Sometimes when we get Jerry Lee Lewis or Little Richard-ish, I'll play like I would with the Stones. But that's Ben's call, if he calls those songs. We never rehearse. Even the first time we played, we didn't. They might come up differently every time. I just sit there. I don't know what he's going to play next.'

There was one city that Charlie would have loved to play with the quartet, and it was deep in his musical DNA. 'I dearly wanted to go to Chicago,' he said, 'because that's where this music comes from. Yes, the same thing happened with the Stones. We ended up in Chicago playing Chicago blues to an audience bigger than Muddy Waters had.' He laughed. 'As Keith will always say, that's what it's about, really. It's about handing it on, and some young kid copying him and playing him, or him copying some old bloke in a rice field.'

One gig they did make was in the Dolomites, described by Charlie in his inimitably dry way. 'It was really weird, right up in the mountains, with the church and chirping birds and snow, and you sit there and think: "Who's going to come to this?" We're playing in a concert hall with a slope, nobody's there, two old women are walking down to get a loaf of bread. And by the time seven o'clock comes, it's completely packed. They love it.'

It was while touring with the ABC&D that Charlie broadened his friendship with Holland, who would sometimes appear on the shows as the third piano player. 'When we were in Austria, that's when we got to chat more,' says Holland. 'When he was touring with the Rolling Stones, it's the biggest touring machine on earth. They've been at it for years, it's well oiled, and they've got people that deal with the whole thing.

'But when he was out with the ABC&D of Boogie-Woogie, there was none of that. Sometimes it would be a little chaotic, and there wasn't somebody to check your room out. But not once did Charlie ever get any angst about it. He was constantly amused at the chaos. I learned a lot from him about staying laconic and calm, that there's no point in getting excited. Whatever happens, that's not going to help. That was his method of doing it.

'Charlie loved playing with Axel and Ben and Dave because he really loved that boogie-woogie music. He understood better than anybody the connection between that music as part of early jazz and how some of it morphs into popular rock 'n' roll. And the people came because they could see its connection with the Stones' great boogie music, which has that effect on the human spirit that makes you want to dance.'

That, says Holland, is why Charlie happily agreed to tour, pushing 70, as a busman's holiday from … touring. 'He did it because the Stones had long breaks in between. If you're a musician, you need to keep your hand in. You can't just practise at home, it's not the same exercise at all. And he enjoyed travelling with his old friend Dave and we all had a good time together. He and Dave would be wrapped up in a blanket at the back of the bus like a couple of pensioners enjoying themselves.

'I remember there was one time in Hamburg, when we stayed at the Atlantic Hotel, which is a very grand hotel he'd been staying at for years. There are not many people who are truly international people like the Rolling Stones. They've been going a long time and they play in all these cities, so they make friends around the world. So he had some Austrian guy who was to do with racehorses, he was a larger-than-life figure. We had breakfast and it went on about four hours.'

Holland concludes: 'I could see, as Charlie's friends appeared out of the woodwork as we travelled around, how he collected people that were like out of glamorous 1970s films in Switzerland, Germany and France. They would come to the boogie shows with their dinner jackets. It was an amazing mix. There'd be a bloke who was like an ex-convict, like a German villain, who would turn up. You couldn't work out what half these people were, but they all loved Charlie.'

BACKBEAT

A Gift for Giving

Charlie Watts was entirely relaxed about spending large sums of money on his own diversions, in part because he also spent vast amounts doing the same for his friends, and showing them how much he loved them. His gift for drumming was complemented by his gift for giving.

Everywhere you step in the world of the Rolling Stones, you speak to friends and fellow travellers who benefited from Charlie's extreme generosity, dispensed entirely without pretension or fuss. Sceptics may argue that it's easy to be magnanimous when you have millions in the bank, but the music industry is not over-populated with artists who stop thinking about themselves long enough to notice those closest to them, much less to remember *their* respective passions.

Dave Green, his friend from as far back as those short-trousered days of Wembley prefabs and ration books, has a typical story. 'He was so generous,' he says. 'He turned up at Pizza Express in Soho, and he had this bag with him. He said, "I got this for you." I'm very interested in polar exploration. One of my collecting hobbies is books on the subject, and he knew about that.

'He'd bought me these four amazing volumes of the *South Polar Times*, which were reproductions of the paper that was produced in the Antarctic by Captain Scott's expedition. Of course I could never afford to buy these things, and he just turned up with them.' Written by the members of the party to relieve the boredom on those long, cruel winter nights, the journals combined puzzles and cartoons with more specialised treatises on seals, whales and penguins.

'I know exactly where he got them,' says Dave. 'When Charlie moved to Pelham Crescent, one of the branches of [rare book firm, and member of the Antiquarian Booksellers' Association] Peter Harrington was just around the corner. There was a chap in there called Glen, who I met for the first time at the celebration of Charlie's life at Ronnie Scott's [in December 2021], which was a wonderful night.

'He was a lovely guy,' Dave continues, 'and it was such a pleasant thing to meet him, because now I know who got all this stuff that Charlie gave to me, including some photographs of Scott LaFaro. He played with Chet Baker, who was one of my heroes on the bass, and I'd never seen them before. You know about Charlie's P.G. Wodehouse [first edition] collection? Glen got all that together too. That's what Charlie was like. He very nonchalantly gave me these amazing books.'

One hopes that part of the enjoyment of hearing such tales is in their very incongruity. There's Charlie lugging books about Antarctic explorers to his lifelong mate at a jazz venue. Now here he comes buying prehistoric swords wrapped up in brown paper. If it fitted the rules of collectability, either for himself or his friends, he was there.

Bill Wyman was this next happy recipient. His slow-motion departure from the Rolling Stones, which finally became official in 1993, left him at liberty to pursue myriad new activities, but he remained, literally, on the greetings card list. 'We always bought each other presents, birthdays and Christmas, and we still do,' he tells me. 'I still get a case of wine from Mick, and Keith sends caviar to us. We send things to each other and we always have done.' When Wyman turned 75 in 2011, the band sent him 75 roses.

But Charlie's munificence with his old friend was another thing again. 'I got into archaeology in the '90s, in my house,' says Bill, 'because workmen found something in the grounds and I thought, "There's got to be other stuff here." They found a ceramic drinking pot from the 15th century. So I bought a detector and started detecting, and I found a Roman site up the road that no one knew about. I found hundreds of Roman coins and brooches, all kinds of stuff.

'When Charlie found out, he started going to these places and buying these archaeological items, which were ridiculously expensive. Of course, he was earning tons of money then. I'd left before the big money, just with a small amount to get along with, and happily. The last tour I ever did, tickets were like £29.95 or something. They went into this huge money-earning situation, and so he did have the facilities.

'He'd come round just before Christmas, I'd give him his Christmas present and he gave me this long thing, it was quite heavy, done up in newspaper and brown paper, with sisal string, and he'd say, "Look after it, because it's a bit special." So I'd say, "OK, Charlie," and I'd put it away. Then we'd go to the country and I'd put it under the tree, and then at Christmas [Bill's wife] Suzanne would say, "You'd better have a look at what Charlie got you." And I opened this thing, and it was a complete Bronze Age sword from 1,000 BC.

'Then the next Christmas, he'd buy me a glass Roman bowl, and another time Bronze Age axe blades, dated 1,500 BC and 800 BC, and another year all these decorated Roman brooches, all inlaid. I've got a ton of stuff. He gave me a sword from the first century, and a dagger which had been found in the Thames, from the 1600s.

'I always kept saying, "Charlie, you can't buy me this stuff, because I can't buy you the same quality." He said, "You ain't got no money, so it doesn't matter." Which wasn't true, but ... so I'd find cricket things for him, and give him stuff like that, which he always loved. So I was able to satisfy his collections a bit.'

It would be an icy heart that refused to be warmed by the repeated evidence of mutual affection among Charlie and his bandmates. 'We used to give each other really nice things, and we'd research what each of us would like,' says Mick. 'He would like silver, and he would give me all kinds of strange, valuable ornamental pieces. He gave me a Little Walter picture with his signature underneath, and I would give him Louis Armstrong programmes, signed by all the band.'

Ronnie recalls: 'Every Christmas, every birthday, there'd always be a handwritten dedication from him and a lovely present, whatever it may be, whether it was a beautiful expensive sweater or a jacket. He'd always buy me beautiful stuff like that. I've got a beautiful box at home that I always use, with Chinese dragons on it. It's an absolutely gorgeous work of art. I bought him odd things, like pepperpots from the 17th century, something off the wall like that. His choice of presents was always very tasteful.'

Chuck Leavell, seasoned keyboard maestro and music director for the Rolling Stones' extended live ensemble, shares a story that encapsulates the drummer's selfless and observant consideration for his friends and bandmates. Reaching the end of a European tour in the late 1990s, Leavell was looking for a Border collie as a birthday gift for his wife Rose Lane.

'I mentioned it to Charlie, and he said Shirley was president of the Border Collie Society and would I like him to investigate,' he remembers. 'So he came back and said, "I've found you two. If you don't want them both, I'll take one. They're sisters." With the last show of the tour taking place in Zurich, Charlie had a Stones staffer drive to the farm near his own in Devon, where the dogs were staying, and got them sent to Switzerland.

'We went and picked them up, and they were just the cutest puppies in the world,' says Leavell. 'I took the dogs around to everyone in the band. There were some family members there and everybody ooh'd and aah'd about these

Border collies, Molly and Maggie. We kept those dogs until they both passed away, eventually, probably close to 15 years. Charlie and Shirley would always ask, whenever we'd see them, how are the dogs, and we'd give them a report.'

Tony King, a key part of the Rolling Stones machine both at home and on the road for a quarter-century, formed a particular bond with Charlie. 'On the last tour that I did, which was *A Bigger Bang*, we spent a lot of time together,' he says. 'He knew I'd taken the trouble to do that, and after the tour he gave me a lovely box, and inside was a Tiffany watch. I had to get it valued for the insurance, and it was worth £7,000. I've still got beautiful handmade towels that I got from him, and linen sheets. This ring, Charlie and Shirley gave me for my 50th birthday. It's my favourite ring and I always wear it.

'The thing about Charlie and Shirley was that they had impeccable taste,' says King. 'So if they gave you something, not only was it in good taste, they always picked a side of your personality, and something that went with you. They were very clever with that, they were a great team, and Seraphina inherited that, too. She's very thoughtful. She gave me some beautiful tulips when [in March 2022] I turned 80.'

Glyn Johns also cherishes his gifts. 'I have two things that Charlie gave me,' he says. 'One is a beautiful antique map of Surrey, which is where I was living at the time, which he gave me for one of my weddings, and also a tie he bought me. We were in San Francisco, we must have gone for a wander or something, just to get out of the hotel. Anyway, I ended up with this fabulous tie, which is actually my favourite.'

Charlie would also prompt those around him to be generous. In 1968 Stones chauffeur and 'fixer' Tom Keylock told the *NME*: 'I've always wanted to buy something for Charlie. He's so difficult, though. I mean, things like LPs and such don't mean anything, and then I saw this handsome horse carved out of one solid piece of wood. I gave it to him yesterday. I've never seen anyone so knocked out.'

Even if Jools Holland were the type to be star-struck, which he very much is not, his decades of experience working and playing with the biggest artists in the music galaxy have helped him keep calm and carry on in most circumstances. But even he confesses to a distinct warming of the heart when he found himself on the gift list of a man he had admired since he was watching from afar in the 1960s, listening intently at 45rpm.

'He liked Horatio Nelson,' says Holland. 'He was studying 18th-century battles or something, so I gave him a bust of Nelson that I'd found somewhere. Same as him, I'm always looking for stuff. He was very pleased with that, and he was very kind, because he then gave me this playbill. He gave me a few fantastic gifts. I saw him and he said, "I've got a present for you."

'He knew I liked Fats Waller,' the pianist continued, 'and like me he collected some of the early jazz photographs, signed by artists. He had things like the Count Basie Orchestra in 1948 or whatever, signed by everybody in the orchestra. That doesn't have a huge financial value, but it's an amazing thing. I told him I had a few of those, I've got one of Louis Armstrong and Duke Ellington. I rather like getting them from time to time.

'The playbill was from 1937 and it was for Fats Waller when he visited London, appearing at the Finsbury Park Empire. It was a variety show – there'd be three shows a night, he'd go on and do two songs, then there was a master of ventriloquy, a master cartoonist, the something twins who were acrobats. It was the end of the music hall, really. Charlie pointed out that Fats was billed as "America's top rhythm pianist", and a lot of people forget that the piano is a rhythm instrument. It's like the drum kit.

'On the back of the playbill, there was a little thing from Waller's trip at that time, where his tour manager had advanced him £200 in cash. Because it was official, he'd signed it "Thomas – his real name – 'Fats' Waller, sum received, £200 cash", and he was staying at the Savoy. Charlie said, "Can you imagine how much 200 quid was?" That was a new car. You could probably have got a house somewhere for that. And he said, "And he'll have got through that in about a week. Nothing's changed in music, has it?"'

Then the rare book firm, from Dave Green's story, popped up in Holland's memory too. 'Here's the bit that was really touching. I really did almost cry when I discovered this. At the memorial to Charlie at Ronnie Scott's, one of the people there was from Peter Harrington's, which was up the road from Charlie's house in London. When Charlie gave me the playbill he said, "I want you to have this. I bought this, and if it had a photograph of Fats, I'd like it. But I realise it's not really for me, because I want something with a picture on it. So I'd rather you had it, because it doesn't really fit into my criteria of collecting." Saying it was like an overspill thing that he didn't want. "Oh Charlie, that's so kind of you, thank you."

'At the memorial, the bloke from Peter Harrington who used to sell Charlie books and things [said], "We got a couple of things that he got for you." I said, "Yes, I've got this wonderful signed Fats Waller playbill with a little docket for his money. Such a fantastic historic piece, and Charlie said he'd got it and then it didn't fit in to his collection." And the fellow said, "No, no, that's not what happened. He asked me to find something with Fats Waller on it for you, because you said you couldn't find anything. I found it for him and he gave it to you." It was so Charlie-esque. He made so little of it, instead of saying he specially found it for you. I did well up inside and had to leave the room.'

The kindness continued on their next meeting. 'He had a couple of books for me,' says Holland. 'One of them is so rare. It was a little book about Pete Johnson, the boogie-woogie piano player, by somebody who met him before he died. It was almost self-published, in the '50s sometime, when Pete was old.

'The other one that really amused me is that we'd been talking about Edgar Lustgarten, who used to do the police series.' TV viewers of a certain age will remember that the British broadcaster and crime writer hosted the series *Scotland Yard* for eight years from 1953, and *The Scales of Justice* from 1962 to 1967.

Continues Holland: 'Charlie said, "I loved those so much, because he'd be sitting behind his desk in this lovely room." I said, "I loved that room!" Lustgarten would say, "Murder's an extraordinary thing. Everybody thinks they know the perfect murder, but they don't …", and then it would cut away and the Wolseley comes out of Scotland Yard. It was only half an hour long, and we just loved it, and his room.

'I said, "You know Charlie, in my little place in London, I've studied his room to see how he's got things. I want to live in that room." You just tried to create this posh 1950s room that Edgar Lustgarten lived in. Charlie thought that was so funny. Then the next time I saw him, he got me a signed, and very rare, Edgar Lustgarten first edition. It was very touching that he thought of those things.'

Equally affecting, and a lasting nod to their cherished friendship, is a tiny detail in Holland's huge model railway at his home in Kent. He proudly sent me close-ups of a section that features reproductions from Charlie's youth. 'I've got a model of him and Dave Green's prefabs in there,' he says. 'I showed him a photo and he was really amused by that. I said, "I've got my old man's shop and your prefabs.

Dave's next door and one inhabited by we don't know who, after that." He never saw it, sadly.'

Charlie's thoughtfulness extended around the world. In 2011 an online admirer on a Stones message board told the story of how his mother-in-law knew the Watts family when Charlie was young, and wore Charlie's sister Linda's wedding veil when she herself got married. She remembered young master Watts coming over for a cup of tea, before the families lost touch and she moved to Adelaide in the late 1960s.

Forward a generation, and her daughter wrote to Charlie, including photos of the wedding. One night, just after midnight, the telephone rang. It was Charlie, saying he had received the letter, would write back, would call again, and apologised for waking them up. 'My wife and I are still in shock,' wrote the fan. 'He is a thorough gentleman.'

Another time, Mark Smallman, frontman with tribute band the Rollin' Clones, told the tale of how their drummer, in a moment of advanced optimism, invited Charlie to his birthday party. He received a handwritten letter back, saying, 'Thank you very much, I'd love to come but I've got a family commitment. But I wish the Rollin' Clones every success. Yours sincerely, Charlie Watts, drummer, Rolling Stones.'

8

The Long
Road Home

In the 2000s there was a new addition to the Stones' touring party. She arrived as a very young visitor and, later, became Charlie's own aide. In 1996 his daughter Seraphina had given birth to her own only child, Charlotte, by her first husband, Nick. 'I remember so vividly when Charlotte was a young, young child and her coming out occasionally on tour,' says Chuck Leavell. 'Charlie just doted on her, and would hold her hand and take her up to the drums and spend time with her.'

Charlotte would occasionally be brought out by Seraphina as a toddler, and has memories of the *Licks* itinerary of 2002–03 and *A Bigger Bang* of 2005–07, before she grasped the scale and significance of what her granddad did for a living. 'I went to school all over,' she tells me, in a rare interview. 'England, Bermuda, America ... in the middle school around age 11, 12, we'd go back to London through Bermuda, or from Bermuda to Boston, and I'd go on summer break and go and see them on tour.

'I remember other students asking me to bring back signed drumsticks. In Bermuda you'd always ask your friend to bring back something from abroad, so it never seemed like a big deal. I was about 11 when *A Bigger Bang* ended, so I hadn't quite figured it out yet. They all got back together when I was 16, so I was much more aware by then.'

What she was especially aware of was the sheer pulling power of these immortals, and their reach across all musical divides. The guests on the *50 & Counting* tour were of high calibre and with considerable credibility, as always with the Stones, all the way back to Ike & Tina Turner, B. B. King and Stevie Wonder. The new London shows featured cameos by the likes of Mary J. Blige and Eric Clapton, as well as old boys Bill Wyman and Mick Taylor. In the States it was Bruce Springsteen, Katy Perry, Taylor Swift and another collaborator that put it all into context for the teenage Charlotte.

'When I went to see the 2012 anniversary show in New Jersey, Lady Gaga was the guest,' she says. 'I'd grown up when she came out, and she was the biggest thing in the world. That was my generation. And the fact that she was the guest was like, "Oh, OK. This is quite a bit bigger than I'd realised."

'It had just seemed like this fun thing we would do on summer holiday. At the same time, it was kind of a sad thing that Pa would be away, but I didn't have an idea of the scale until we got to those reunion shows.' (Charlie is 'Pa' to Charlotte, just as he is to Seraphina.)

'It was like, "What do you mean Lady Gaga was in a trailer at the side of the gig, and Pa had this dressing room! What's going on?! OK, I get it now." Those were some mega-shows. They had a lot of guest artists. It was always fun to pop your head into the VIP room and see who was there."

Charlotte, who like her grandfather excelled as an illustrator, also went on to work as a fashion model, her tongue and lips tattoo sometimes visible on her forearm. She was 17 when she started travelling with her granddad, around the time of the *14 on Fire* tour, named for the year, not the number of shows. What started as a visit turned into an official role.

'They had rehearsals in Paris for the start of that tour,' she says. 'I'd come out for Valentine's Day to see everybody, and they were about to start the Asia and Australia leg of the tour. Pa had said, "Here are the dates. If you want to come to any of these, let me know," and I saw that there were three in Japan, which was the most shows in one spot. I got out there and fell in love with the country. It was the first time I'd been on tour without my parents around or any of my mates.

'So I was just with the crew and with Pa, and after two weeks I was really sad, packed up ready to go back to England. I came to say goodnight to him, because I had an early morning flight and he said, "Do you want to stay?" and I was like, "Really? I'd love to." The next tour he said, "Would you like to come with us?" and then by the third one, it was, "You *are* coming with us."'

'It drove Seraphina nuts,' says Chris Kimsey, 'because Charlie would let Charlotte do anything and everything she wanted to do. It was quite lovely to see.' Seraphina puts it slightly differently. 'On the tour, you see the same people year after year. And it's the same people that my daughter was going out on the road with that I did at the same age.

'So when she started to work for my dad, with my dad, I said, "You can't get up to anything, Charlotte, because these people remember me. So bad luck, they've seen everything!" It's funny. I said, "I feel quite old now, that's my 21-year-old daughter there!" It's a huge machine. It's not the 100 Club anymore.'

Don McAulay, Charlie's drum tech, got close to Charlotte as she became a tour fixture. 'Charlie loved to show Charlotte the world,' he says. 'I don't think he would have toured as long as he did from that 50th-anniversary tour otherwise. He always asked me to look after her and make sure she was OK. She's like my little sister.'

That family line, and the incredible continuity it engenders, are among the most powerful measures of the generation-melding permanence of the Rolling Stones. When it passed from mother to daughter, it certainly gave Seraphina pause to compare Charlotte's sense of responsibility with her wildness at the same age.

'I got sent home from the tour – my mother requested I come home and my father sent me home because it was so stressful,' confides Seraphina. 'I was quite naughty. Charlotte never got sent home. I ran amok. I was 21, and he was worrying too much about what I was getting up to. My mother said, "Send her home now. I'm not having that."

Charlotte was good. She got employed in the end, so I was very proud.

'Charlotte earned her respect on the road. I didn't work, I was just in the back seat watching. She got to know everybody. I just hung about and showed up, and sat around. I was there for six weeks, swanning about and sitting watching everything.'

'I started straight away trying to find a way to be helpful,' says Charlotte. 'I would deliver the day sheets. That was the only thing anyone would trust me with, so I took that *extremely* seriously. I made up a dance and a song for it. Eventually, Cheryl Ceretti, who was in charge of media, very kindly offered me a position helping her out. So I would deal with the meet and greets and support acts, get pictures for Instagram and stuff like that.

'On paper they said I was "Executive Assistant to Charlie Watts". I thought, "I buy him a can of Gillette [foam] every other month, that's not being someone's executive assistant." I was in the media department actually doing stuff, but on paper it said I was his assistant, which was a non-job. He never had one. He didn't ask for anything. I had to convince him. "I'm already going to the pharmacy." "Well, don't go for me ..." "I'm already going."'

Charlotte also took responsibility for making Charlie's predictably modest and perfunctory dressing room on the tour into something more homely, augmenting it with jazz posters, a CD player, additional refreshments, anything to make it more welcoming for the granddad she adored.

'People would come to me with ideas and you'd slowly notice these things being added,' she says. '"Let's make it a bit homier!"'

Charlie was back in eastern Europe in the summer of 2009, visiting the Janów Podlaski stud farm to make the largest purchase in the Pride of Poland horse sale. He spent $700,000 on a beautiful, dark dappled grey mare called Pinta, the latest in a long line of Arabians purchased with Shirley. In 1993 they had bought Palba for $100,000; in 1998 Emilda ($200,000); in 2000 Euza ($110,000); in 2001 Egna ($120,000), and so on. (The history of the Polish stud farm itself would have fascinated the drummer: it was established in 1817 by Tsar Alexander I to replenish the Russian cavalry after Napoleon's invasion five years earlier.)

In 2010 extra-curricular work included his parts for Ben Waters' tribute record to his inspiration Ian Stewart, *Boogie 4 Stu*. Released the following year, after the 25th anniversary of his passing, it was just the kind of rhythm and blues party Stu would have dug, and included a lesser-known gem in the Stones' latter-day catalogue, albeit one on which all their contributions were recorded separately: a rousing take on Bob Dylan's 'Watching the River Flow' with Mick, Keith, Charlie, Ronnie and, appearing with them on record for the first time in nearly 20 years, Bill Wyman.

Charlie also played a 2010 concert with the Danish Radio Big Band, returning to the country where he had briefly lived and worked before the Stone Age began. He was joined by his pals Dave Green and Gerard Presencer, the latter a member of the long-established DRBB by then, after Charlie himself had asked whether they had any openings for recording or performing. Four days of rehearsals were followed by a concert in the National Concert Hall of Denmark, broadcast on Danish National Radio. It wasn't until 2017 that its appearance as an album signified Charlie's last release in his name during his lifetime.

It was also in 2010 that the Stones, and notably Mick, took a moment to look over their shoulder, with the first in what became a series of deluxe album reissues. The newly augmented *Exile on Main St* added ten extra tracks, most of them frequently bootlegged in various forms but now gaining their first official release. Remarkably, almost all of them contained some new vocal overdubs by Mick, who observed matter-of-factly that his voice, like his 28-inch waistline, was the same as in 1972. Keith also added some guitar parts and even Mick Taylor returned to active service to play on 'Plundered My Soul'.

Charlie, no doubt to his relief, was not required for any such sonic tinkering, but this new wine in old bottles contained some fine performances by him, notably on the colourful 'Pass the Wine (Sophia Loren)', a nod to the percussive, Latin-flavoured stylings of the often-underrated American collective War. The drummer did, however, join in with what was probably the most extensive promotion the band ever undertook for an essentially old record, moaning good-naturedly: 'It's 40 years old, some of it. No wonder I can't remember a lot of it. It's like, "You had red socks on." "No, I had blue socks on."'

So it was, with the muscle of Universal Music behind it, that the album not only reconnected with an old generation, but introduced itself to a new one, returning to No. 1 in the UK 38 years after it was first there. Next time I saw him, Charlie was delighted. 'I loved it when they said, "You're No. 1,"' he said. 'Mick and I thought it was going to be about ten 50-year-olds buying it. It's amazing, really.'

The same deluxe augmentation would subsequently be afforded fellow high markers *Some Girls*, *Sticky Fingers* and *Goats Head Soup*. When I met Charlie and Ronnie together at the Dorchester, supposedly to promote that *Some Girls* package, they were in playful mood. 'Oh God, not you again,' said Ronnie, offering a hug. 'Oh, bliiiimey,' added Charlie in mock surprise. 'I wouldn't have dressed up if I'd known. I put a suit on and everything.' He had, too: a black pinstripe with a crisp white shirt.

Charlie Watts turned 70 in June 2011 as Mick stuck plasters over the open wounds caused by some less than complimentary observations in Keith's million-selling *Life* memoir. Charlie stayed well clear, occasionally being driven from Devon into London, one time to play with the ABC&D at Pizza Express, another to attend the launch of jockey Frankie Dettori's Cavallino restaurant in Chelsea. That was a rare night in the celebrity role he hated, alongside Ronnie and a miscellany of names including Mike Rutherford of

Genesis, Roger Taylor of Queen, and sportspeople Boris Becker and Carlo Ancelotti.

Before the end of the year, the Stones had reconvened for a no-pressure jam session, with an eye on the calendar. Their golden anniversary was on the horizon. Ronnie said he wanted a 'year-long royal wedding', and even Charlie was sounding close to keen on something, still to be identified, to mark 50 years. 'It would be a nice thing to do to finish it off with, or to start a new venture,' he said. 'Well, we're a bit old to be starting new ventures, but it would be nice to do something next year.

'Once you're sitting up there doing it, it's fine, but we will not, and I certainly won't be doing, a two-year tour. We physically can't do it, I don't think, at our age. But I played two weeks every other day [with ABC&D], and I don't see any difference. The Rolling Stones are a whole 'nother project, meaning it costs a fortune for us to say, "Let's go and play there." It's not me and Ronnie playing next door, it's a big bloody thing, and whether that gets together I don't know.' It did, and this time it would be spread over a 'mere' nine months.

Rumours sprouted about the band playing at the 2012 Olympics in London (incorrect) and at Glastonbury (premature), and in February Keith said that the Stones simply weren't ready to tour in their anniversary year. But they surprised him. After playing together in a New Jersey studio in May, and a few extra-curriculars thereafter, there was a flurry of activity. For the 50th anniversary of their first-ever gig at the Marquee, the Stones convened at the site for a new photograph, this now being an event in itself.

But it was becoming clear that the big birthday would be more than just a new band shot, a photo exhibition and a book. In August they were in Paris for what Keith called their fastest-ever session (in modern Stones history, at least) of two songs in three days. Rehearsals followed. *50 & Counting* was on, and even Charlie approved, although he confessed he had considered retirement yet again.

The tour crowned their half-century with what was a handful of tea parties compared with their former enormity: a mere 30 shows in Europe and North America combined, with box-office grosses of 'only' $148 million. But they did it right, complementing the tour with the *Crossfire Hurricane* documentary and the *GRRR!* compilation, its two new songs including Mick's muscular, potent 'Doom and Gloom'. At 71, their drummer was still the steel girder the whole mighty edifice was built on. At the same time, his traditional detachment from the commercial world was now blended in the new digital marketplace with befuddlement.

'I've lost track of recording,' he confessed. 'You do "Doom and Gloom", and what does it do? Did it sell, or what? What they're good for is, you've got another new song to play, which makes the show a bit interesting. I don't know where they go. I lost track of the recording industry, and I've got enough records, thank you. I don't know, I don't mind it, I always enjoy studios [but] I prefer playing live, I prefer the thrill of that.

'Studio work's a bit ... now, if they don't like you, they'll take you off and put something else on. That's what they do, you know. And if you make a mistake, Pro Tools straightens it all out. Once upon a time you had to start and finish. What you did was what was on the record. We still *record* like that, I might add, but it's not really kept like that. Engineers can do what they like. It's a producer's world now, more than it ever was.'

As the industry became digitised, Charlie was perfectly happy to admit to me in 2013 that he not only didn't listen to the band's records, he didn't know where or how they were sold. 'I don't hear them, I don't know where you go to get them,' he said. 'I don't have one of these,' he said, pointing at my mobile. 'When you had Stax Records, nearly all the artists that came out on Stax I would listen to, then Motown. Now there [aren't] any of those labels. There isn't a Big Thing anymore. What are we on now, Universal. That's got loads of things on it, and they've bought everybody.'

I mentioned that it seemed somewhat incongruous that the band were now released on Universal's Polydor label. Classic response: he didn't know they were. 'I've got no idea, to be honest with you. Mick would be very au fait with all that. The last record person I knew was Ahmet Ertegun, and that to me was a record person. He went to a club, heard someone sing and asked them if they wanted to sing on a record.

'You see bands all the time, going down on the train, I do, going down to Exeter University, and you wonder if they're any good, because you immediately think they're trying to be Bob Dylan. But the reality is, they might be bloody marvellous.'

The tour debuted with two sellouts at The O2 in November, as the band stepped back to year dot (plus one) for the first performances of Lennon and McCartney's 'I Wanna Be Your Man' for 48 years. 'It took us 50 years to get from Dartford to Greenwich,' Mick told an excited crowd of close to 20,000. Mick Taylor's return for the epic and episodic 'Midnight Rambler' ('It was great, wasn't it?' said Charlie) was an inspired bridge to the late 1960s, and as I wrote for *Billboard*: 'The grins and pats on the back from Messrs Richards and Wood were heartfelt proof that it was pretty special for them too. With Charlie Watts keeping up an almost impossibly vigorous backbeat, the show was now en route to glory.'

'I thought the O2 shows were real fun for people, and for us,' Charlie told me. 'Bill's great to have anyway, he's a very funny person, always has been and always still is. So him and Mick Taylor playing was great. I wasn't in a cage this time, they took 'em down, which is a bit scary to begin with. I didn't tell them that. They were put up originally to keep guitars out and the drums separate, really, but it's much nicer with them out of the way, you can communicate better.

'You get used to anything, actually. I mean, I bang on endlessly about playing in clubs and how wonderful they are, but actually you get quite used to [big shows] ... once you're up there, it's like a club anyway. There's only the four or five of you, Darryl's there and Chuck's there, Ronnie and Keith, that's it. That's all you see, really.'

In March 2013 prolonged murmurings that the Stones were finally bound for the Glastonbury Festival came to fruition. Everyone was super-excited, except for one person. Off the record, Charlie told me that he was against it, but had been outvoted; everyone else, and crucially their kids, were in favour. 'All my kids and lots of people all over the world will be pleased that we're finally doing that,' said Ronnie, anticipating their arrival and the traditional challenges of the English weather. 'Even the helicopter's got wellies on.'

Once Charlie was there, of course, he enjoyed it just fine, as he did the band's return to Hyde Park the following week, and again a week after that, 44 years after their famous first time there. 'I had a really good time in both places,' he said, adding sheepishly: 'I've got to learn to shut up about things. That's typical of me.' Indeed, as far back as 1998 he had expressed the wish that the band would still be going in 15 years, so that came true, and more besides. Thus he had the great pleasure of playing again with Mick Taylor, on both 'Midnight Rambler' and 'Satisfaction', and the feeling of a musical institution being passed down to another new generation was palpable.

In between the two Hyde Park shows, Charlie was on another, rather smaller stage, at the Lyric Theatre, sitting in with live bandmate and saxophonist Tim Ries's Rolling Stones Project. The lineup was like an extended group show, also featuring Chuck Leavell, Darryl Jones and Bernard Fowler, and Charlie was clearly in his element. He sat in with Ries for several more shows in the ensuing years.

In 2014 he was in the YouTube clip that Mick filmed with his friend, collaborator and Stones live band member Matt Clifford, to introduce a press conference by the reunited Monty Python team, publicising their run of shows at The O2. Game for a laugh and a little self-parody, as he is more often than he's given credit for, Mick pretended to ridicule 'wrinkly old men' going out to make a buck. Charlie slouched on the hotel room couch, offering a look of priceless mock horror – one that befitted a proud technophobe – when Mick mentioned YouTube.

'Mobile phones I think are a pain in the arse, but most people think they're fantastic,' Charlie said to me in the late 1990s. 'I don't know what Mick would do without one. But I cannot stand them. But I think I'm more of a dinosaur than he is.'

'We used to make jokes about it,' says close friend and Stones confidant Tony King. 'He'd say, "Are you downloading that then?" and come out with all the phrases to try to sound modern. But he used to say it with tongue firmly in cheek.'

When the 2020 documentary *The Tree Man* celebrated Chuck Leavell's dual roles as A-list musician and tree farmer and conservationist, all of the Stones were interviewed for it. 'Charlie, as usual, didn't have a lot to say,' he laughs. 'One of the clips that our filmmaker Allen Farst used, he asked him, "What can you tell me about Chuck?" and he said "He's a great ... emailer." Because I'm a pretty fast typist, and I can be on the plane, entering database information, doing communications. He said all the time "What are you *doing*?"

'I will say this,' adds Leavell. 'Being of Southern upbringing and the traditions that we have, letter-writing is a pretty big thing that we're taught from a young age, so I've written letters to Charlie and to all the guys, especially early on. I think Charlie especially appreciated it. He would always mention that. That's the kind of communication he enjoyed.'

Charlie took pleasure, though, in recognising that he wasn't the only band member who sometimes resisted even simple communication. Once, describing life in between Stones duties, off the road and away from the recording studio, he revealed: 'You'll suddenly get a fax fly through from Keith, 'cos he won't use the telephone, you know. Hates them, but I can see why.'

With the new momentum of the Stones as a live force, soon they were back out for the *14 on Fire* and *Zip Code* tours of 2014 and 2015, then south of the border for *América Latina Olé* in 2016. The year also featured a mini-US tour in the autumn, by which time the physical challenges that would confront any rock drummer, never mind one who had now turned 75, were becoming more tangible, the more so when the extended *No Filter* began in

2017. But Charlotte, in particular, was there to remind him of home.

'The last few years on the road, I didn't think of it this way at the time but a lot of people told me that it made a really big difference that I was there, because it meant a bit of home was there,' she says. 'I'm extremely grateful that I could be there with him. On the days off, we didn't spend a great deal of time together. I'd come and visit him in his room, and he'd be tapping his foot saying, "Go and have fun," like "We're in a city, go and explore. Are you going shopping? Are you going out with your mates? Don't sit around here for me, I'm just chilling."

'I used to sit with him on the plane, and I'm so scared of flying that I'd have panic attacks, every take-off. He'd get a bit frustrated because he didn't know what to do to help me. So I started sitting at the back for take-off and landing, and he'd come and sit with me, I'd come up and hang out with him. We would mostly travel together, so we'd be in the car or the plane.

'On days off, my favourite was when we'd go to a museum. We did a lot of aviation museums in the last couple of years, because I was mad on Concorde, still am. So I'd get to see that, and he'd get to see all the Second World War planes. He collected all that stuff, and his father and grand-father fought in the wars, so he wanted to see that. It felt really good to have some common ground, that I wasn't dragging him around, or he didn't feel he was dragging me around somewhere that the other one didn't want to be.'

Says Chuck Leavell: 'As she got older, Charlotte became very much an integral part of our entourage. Her art was used on posters and everything, and Charlie was so proud of her. She was about the only one, with the exception of maybe the security guy that worked for him, that could knock on his door at the hotel and get an answer. He was very private that way. Charlotte became a constant for us.'

Speaking after Charlie's passing, Keith muses: 'I realised I never actually visited where Charlie lived. I never got down to Devon, even though I was in West Sussex. That was another weird thing. He really didn't want to mix home life with the work.' Did they talk much about family on the road? 'Not a lot, but nobody does much. "How are the kids? Long as they're all right and your old lady's OK ..." But he was obviously attached to Charlotte. When he was playing grandpa, it was a touching sight. It was a connection. She did a great job.'

'There's a sense of family and comfort, and it's still the same crew that I grew up with,' reflects Charlotte. 'In terms of the generations of the kids, it's almost like there were different groups every couple of years. Georgia May, Lukas, Gabriel [all Mick's children] and I were all a bit separated out by our age differences.

'You get Theo [Keith's daughter Theodora] and Lizzy [Jagger] and that whole group, they're in their 30s now. They're all within a year or two of each other. So I didn't see the kids a whole lot on tour. I spent a lot more time with the crew, and it would be like, "Oh, one of them's coming out, it'll be fun." But I wasn't part of one of those generational groups of the kids.'

Lisa Fischer, touring with the Stones as the finest female backing vocalist they ever had, says: 'I think that was a saving grace for Charlie. Having Charlotte on the road was beautiful, and he was so protective of her but without being stifling. He would basically say, "Don't influence her, in any negative way." We were like, "We would never do that, we love her." There were a lot of people always looking out for the kids. They'd come in and out of my dressing room and hang out. Being the only girl, it was always the girls' hang room. They'd come and talk about their boyfriends, that kind of stuff.'

Family, reflects Fischer, has long been a crucial part of the Stones' massive touring machinery. 'Huge,' she says. 'And how involved they all were and are with their kids, still. Not only as parents and grandparents would they be watchful, but if the people that were their personal assistants and security and anyone that worked on the tour saw anything that looked awry, they'd be on it. So they were well cared for.

'A lot of people think, "Oh, this is not a good place for them to be." But there'd be games for them to play, trips planned for them or family outings on days off. Some of the kids actually attended school on the road, they had their tutors. So it was really a healthy, balanced environment, considering it was a moving city.'

The touring band's city-to-city and country-to-country flights were something to witness too. 'All the way down,

Pa would say hi to everybody and all the way back up, every flight,' says Charlotte. Leavell remembers: 'We would get on the private plane – and Keith would do this a lot too – but Charlie would always make the rounds. There's obviously protocol. The crew get on first, then the band, then we wait on the principals. But he would always walk up and down the aisles and ask everybody how they were doing, how was their day, what did you do last night. So personable, and it always brightened you up that Charlie Watts wanted to have a conversation with you.'

Charlotte fondly describes her granddad's eccentric travelling habits. 'I've got a folder on my old computer just titled "Pa climbing",' she says. 'Whenever we would travel, he would always leave his bag, like we'd be in the Viano – the Mercedes with the seats facing each other in the back – and he'd leave his hand luggage in the back, or on a train or a plane in the overhead. I have this series of photos of him climbing on the chairs to get into the bag.

'Everybody else would just get the bag down, but there's him climbing on various transport chairs to get his stuff. I'd be like, "Will you get *down*!" and he'd say, "I'm getting my stuff." It was so funny. He'd be equally horrified if there was going to be turbulence. Everybody on the plane would be like, "What is he *doing*?" "Just ignore him."'

Each fellow Stone has priceless memories of their touring rituals, both on show days and during downtime. 'You never liked to look too deep, because you knew he wouldn't allow you in past a certain point,' says Ronnie. 'What he gave you was just enough, and maybe a bit more if you sat with him for a while. He would always come into my room before every concert and have coffee with me, then he'd sit down and have a chat.

'Then he'd go away, come back for another cup and we would compare how cold we were. We always went sub-zero. Our hands were freezing, and our faces. Everyone would go, "Look at you two." The two Geminis, we always went down in temperature. That was our way of getting stage nerves. With the apprehension of going on, we got cold. But it was lovely that we always shared that.'

Mick reveals that in recent years new technology came to the rescue during an amusing moment of uncertainty in rehearsals. 'Charlie and I used to joke. I'd say, "No, it's not 'chh-boom-boom', it's 'boom-boom-chh'." On stage, until the very end, with "Beast of Burden", Charlie would get it the wrong way around. "It doesn't sound right, Charlie, what you're playing. Whatever it is, it isn't what you played on the record. So just listen to the record.' And I'd play it on my phone, and he'd go, "Oh yeah."'

'A big part of what I did,' says Don McAulay, 'was just watching him on stage, as a man of very few words, getting to know who he is so that whatever his movements were, I could understand his body language. I remember when my father was going through something, and they knew each other. You know how humble and cool Charlie was. One time in a show when they were playing "Waiting on a Friend", which is a very simple part, he called me over. I'm thinking something's wrong. And he said, "How's your dad?" In the middle of a show.'

'You never saw him at my so-called infamous parties,' adds Keith. 'He wasn't that kind of guy. He was what he was, he was a quiet guy, very interested in loads of things. He was always drawing. Sometimes I would just sit there and watch him for hours. They used to have these vibrating machines next to beds in American hotels [for the uninitiated, this was the coin-operated device called Magic Fingers, mounted to hotel beds, which provided 'tingling relaxation and ease' for a quarter].

'I remember about two hours where he just drew this thing, got it wrong and started again. It was amazing to watch, and I don't think a word passed between us, without any discomfort or anything.'

Late in 2015, in the band's fastest recording sessions for aeons, they were at Mark Knopfler's British Grove Studios to cut *Blue & Lonesome*. It was a glorious, spontaneous and simmering return to the raw muscle of their salad days, full of sensational performances of expertly chosen set texts by their North Star artists like Howlin' Wolf, Magic Sam, Little Walter and Eddie Taylor. It went straight to No. 1 in the UK, and it was the last Rolling Stones studio album of Charlie's lifetime.

In March 2016 there was yet another example of his magnanimity as the Stones prepared to make their way to Cuba, for the little matter of a free show for perhaps

450,000 people in Havana. As quietly as you like, Charlie dropped in with Bernard Fowler and Tim Ries to the University of Miami's Frost School's weekly jazz session.

Every Monday, about 100 aspiring jazz musicians gathered at the school, normally to hear student or faculty groups perform. This fortunate group witnessed Ries's new big band charts of 'Under My Thumb' and 'You Can't Always Get What You Want,' before Charlie played a side-by-side shuffle on 'Honky Tonk Women' with drumming scholar Marcelo Perez. 'You should have seen the faces of the students when he walked in,' Dean Shelly Berg told the University website. 'It was complete disbelief. There's a lot to learn from the person Charlie was. He proved that fame doesn't have to change who you are as a person.'

Later that year came *Desert Trip*, the two-weekend event on the Coachella Festival site in Indio, California. With the Stones on a juggernaut bill with Paul McCartney, Bob Dylan, The Who, Neil Young and Roger Waters, it was little wonder that it became known as 'Oldchella'. During the stay, Lisa Fischer played a solo gig nearby and had some surprise visitors.

'Charlie, Ronnie and Keith came to a show I was doing while the Stones were out in the desert,' she says. 'I was in shock, because I knew they had shows. I was like, "I'm not going to see any of them." And they all came, which was so sweet. I know Mick couldn't come because he had to rest, but they had a little bit more freedom.'

Charlie turned 77 on the road as the Stones played the Ricoh Arena in Coventry in June 2018. Always a picky eater, his diet was of concern to both family and bandmates. 'I would always be on at him about eating,' says Mick. 'Especially in the latter days when you could eat perfectly well, and I would force him to come out and eat with me at night. You get bored sitting in your room, and there's no one going to encourage you to eat, so you eat less and less.

'Me and Charlie are probably putting out the most energy [in the show], and he was probably putting out more than I am. You don't get to stop, and you can't fuck up. If I don't want to run to the other side of the stage, no one's going to tell me I have to. If Charlie stops playing, then you're fucked. You have to have a good diet, and you have to be looked after, and for whatever reason, he wouldn't eat properly and manage his diet.' It was a long-term habit. 'He never ate very well,' says his sister Linda. 'The only thing he used to love to eat was fish.'

Ronnie remembers Charlie's continuing bafflement at his and the band's popularity. '"Why me? Why us? Here we are, still going." *Every* tour he'd say that to me. "Why do people keep showing up?" I said, "Charlie, there's something, when we all get together, people just come out of the woodwork. It's as simple as that, you can't explain it."'

'The last couple of tours, he was feeling it,' says Keith. 'It wasn't just a case of "I don't feel like it anymore." He was having to really work those shows, and he'd be pretty beaten up after every one.' But, adds Don McAulay, 'I didn't notice any decline in his playing. It was harder to tour, but I saw him get more inventive as a player.'

In January 2019 Charlie was in Los Angeles for the 90th birthday party of one of his most respected peers, Wrecking Crew drum titan Hal Blaine. McAulay records that it prompted discussion of another starry gathering some 55 years earlier, after both drummers had played on the famous *T.A.M.I. Show* that James Brown made his own. A particular memory of that night was another Wattsian classic.

'Hal grabbed Charlie, Bill Wyman and it might have been Andrew Loog Oldham,' McAulay recounted of that 1964 gathering, 'and they were driving through the Hollywood Hills in Hal's beautiful convertible, to his place for a party. It was the year the automatic garage door-opener came out, and the first time anyone had one. Charlie didn't know anything about it.

'So as Hal is going towards the house, he's not stopping, and the garage door is still closed. All of a sudden, Hal reaches down, hits a button and the door opens out. They freaked out. All these big stars were at the party after the show, and Charlie supposedly had no interest in them, he just kept opening and closing the door. "Where's Charlie?" "Oh, he's in the garage."

Ever the student, he used downtime on 2019's North American leg of the *No Filter* tour to visit a drum exhibition at the New Orleans Jazz Museum, then the Louis Armstrong House Museum in Queens, New York. He was photographed at Satchmo's desk, quite a thrill for someone whose time-machine dream would have been to see him with a big band at the Roseland Ballroom in Chicago. If he wasn't dressing up to the nines to see Ellington at the Cotton Club, of course.

Another time he visited the Motown Museum in Detroit and its famous Snakepit studio, where McAulay says Charlie knew everything about it before they even arrived. Charlie was still distributing lovely surprises to his bandmates during that tour too. Says Chuck Leavell: 'I had released an album called *Chuck Gets Big*, with the Frankfurt Radio Big Band. During that tour I arranged a show at a theatre in New York. Charlie had heard the record and really liked it.

'Of course I invited him to the show, and he came. He sat in on "Honky Tonk Women" along with a few of the others in the band. Our singer Sasha Allen was there. It was just such a generous thing for him to do, and he raved about it afterwards, which of course made my day – made my life – that he thought it was a good show.'

The *No Filter* itinerary finally drew to a close on 30 August 2019, when 40,768 people saw Charlie Watts play in public with the Rolling Stones for what turned out to be the last time. The show, already rescheduled once for Mick's heart surgery and then moved back a day in hurricane season, took place at the Hard Rock Stadium in Miami Gardens, Florida. 'One hell of a hurricane party,' drooled the *Miami New Times* of the rain-soaked show.

'Watts, looking shy and slightly detached, perched behind his minimalistic drum set,' wrote Wendy Rhodes in her review. It was a comment that could have applied to any one of his couple of thousand performances with the group over 56 and a half years. Then, she added, the closing 'Satisfaction' 'saw every bandmate, even Watts, laughing, playing, and appearing to have the time of their lives'. No one knew it, but with Covid-19 about to rewrite the world, it was a final image to savour.

Also in 2019 there was one last family holiday back in France for Charlie, Shirley, Seraphina and her husband Barry. 'We still have that house that I grew up in, and we were there, just the four of us,' says Seraphina. 'I'm so glad we did it, it was the most fun trip,' adds Barry. 'This little farmhouse in France gets three TV channels, all French. Seraphina and Shirley speak French. Charlie and I do not.' Seraphina smiles wistfully. 'We were crying with laughter at all these French films. It was so good to have had times like that.'

Even during lockdown, Shirley's work with rescue greyhounds went on, as she and Charlie adopted another from the Forever Hounds Trust in May 2020. These were strangely quiet, stationary years for a man who had spent five and a half decades in a suitcase. But there was contact, as if interplanetary, through the new reality of the live stream, with four Stones in four rooms playing 'You Can't Always Get What You Want' for Global Citizen's *One World: Together at Home* virtual concert. Soon afterwards, there was the spirited new track 'Living in a Ghost Town', started in 2019 and with Charlie keeping a near-reggae beat, its lyrics adapted by Mick for the dark pandemic days.

Charlie's 80th birthday in June 2021 was a cause for celebration among all of his admirers. But friends who telephoned with good wishes, such as Dave Green and Jools Holland, found him a little below par. This time, Charlie Watts was behind the beat.

9

Forever the Wembley Whammer

The first official notification that Charlie was even one degree under came with the August 2021 announcement that he would not make the beginning of the Stones' delayed but renewed *No Filter* tour of North America, due to start in late September. He had undergone a successful operation but needed more rest and recuperation than rehearsal schedules would allow. 'For once, my timing is a little off,' he said in the press statement.

Charlie had earlier expressed his trademark hesitancy about the new itinerary, but not for the usual reasons. 'He was slightly reticent about going on this last tour because he wasn't feeling very well,' says Mick. 'He said, "But you're the cheerleader of the group and if you say I should do it, I'll do it, of course I will, I'm happy to."'

Steve Jordan, hugely distinguished drummer, producer, close compadre of the whole group and Keith's longtime bandmate in the X-Pensive Winos, was the one, the only deputy. The official line that the band were anticipating Charlie's full recovery, and for him to join the tour later, was genuine. 'We were hoping it, and so was Steve,' says

Keith. 'He said, "I'll keep the chair warm for you, Charlie," not expecting that it would be permanent. But they were two good friends, and it was the most amazing piece of luck for us. Charlie always said to me, "If any reason should *ever* occur that I'm not behind the drums, Steve Jordan is your man." He sort of named him as Crown Prince.'

'I saw Charlie in the hospital,' says Ronnie, 'and he was telling me that Steve would definitely be the one to hold it until he could get out on tour. We watched the horse racing, and of course he loved Frankie Dettori. The last few days of his hospitalisation, he was like, "I don't like this," because he went to a certain level of treatment, then they decided to do some extra work on him.'

The gracious Watts family, who gave me their time and their memories so generously for this book, have chosen to keep the precise details of Charlie's death a private matter, save to say that after a successful operation, there were unexpected complications after surgery, leading to a rapid decline. Seraphina, Barry and Charlotte stayed with him day and night, and Seraphina was able to be with her father at the end.

Mick reveals: 'I was speaking to him in hospital, and because he was so untechnical I sent him a big iPad to watch the cricket on. I set it all up with the apps and he watched some of it on that. But Ronnie had had a similar illness and got better, and that's why I guess I was so confident Charlie was going to do the same thing. It was all so quick, that was the shocking part of it. One minute I was speaking to him about the tour and what the logo was going to be, and the next minute he was gone.'

Charlie's death on 24 August 2021 prompted overpowering, long-lasting lamentation among millions of people who never even met him. Images of his near-60 years of active service were posted on social media in their millions for months, and his passing was described like a family bereavement. He would, of course, have been hugely embarrassed about the fuss.

'Then it was having to just carry on,' says Mick. 'Well, we didn't have to, but it just felt like we should, and Charlie said we should. He said, "You should do the tour anyway." Because it had been delayed [by the pandemic], remember. "You can't cancel it again."' True to his selfless character, three days before he died, Charlie spoke to Don McAulay and was full not of self-pity, but of apologies that he wasn't on the tour. 'He was a very easy man to love,' says McAulay simply.

'We were already well into rehearsals when we got the news,' says Ronnie. 'We had a day off and thought, well, Charlie doesn't want us to sit around and mope. We'll just get on with it. That was it. We just took off and carried the message that Charlie would have loved.' They did so to some of the most lionising reviews of the band's recent history. Jordan told *Rolling Stone*: 'My goal was to bring back some of the stuff from the records, and then reference what I think of as one of the hottest live periods for the band. For me, that was from about 1971 to 1975 during the Mick Taylor years, where Charlie was incredibly on fire.'

Late in 2021 Charlotte forced herself to see the last three shows of the run, including with a good friend in Detroit. 'It was an important one for me,' she says. 'It was my first show without him and she was there to hold my hand. It was nice seeing everybody and it was a good realisation that he's not here.'

Ringo Starr wrote of one image we wouldn't be seeing. 'Charlie was a great guy, a lot of fun,' he said on hearing of his old friend's passing. 'I had a party in the '70s and Charlie came and so did John Bonham, so we've got three drummers just hanging out. Bonham got on the kit, and since they weren't attached to the ground like they are on stage, Charlie and I are holding the bass drums for him as he played. What a photo that would have been.'

Pete Townshend also wrote movingly: 'Charlie Watts wept at Keith Moon's funeral. I wish I was capable of such tears today. Instead I just want to say goodbye. Not a rock drummer, a jazz drummer really, and that's why the Stones swung like the Basie band!! Such a lovely man. God bless his wife and daughter, and I'll bet the horses will miss him too.'

'Legacy' is a word that would make him splutter with indignation, but the Wattsian time signature written across more than half a century of popular music is magnified and amplified by the sheer span of favourite performances he left. 'They're all outstanding in my book,' says Glyn Johns.

'The obvious one is "Honky Tonk Women" because it starts with him and a cowbell. But I wouldn't pick one above any other. He's never let the side down on anything. He never blew a take, I can tell you that.'

Mick especially remembers his stellar drumming on *Get Yer Ya-Ya's Out!*. Tony King favours his dramatic break-down on the *Steel Wheels* song 'Rock and a Hard Place'. Charlotte loves 'Midnight Rambler' and 'Sympathy for the Devil' on stage, and on record the *Undercover* track 'Too Much Blood' and the latter-day single 'Don't Stop'. 'There's a video of them behind the scenes doing that, and him wearing this baby blue jumper,' she says. 'Also, I never wanted the *tour* to stop, so I'd listen to it between tours and be missing everybody and saying, "Come on, let's go again." It was the best of my life. I can't listen to it now. But one day.'

Dave Green remembers getting the news of his oldest friend's death while he was in his car. He had been working on a version of 'The Flower Is a Lovesome Thing', by one of Charlie's favourites, Billy Strayhorn, as remade with his pals from the ten-piece band at Ronnie Scott's. 'I'd forgotten what was in the CD player,' he says. 'This track came on, and it was tears. It's a slow ballad, a beautiful song, and it was the first music I heard after Charlie died.'

For Charlie's former Zildjian compadre John DeChristopher, it always comes back to '19th Nervous Breakdown'. 'It's almost like he's channelling Elvin Jones or a bebop drummer, it's so technical and feels so good,' he says. 'It's the perfect blend of what makes Charlie so special.

Then on something like "Winter", his playing is exquisite. There were no rules for him. It was whatever it takes to make everyone sound good.'

'He was unique in what he brought to the Stones,' adds Dave. 'It was never a pre-ordained concept of how to play with a rock band. He just played the way he felt the music. He never had that showy element. He was very self-effacing, just playing for the music.'

'I have to say I really loved him,' says Jools Holland. 'I felt great sympatico with him and he was very kind to me. He was like somebody from another age, but at the same time completely connected to the moment. He lived the dream.'

'"Enigma",' I say to Keith, 'is an overused word, but you can use it for Charlie "Boom Boom" Watts.' 'You can,' he agrees. 'It's the most fitting word. He could create his own world, Charlie, in his own way. It's difficult to define. He was a mystery to me. Always will be, in many ways. But at the same time, you live with a guy, especially in the '60s … we lived that way basically for four years, where we were just around the corridor from each other.'

Admirers of extremely famous people often make the selfish error of thinking they have the copyright on grief. Processing the departure of an artist you admire greatly, who has been in your life as long as you can remember, is highly emotional, but it can be nothing compared with the loss of a husband, a brother, a father, a grandfather.

'He rang every single day,' Seraphina remembers. 'He rang my mother and then he would ring Charlotte and me. When I go to the main house, it's like he's still away. He's on tour. I said that to my mother the other day. It just feels like he's going to call any minute.'

'From very early on,' says Charlotte, 'I was like, "I can't get too attached to this world, because it is what it is. It's got to end one day." But to be given that opportunity, it's still hard to believe that's over. That's the amazing thing, to be so lucky in so many ways to have such a wonderful person in my life.'

She paraphrases her friend Don McAulay's description of how Charlie saw life. 'It was like he invited us into this world with very much a sense of, "This is all kind of make-believe. Enjoy this while it lasts, but none of us should get used to it, because everybody has to go home at the end of the tour." Charlie Watts has indeed gone home at the end of the tour, but close your eyes and he's up there creating his firework display behind that tiny kit, smiling that dazzling smile and thrilling us all, one beat at a time.

Afterword

1 June 2022, the Wanda Metropolitano Stadium, Madrid. Impossibly, the dice are still tumbling, and more than 50,000 manic Spaniards are there to reopen rock's longest-running party. The Rolling Stones are starting the European tour that marks their 60th anniversary, and one man dominates the gigantic screens.

Images from Charlie Watts's decades of service are cheered to the skies, before his friends of a lifetime play on in his honour, cheating nature, gravity and any other law you can think of with a show that, true to Stonesian lore, might fall apart at any minute, yet builds in magnificence into a thing of wonder.

The uncharitable thought occurs that if tonight's opening acts set the clock ticking now, then to match the shelf life of the headliners they will need to be treading the boards in the year 2082. Led to victory by a frontman whose physiological clock apparently stopped sometime in the 1980s, the Stones dish out classics for fun, with the remarkable addition, for the first time on any stage, of a storecupboard extra that now finds itself as a centrepiece, 'Out of Time'. Which they certainly are not.

At the drum stool, Steve Jordan plays brimstone beats with faultless poise, in the full acceptance that in some strange way the night belongs to the man who isn't there. 'Steve is so good about it,' Mick tells me. 'He's studied what Charlie played on stage, and what he played on the record. He's not slavish to it. But if you don't know who's behind you, sometimes you could think, with the intro of "Paint It Black", for instance, it's Charlie. It's uncannily the same.' Charlie is still good tonight.

Picture Credits

While every effort has been made to trace the owners of copyright material reproduced herein and secure permissions, the publishers would like to apologise for any omissions and will be pleased to incorporate missing acknowledgements in any future edition of this book.

Endpapers: Fiona Adams/Redferns/Getty Images
Plate 1, 2 (bottom), plate 7 (top left): Courtesy of Linda Rootes
Plate 2 (top): Courtesy of Claire Deacon
Plate 3 (top), plate 11 (bottom): Courtesy of Dave Green
Plate 3 (middle): Courtesy of Brian and Ann Jones
Plate 3 (bottom): Estate of Charlie Watts
Plate 4 (top): Popperfoto via Getty Images
Plate 4 (bottom): Archive Photos/Hulton Archive/Getty Images
Plate 5 (top): TV Times via Getty Images
Plate 5 (bottom): Pictorial Press Ltd/Alamy Stock Photo
Plate 6 (top left): Daily Mirror/Mirrorpix/Mirrorpix via Getty Images
Plate 6 (top right): Trinity Mirror/Mirrorpix/Alamy Stock Photo
Plate 6 (bottom): Stan Mays/Daily Mirror/Mirrorpix

Plate 7 (top right): Keystone Features/Hulton Archive/Getty Images

Plate 7 (bottom): ABKCO

Plate 8 (top): Sunday Mirror/Mirrorpix/Mirrorpix via Getty Images

Plate 8 (bottom left): Evening Standard/Hulton Archive/Getty Images

Plate 8 (bottom right): Robert R. McElroy/Getty Images

Plate 9: Keystone/Zuma/Shutterstock

Plate 10 (top): The Estate of David Gahr/Getty Images

Plate 10 (middle): Aaron Rapoport/Corbis via Getty Images

Plate 10 (bottom): Mirrorpix

Plate 11 (top): Trinity Mirror/Mirrorpix/Alamy Stock Photo

Plate 12 (top): Courtesy of Tony King

Plate 12 (middle): Lawrence Schwartzwald/Sygma via Getty Images

Plate 12 (bottom): KMazur/WireImage/Getty Images

Plate 13 (top): Christian Charisius/Reuters Pictures

Plate 13 (middle): © Jools Holland

Plate 13 (bottom left): Action Images/Paul Childs Livepic/ Reuters Pictures

Plate 13 (bottom right): Kacper Pempel/Reuters Pictures

Plate 14 (top): Sean Hansford/Manchester Evening News/ Mirrorpix

Plate 14 (bottom left and right), plate 15, plate 16 (top left and right): © Don McAulay

Plate 16 (bottom): © John Christie

Index

INDEX

Summer of Love 104, 110
Sunday Night at the London Palladium
105
Super Bowl XL (2006) 265
'Sympathy for the Devil' (Rolling
Stones) 116, 200, 329

T.A.M.I. Show 92, 318
Tattoo You (Rolling Stones) 93–4,
171–2
Taylor, Dick 30, 40
Taylor, Eddie 14, 315
Taylor, Mick 72, 113–14, 117, 126,
128, 136, 200–1, 296, 301, 306, 307,
328
Teuchtler Schallplattenhandlung und
Antiquariat, Vienna 243–4
Their Satanic Majesties Request
(Rolling Stones) 106
'This Place Is Empty' (Rolling Stones)
264
Thomas, Dylan 235, 258
'Too Much Blood' (Rolling Stones) 329
Top of the Pops 51, 52
Toronto, Stones rehearsals in 208,
217–18, 258–9
Tour of the Americas (Rolling Stones)
137
Townshend, Pete 150, 177, 256, 257,
328
Tracey, Stan 23, 186
Troubadour, Earl's Court 22, 30, 37
25 x 5 (film) 191–2

'Undercover (of the Night)' (Rolling
Stones) 176
Undercover (Rolling Stones) 176, 329
Urban Jungle tour (Rolling Stones) 191,
200, 201–2
U2 199–200, 201

'Ventilator Blues' (Rolling Stones) 127
Virgin Records 208
Voodoo Lounge (Rolling Stones) 211,
214

'Waiting on a Friend' (Rolling Stones)
93–4, 314–15
'Walking the Dog' (Rolling Stones) 102
Warner Brothers Records 21
Was, Don 217, 264
Wasserman, Paul 180, 181

Waters, Ben 273–4; *Boogie 4 Stu* 300
Watts at Scott's 262
Watts, Charles A. (grandfather of CW)
5
Watts, Charles Richard (father of CW)
4, 5, 7, 11, 19, 155, 171
Watts, Charlie: *A Biography by Charlie
Watts* 101–2; bands/groups *see
individual band/group name*;
'beloved' status 257–8; birth 4–5;
birthdays 29, 302–3, 317, 321;
cancer 262–3, 270; cars 236–40;
Charles Daniels Studios tea boy 21–2;
Charles Hobson and Grey job 24;
childhood 4–20, 155; classical music
fan xi, 258; collector xxi, 88, 106,
111, 138, 162, 163, 231–45, 254,
282–3, 284, 287–8, 289, 310; cricket,
passion for 10, 26, 79, 205, 240–3,
284; culture trips 225; death xxi, 42,
155, 156, 325–8; Denmark, design
work in 23–4, 65, 86; design
consultant, uncredited Rolling Stones
118, 124, 173–4, 199–202, 219,
260–1; diet 184, 317; draws bed in
hotel rooms 221; drum loops, plays
along to 216–17; drumming, begins
11, 14–15; fame, on 59–61; family
and *see individual family member
name*; festivals, on 271–2, 307; first
editions 233; Flower Power, dislikes
104, 110, 140; gentleman, as
18th-century 267–8; gift-giver/
generosity xxi, 256–7, 281–91;
graphic design artist 14, 19–20, 21–4,
38; Grand Tour of Europe 267;
homes *see individual house or place
name*; humour xii, xiii–xiv, 72, 91,
166, 192, 220; husband, devoted
69–75 *see also* Watts, Shirley;
introduced in Stones live show
249–51; legacy 328–31; live
appearance as Rolling Stone, last
319–20; logos, Stones and 124, 157,
327; loner 226; magazine cover, first
solo 87; media, wariness of 108;
memorial 193, 282; musical taste xi,
9, 12–13, 15, 16, 17, 19–20, 77–8,
93, 127; musicianship, Johns on
89–90; narcotic madness, 1980s xxiii,
179–89; OCD traits/fastidiousness
48–50, 232; punk, on 140–1;